MANIAS AND DELUSIONS

Cover: An altered photograph transforms Nazi leader Adolf Hitler into a nightmarish vision, disintegrating against the garish background of a grinning Bali mask.

MANIAS AND DELUSIONS

By the Editors of Time-Life Books

TIME-LIFE BOOKS, ALEXANDRIA, VIRGINIA

CONTENTS

FEARSOME FABRICATIONS

The real world abounds with fearsome schemes and clever conspiracies—one need not be a lunatic to feel the cold breath of fear. And yet, part of the human constitution, it appears, requires that we fabricate alternative realities in which little or nothing is true, but all is fervently believed and feared.

Frequently, the terrifying core of such belief is merely the unknown, and the fiction is just a way of explaining what one has experienced or observed. Sometimes people reshape reality in order to accommodate events that are beyond their understanding or control; sometimes a burden of grief or guilt alters their perceptions, or they become mired in the skewed belief that authority is evil, all knowing, and in perpetual conspiracy. No matter the motive, culture, or epoch, these notions trigger the deepest of human fears.

Beyond such excursions into needless terror, however, lies a more sinister domain of determined ignorance, implacable hatreds, and irrational fright focused upon the differences of others and the latent hope that someone else can be blamed for the flaws of a society. Here, one leaves the rational world very far behind. Whatever clinicians may call the condition, it deserves the terrible name of madness.

Child's Play

On a September night in 1590, Lady Susan Cromwell dreamed that a vicious black cat was about to strip the skin and flesh from her body. She thrashed and moaned in terror until her daughter-in-law woke her and let her escape the murderous claws. The black cat, she gasped, had been sent by Alice Samuel, an old woman she had just accused of being a witch. Lady Cromwell's tormented fantasy fit the times. The witch craze that had gripped Europe for close to two centuries was at its peak. The fear of witchcraft was rife, and so was the fear of being charged with the offense—those found guilty were condemned to death, often after horrible tortures.

Earlier that day, Lady Cromwell had become convinced that Alice Samuel, one of her poor tenants in the Huntingdonshire village of Warboys, had made a pact with the devil. Lady Cromwell had called upon her good friends in Warboys, Master Throckmorton and his wife, to inquire after the family's health. There was good reason for her concern. Since the previous November, the Throckmortons' five young daughters—Joan, Mary, Elizabeth, Jane, and Grace—had suffered from mysterious fits. They shook and sneezed uncontrollably, screeched, swooned, and were assailed by horrible visions—not of evil spirits, but of an octogenarian neighbor the villagers called Mother Samuel.

First nine-year-old Jane, then the rest of the sisters, had accused the old woman of being a witch. She caused their fits, they claimed, and meant eventually to kill them. Elizabeth swore that Mother Samuel had forced a mouse into her mouth, supposedly a witch's technique for introducing an evil spirit into a victim's body. While disturbed by the accusations, Throckmorton and his wife were loath to credit their daughters' diagnosis of their fits. Even after the hysterical contagion had spread to her seven women servants, the mistress ignored their pleas to use her influence and have the witch burned before she killed the lot of them.

But Lady Cromwell was quicker to pass judgment than her friends were. On the day of her visit, one girl after another fell into a fit. Summoning Mother Samuel to the Throckmortons' house, Lady Cromwell turned upon the old woman and called her a witch. Then she picked up a pair of scissors and snipped off a lock of the crone's hair, ordering that it be burned. According to folklore, such an assault could sap so much power from a witch that Satan would abandon her. Stoutly denying Lady Cromwell's charge, the bewildered woman exclaimed, "Madam, why do you use me thus? I never did you any harm as yet." Those two words—*as yet*—would resonate in memory.

That same night, Lady Cromwell had her terrible dream of the cat and soon began to experience Throckmorton-style fits that lasted for more than a year. In early 1592, she died. In retrospect, it appeared to some that Mother Samuel had foreshadowed her enemy's death, but no charges were brought against her then. Henry Pickering, the girls' uncle and a Cambridge University don, had no doubt whatsoever that the old woman was a witch. She must confess and repent, he told her—otherwise, he would supply the fire and the wood with which to burn her at the stake, and "the children should blowe the coales." No match for such adversaries, and frightened of what might befall her, the old woman began to avoid the Throckmortons.

The girls meanwhile made the place a virtual bedlam, prattling like infants, poking their heads into the blazing fireplace, falling in and out of fits on a moment's notice. They talked obsessively about Mother Samuel and the spirit that, they agreed among themselves, was tormenting them at her bidding. This demon took a variety of forms, they said, but its most common avatar was a drab, dun-colored chicken. Perhaps frustrated by their victim's absence, in the late fall of 1592 the hysterical quintet was taken with a perverse fancy: They could be cured

only if Mother Samuel was with them. Without her physical presence, they warned, their disorder would only worsen. Mr. Throckmorton and Mother Samuel's husband, John, forced the old woman to agree, and she was duly installed in the enemy household.

It took the cruel girls only a few weeks to break their reluctant companion and seal her fate. Dogging her footsteps from morning until night, they threw fits and jabbered about the dun chicken. Day in and day out, the five hysterics repeated to their captive the exact day that she would confess—the Tuesday following Twelfth Night, in early January. Mother Samuel confessed well ahead of the girls' schedule.

A day before Christmas Eve, she asked Mr. Throckmorton's forgiveness for harming him and his children. "Master," she said, "I have forsaken my maker and given my soul to the devil." Having slept on her confession, however, she retracted it the next day. Mr. Throckmorton rejected the disclaimer and after years of indecision, instituted official proceedings against her. The implacable daughters then brought the fatal charge: Mother Samuel had used her witchcraft to murder Lady Susan Cromwell.

By now, the old woman had embraced the delusions that had imprisoned and broken her. She believed that the Throckmorton girls had been bewitched by *someone*—

herself, for all she could tell. To the authorities that questioned her, she affirmed that she had killed Lady Cromwell. To seal her pact with the devil, she had joined with him—in the guise of a man calling himself William Langland—in sexual intercourse, and Langland had given her the evil spirits with which to execute her malicious plans. There had been six demonic dun chickens in all, she confessed. Lady Cromwell's killer was named Catch, and his mate Pluck had bewitched the Throckmorton girls. The lot of them had pecked blood from her chin and often lived inside her body.

Even this was insufficient for the Throckmorton daughters. They broadened their accusations of witchcraft to include John Samuel and the hapless couple's pretty daughter, Agnes. On April 5, 1593, the three were tried and condemned to death by hanging—the jury was unmoved by John's and Agnes's protestations of innocence. The doomed trio passed into history as the Witches of Warboys.

But not everyone in Warboys believed that justice had been done. A few people grumbled that "fair words" had been used to trick a simple old woman into confessing crimes of which she was innocent. As for the Throckmorton girls who had played on adult fears to such effect, their fits vanished with the death of Mother Samuel. □

Condemned and hanged as a witch in 1593, the falsely accused Mother Samuel welcomes Satan with a wave of her wand in this illustration from a 1715 history of witchcraft. She is attended by demons in animal form.

Sealed Orders

If any members of the Congregationalist First Church of Charlestown, Massachusetts, were wont to doze during sermons, the sensational message delivered by the Reverend Jedidiah Morse on May 9, 1798, would have roused the drowsiest among them. A secret band of wicked, artful men, he warned his parishioners, had laid a plot to destroy every altar in Christendom and every legitimate government. Their emissaries were already at work in the United States, worming their way into schools, literary societies, political clubs, newspapers, the post office—indeed, any agency they could use to erode patriotism and religion.

The Order of the Illuminati, as the conspirators called themselves, had enjoyed the first fruits of their labor in France. Carefully orchestrating the course of the French Revolution, they had promised the people liberty and equality but, in a diabolically calculated turning of the tables, had given them instead bloody political strife and civil war. King Louis XVI had been beheaded, the Reverend Morse reminded his flock, and he noted with a certain reluctant sympathy that the Roman Catholic church had been expropriated and its priests murdered or driven into exile. Then, transformed into the engine of the Illuminati, France had gone to war, exporting regicide and impiety to other European countries.

The worshipers at the Charlestown church that spring day were among the first Americans to face the Illuminati threat: The book behind Morse's revelations had been published in the United States only a month earlier. James Robison, its author, was a highly respected Scottish scientist and mathematician, but he had cast empiricism to the winds in *Proofs of a Conspiracy Against All the Religions and Governments of Europe.* The result was a tapestry of facts woven on a paranoid's loom. The work's central figure, an innocuous Bavarian law professor named Adam Weishaupt, was portrayed by Robison as a sinister genius of enormous power.

A follower of such antiestablishment thinkers as the French author-philosopher Voltaire, Weishaupt viewed the Order of the Illuminati as a means of replacing Bavaria's church-state heirarchy with an egalitarian society based on reason. He was, however, no bloody revolutionary. He believed that if he and other like-minded rationalists worked in concert to promote liberal principles, tyranny and superstition would inevitably wither away.

Weishaupt organized the first Illuminati colony of five members in 1776, concentrating his recruiting efforts in Masonic lodges—at heart, social clubs where men could gather to argue politics and philosophy. From its beginnings in England in the latter part of the seventeenth century, Freemasonry had been a magnet to men of an intellectual and a liberal bent, who were drawn to the order's mystic trappings and vows of secrecy. Following the Masonic model, Weishaupt gave his order secrets and rituals of its own. Such trappings made the Illuminati more appealing to Masons; but they also imparted a suspect air to the organization.

The order had grown to perhaps 2,500 members by 1784, when the archconservative duke Karl Theodor became Bavaria's chief of state. He resolved to root out Weishaupt's creation, which he deemed seditious and immoral besides—one document confiscated in a raid on an Illuminato's house defended suicide and atheism, while another described a concoction that would induce abortion. In 1787, Karl Theodor pronounced the order's death knell: An Illuminato who recruited new members would be summarily put to the sword; recruits would forfeit all of their possessions and be banished forever from Bavaria. Weishaupt had seen trouble brewing and two weeks before the ban he fled to safety in Gotha, in what is now southern Germany. His secretive society evaporated behind him, and even he experienced a change of heart: When he died in 1830, Weishaupt was once again a Catholic.

James Robison picked up the threads of the Illuminati saga in the 1790s and added his convictions of conspiracy. Karl Theodor's edict, he asserted, had not destroyed the Order of the Illuminati after all. Its leaders, so skilled in stealth, had merely gone underground, where, like puppet masters behind a curtain, they had used their Masonic dupes to execute their revolutionary plans in France. They possessed secret weapons of their own invention, Robison charged, including a substance that "blinds or kills when spurted in the face" and a technique "for filling a bed-chamber with pestilential vapours."

New Englanders such as the Reverend Morse were primed to take Robison's chronicle of conspiracy at face value. When Morse delivered his sermon in the spring of 1798, anti-French feeling was already running high in the religious establishment and its political alter ego, the Federalist Party. Once enthusi-astic supporters of the French Revolution, they had turned violently against France after radicals seized control. Clergymen blamed imported French radicalism for the tide of religious skepticism then rising in New England. *Proofs of a Conspiracy* now persuaded them that the corrupting flood was no accident.

In the wake of the sensational alarm Morse raised, a storm of sermons broke from other New England pulpits, and newspapers joined in spreading Illuminati fever to every town and village. The editor of the influential *Porcupine's Gazette* declared that every living man should read *Proofs of a Conspiracy*

because "it unravels everything that appears mysterious in the progress of the French Revolution," and the *New York Spectator* informed its readers that they must choose, and quickly, between "INDEPENDENCE and SUBMISSION."

Robison's name was on the lips of every Independence Day orator that summer. In New Haven, President Timothy Dwight of Yale University catalogued the evils the Illuminati had in store for America: They would turn its churches into temples of reason, cast the Bible into a bonfire, grind Christian virtues underfoot, and make concubines of Christian women. On the same day, Timothy's brother Theodore told a Hartford audience that, if he were selecting likely candidates for an Illuminati lodge, "I should in the first place apply to Thomas Jefferson, Albert Gallatin, and their political associates." Gallatin was the liberal Democratic-Republican party's leader in the House of Representatives, and Jefferson, then serving as vice president, was the party's driving force. He was also a deist and a shameless defender of France. The *Connecticut Courant* called him "the foe of man" and an enemy of his own country.

But Jefferson was, as he so frequently was, in good company. Accusing fingers were also pointed at Tom Paine, who had earned the enmity of the orthodox for his harsh critique of religion in the recently published *The Age of Reason*. The *Porcupine's Gazette* revealed that an English-language edition of 15,000 had been printed in France and shipped to ◊

the United States—a French connection that, to some frightened Federalists, was tantamount to proof that Tom Paine was part of the Illuminati conspiracy.

The much-persecuted Quakers, properly known as the Society of Friends, were also singled out. They addressed one another as "friend," a practice smacking of Illuminati-style egalitarianism, and they espoused the "atheistical principle" of brotherly love. Republican political exiles belonging to the American Society of United Irishmen were likewise branded agents of the Illuminati. American Freemasonry escaped widespread opprobrium, however—it was led by the revered George Washington, and thousands of ministers and prominent men on both sides of the political fence were members.

Nearly a year passed, without a trace of an Illuminati cell or its Masonic foot soldiers. Then, as fear of the purported plot was beginning to subside, the tireless Reverend Morse mounted his pulpit once more. His sermon for April 25, 1799, claimed that he had "complete and indubitable proof" of the Illuminati influence in the United States. From fellow Federalist Oliver Wolcott, controller of the U.S. Treasury, Morse had received documents revealing that the Grand Orient—France's chief Masonic lodge—controlled a network of some sixteen American cells plus a seventeenth in Santo Domingo. Predictably, the vast majority of the members—some 1,700 in all, Morse estimated—were French emigrants. Although the documents were the routine business correspondence of a Masonic lodge, a determined reader such as Morse could find dark hints of conspiracy between the lines. For example, a passing reference to a new lodge in French dominated Santo Domingo, scene of a successful slave revolt, mentioned that it was called Perfect Equality—to Morse, a name redolent with insurrectionist intent. From there, it was only a short leap for the minister to conjure a French-led invasion launched from Santo Domingo to sow insurrection among American slaves.

As a wave of renewed anxiety swept New England's populace, the region's Democratic newspapers finally went on the attack. One editor suggested that, instead of preaching a "nine-penny sermon," Morse should have submitted his famous documents to the federal government. The Illuminati scare was, observed another journal, as bad as Salem's former obsession with witchcraft. Robison and his American acolytes were delivered a telling blow when a well-known German historian wrote that Europeans regarded *Proofs of a Conspiracy* as a farrago of falsehoods.

Still convinced that he was right, Morse sought to quiet his critics by investigating the membership of the Virginia Masonic lodge himself. He wrote to Virginia congressman Josiah Parker for information—and got an unwelcome reply. The members were indeed French, Parker wrote, but they were also upright, honest men and most certainly not conspirators. The congressman's testimonial evidently persuaded Morse that the conspiracy consuming him was, in fact, a fantasy of fear. Other true believers soon left off what Jefferson called their bedlamite ravings. By the end of 1799, New England's Illuminati panic, like the short-lived order itself, had disappeared. □

Tooth Wary

For years, public-health officials in the United States had been aware that, in terms of dental health at least, some American cities were more equal than others. In some communities, tooth decay was almost unknown—Hereford, Texas, for instance, billed itself as the Town Without a Toothache. The difference, researchers discovered in the late 1930s, was the amount of fluorine present in the water—the more fluorine, the less decay. Thus, they reasoned, raising the fluorine content of a city's water supply to about one part per million should decrease the incidence of childhood tooth decay. But caution was in order: Fluorine, a pale yellow relative of chlorine gas, is highly reactive—and, in sufficient concentrations, a lethal poison.

In 1945, officials in the Hudson River valley town of Newburgh, New York, announced their plans to begin adding fluorine to the water supply. Newburgh, they explained, was to take part in an experiment to determine whether the addition of a fluorine salt—sodium fluoride—would retard tooth decay among children, without adverse side effects to the general population. Nearby Kingston, where the water would remain unfluoridated, was to serve as the control. A parallel study was undertaken in two Michigan cities, Grand Rapids and Muskegon. The health of residents in fluoridated and unfluoridated communities would be compared after ten years.

Almost immediately, residents of Newburgh began to report such disturbing symptoms as dizziness, "eroded throats," nausea, headaches, and back pain—all attributed to the treated water. Local businesses found the water to be unsuitable as well; a bottling plant manager said that the water was too fizzy, while dye workers claimed that they could no longer match colors properly. Newburgh's public-health and water officials had little sympathy: The equipment needed to feed sodium fluoride into the water supply had been delayed; fluoridation was still a month away. But these early jitters set the tone for the often irrational debate that rages to the present day.

The results obtained in fluoridated Newburgh and Grand Rapids showed a significant reduction in tooth decay compared to unfluoridated Kingston and Muskegon; indeed, Muskegon opted to fluoridate well before the ten-year experiment was over. As cities across America moved to imitate these early successes, however, they ran into a pervasive, unreasoning fear of fluoride. Frightened residents reported everything from dead goldfish to asthma attacks and ruined photographic negatives.

Exhaustive studies by the U.S. Public Health Service and other agencies showed no evidence that there were any significant harmful side effects to low-level fluoride ex- ◊

Women bearing picket signs protest outside Kensico Reservoir in September 1965 as city officials open the valves that would add one part per million of sodium fluoride to New York City's water supply.

posure; in fact, many people lived in areas where the water was naturally rich in fluorine. To many Americans, however, such studies were irrelevant compared to what they saw as an entire population being force-fed a poison. The *National Fluoridation News* claimed that fluoridation in Grand Rapids was responsible for a "large increase" in deaths from kidney disorders and brain abnormalities. In Hartford, Connecticut, fluoridation opponent Lillian Van de Vere appeared at meetings on the issue with her face covered in bandages, explaining that she had broken out after drinking coffee made with fluoridated water. Beyond such unsupported assertions of physical harm, the controversy turned on the matter of human rights.

Many who opposed fluoridation were motivated only by a vague fear that their freedom was eroded when the government introduced a chemical—any chemi-

cal—into their water supply. They viewed the procedure as a veiled threat to their personal liberty; the idea was simply "un-American." One opponent explained that he cared little whether the chemical helped or hurt him. "What I resent," he said, "is a bureaucrat forcing the stuff down my throat." Still others were more concerned that fluoridation resembled a kind of "mass medication," a way of dosing the multitudes that might be the precursor of socialized medicine—in the 1950s, a fearsome symptom of a Communist takeover.

To many, fluoridation was nothing less than a "method of Red warfare"—a Communist plot to drug America into submission. A speaker at an American Legion convention in New York State claimed fluoridation was a "secret Russian revolutionary technique to deaden our minds, slow our reflexes, and gradually kill our will to resist aggression." According to the antifluoride *Americanism Bulletin*, flouridation had already been put to this purpose by Germany's Weimar regime and had been used by the Russians to obtain phony confessions from prisoners. Fluoridation, the *Bulletin* went on, was "more dangerous than atomic bombs." Opposition groups in La Crosse, Wisconsin, and Iron Mountain, Michigan, even suggested that the U.S. Public Health Service, the major government sponsor of the program, was itself a Communist tool.

Such opposition slowed, but could

not stop, the adoption of fluoridation across the United States. In 1956, some 34 million Americans either had or were slated for fluoridated water supplies—about 20 percent of the total population. By 1978, *Consumer Reports* could chide those who had kept the debate alive, calling it a "fake controversy" whose survival represented "one of the major triumphs of quackery over science in our generation." Today, nearly four decades later, some 53 percent of a much larger population has fluoridated water. Still, a good portion of the country has abstained; the 100 million or so citizens with untreated water include residents of such major cities as Los Angeles, San Diego, and San Antonio. Many Americans still fear being poisoned or compromised by their government.

And the argument is far from over. In 1990, the results of an intensive study conducted by the Public Health Service's National Toxicology Program caused a new flurry of debate: Sodium fluoride, the tests suggested, may have produced a slight increase in osteosarcoma—a rare type of bone cancer—in male rats. In the experiment, one of fifty rats fed water laced with forty-five-parts-per-million sodium fluoride—forty-five times the dosage in fluoridated water supplies—developed the cancer, as did four of eighty male rats fed seventy-nine-parts-per-million fluoridated water. When a panel of outside scientists called the conclusion "equivocal," both sides claimed victory. The evidence lacked the statistical significance to propel changes in the status quo but was enough to rekindle the endless debate. As one expert noted, "This has become a religion on both sides." □

Antifluoride radiologist Frederick B. Exner shows a photo of teeth he called "moderately" fluoridated.

MODERATE FLUOROSIS FROM 1.0 P.P.M.
CONFIRMED BY DR. H.T.DEAN

First Lady Eleanor Roosevelt's support of leaders such as Mary McLeod Bethune *(far left)* fueled rumors that black servants devoted to her had laid a plot to discomfit white employers.

Pale Fantasies

However firm its apparent hold, a society's ruling class keeps an anxious eye fixed on the underclasses for signs of rebellion. In 1942, a noxious fantasy spread among white southerners in the United States: Treacherous black domestics were mounting an assault on the existing order. The conspiracy was said to be under the control of so-called Eleanor Clubs, which had been organized all over the South, from Virginia to Louisiana. The supposed leader and financial benefactor of the clubs was First Lady Eleanor Roosevelt, whose advocacy of black causes had already infuriated many southerners. It was charged that the liberal troublemaker inspired near-religious devotion among club members, who called her "Great White Mother" or "Great White Angel." The motto of the Eleanor Clubs: "A white woman in every kitchen by Christmas."

According to the fiction, the club instructed each member to demand higher pay and to refuse double duty. A cook would not clean, and a maid would not cook. Servants were to be called Miss or Mrs., join their employers at the dining table, and use the front instead of the back door. If an employer objected or betrayed a dislike for Mrs. Roosevelt, the servant would resign her job and add the employer's name to the club boycott list.

Inconveniencing white households was the least of the evils that were said to emanate from the Eleanor Clubs. Something else, something dreadful, was whispered that spoke to an underlying fear and hostility: Eleanor Club members were stashing away ice picks and butcher knives in preparation for a violent rebellion. In Florida, there was talk of a Roosevelt-inspired race riot threatening the state.

The predictions of disorder and riot prompted a number of police departments and the Federal Bureau of Investigation to search out Eleanor Clubs, but they came up empty-handed. As time passed and maids and cooks went about their daily business as usual and no bloody attacks took place, white anxieties died down. In 1943, the Eleanor Club madness was gone. □

*B*illed as the oldest professional rumor service in the field, W. Howard Downey & Associates (with branches located in the cities of New York, Atlanta, Chicago, and Toronto) offered to spread false tales on a moment's notice, using nothing but old-fashioned word of mouth—for or against a product, a person, or an issue—for as little as fifteen dollars per day, plus expenses.

Gas Feigns

The epidemic of hysteria that enveloped the town of Mattoon, Illinois, felled its first victims on the night of Friday, September 1, 1944. A woman identified only as Mrs. A was in her bedroom, according to her report to the police, when someone raised the window and sprayed her with a sweet-smelling gas that caused the brief, partial paralysis of her legs. Her daughter had also been sprayed by the pump-wielding intruder, she reported. The police searched in vain for the perpetrator, but two hours later, the victim's husband called to say that he had just come home and had spotted a man running away from the bedroom window.

Four more victims stepped forward after reading in the Mattoon *Daily Journal-Gazette* that an "anesthetic prowler" was on the loose. One couple reinterpreted their recent night of digestive distress. They had blamed their symptoms on hot dogs but now believed that they had been gassed as they slept. After a two-day lull, there was a spate of reported attacks on Mattoon residents. According to the police blotter, the demented gasser struck as often as seven times a night, flitting about the town at will. Terrified Mattoonites wondered who would be the next target of his gas, variously said to smell like gardenias or like cheap perfume. Not even house pets escaped him, for it appeared that three dogs might also have suffered attack. None of the pets had barked, and their victimized owners took that as evidence that the gasser had sprayed the animals into silence.

Despite the boldness of the assailant's forays, he was maddeningly elusive. Posses of armed men and boys roved backyards at night until the police asked them to disband, lest some innocent householder be shot. The state police were called in, and fear of phantoms ratcheted up with each issue of the *Journal-Gazette*, where the mysterious anesthetist pushed even war news to the inside pages. The besieged town's predicament was reported across the country. When servicemen from Mattoon read about what was going on in overseas editions of the military newspaper *Stars and Stripes*, they wrote home for news of their womenfolk.

In fact, twenty-six of the twenty-

eight reputed human victims had been women. The symptoms—paralysis, nausea and vomiting, palpitations, a dry mouth and throat, and occasionally a burning sensation around the mouth—were dramatic but transient: They disappeared so quickly that only four people saw a doctor. All four were diagnosed as textbook cases of hysteria. Little was said officially about the subconscious impulses that made the patients so receptive to the phantom anesthetist delusion.

As days passed and no one could lay hands on the mad gasser, the townspeople began to doubt his existence. When no further reports of gassing followed the final one, on September 12, the *Journal-Gazette* ceased its breathless stories. The threat that just a few days earlier had seemed so real began to dissolve. The telephone fell silent at the local police station, and, after a fortnight's madness, reason returned to Mattoon. □

Appetite for Anxiety

An anonymous typewritten leaflet—passed from friend to friend, stuffed into mailboxes, and posted in schools, factories, offices, and clubs since 1976—has infected France with a fear of food, long a national obsession. The leaflet warns that an appalling conspiracy threatens the nation's health. Food and beverage manufacturers, with the government's complicity, are peddling products containing additives claimed by the anonymous author to cause cancer and other serious disorders. The tract goes on to say that the evidence of this nefarious activity has been willfully ignored, even suppressed.

Whether the attack was powered by paranoia or cool-headed deception is a mystery. Whatever the motive of its author, the leaflet claims as its origin a famous center for cancer research in the Paris suburb of Villejuif. To the layperson, the leaflet reads like an authentic scientific laboratory report. It is replete with impressively authentic numbers—the three-digit E (for Europe) codes that Western European manufacturers use routinely to identify additives on food labels for their international, multilanguage market. But there reality stops. According to the one-page document, of 100 additives blessed by the government, 17 cause cancer and 27 more are suspect. Moreover, virtually no part of the body is immune to some ill effect from the substances, from rashes to gallstones to an inability to digest ice cream.

Exhorting consumers to boycott products poisoned by these additives, the Villejuif leaflet indicts various brands of soft drinks, mustard, orange juice, apéritifs, and other food and drink. A favorite cheese of children, parents are told, is laden with a potent carcinogen. "THINK OF YOUR CHILDREN'S HEALTH!" the leaflet exclaims.

The Villejuif cancer institute, the French Ministry of Health, and unhappy corporations singled out for mention have denied the leaflet for years. Studiously rejecting the denials, consumers have retyped, revised, photocopied, and passed on the flyer. The original's progeny have been read by members of at least half of the nearly 21 million households in France. How financially painful the resulting boycott has been is impossible to pinpoint, but surveys suggest that the leaflet has persuaded more than a fifth of its readers to shun at least some of the brands it condemns.

In recent years the Villejuif leaflet has gone international and intercontinental. Translated versions are being passed from hand to hand in Great Britain, Germany, and Italy, and in the Middle East and Africa. Given this growing currency, the Villejuif leaflet would seem to possess a kind of authority—and yet it discredits itself. Its "Most Dangerous" slot goes to the substance coded E330, used in some cheeses and beverages, and naturally abundant, especially in such fruit as oranges and lemons: citric acid, a key element in all animal and plant metabolism. □

Tropical Storm

For a few short months, Brooklyn bottler Eric Miller savored the success of his newest soft drink, Tropical Fantasy. A bargain at half the price of well-known soft drinks, it was soon selling briskly in New York City's poor neighborhoods.

Miller's strategy of concentrating on areas where a low price would appeal to thirsty customers paid off nicely, and the chance of Tropical Fantasy overtaking its competitors looked bright. But to Miller's dismay, sales hit the brakes, then went into reverse. He soon learned why from grocery-store owners: An unsigned flyer being passed around was turning customers against Tropical Fantasy, along with several other inexpensive brands. Their actual manufacturer, the flyer asserted, was the Ku Klux Klan, which was lacing its sodas with stimulants that would render males sterile. Klansmen, it suggested further, had designed their sales plan cunningly to reach its intended victims. "They are only put in stores in Harlem and minority ar-

eas," the handbill noted. "You won't find them down town. Look around." A convincing touch was the totally false claim that the television news program "20/20" had reported on the link between the Klan and Tropical Fantasy.

Fearing that they were targets of a genocidal plot, former customers turned against Tropical Fantasy. A few were so furious that they went after store owners and route men with baseball bats and bottles.

By the spring of 1991, the scurrilous report had slashed Tropical Fantasy sales by 60 percent over the preceding fall. But the embattled bottler fought back. He circulated a flyer of his own defending his soda and gave interviews to radio stations. The federal Food and Drug Administration pronounced the notion of sterility stimulants "outlandish." A Klan imperial wizard, James Farrands of Sanford, North Carolina, also weighed in, declaring, "The KKK is not in the bottling business." Miller also got a big boost from New York's black mayor David Dinkins, who appeared on television enjoying a cold Tropical Fantasy.

Eric Miller bested his unknown enemies—possibly some rival soda sellers—with his antismear campaign and broad support. No longer fearing a conspiracy, customers came back to give Miller's tale a happy ending. By the fall of 1991, the business of slaking New Yorkers' thirst was once more turning a profit. □

Extra Ingredients

Preparing food for the public carries the risk that sometime, somewhere, something will go horribly amiss—and justify a persistent human fear that purity must inevitably be poisoned. When the moment comes, either in reality or in the fantasies of consumers, anxieties about contamination fly out into the world on the swift wings of rumor. Sometimes the incident is actual—vermin may really have been found in soft-drink bottles or southern-fried. More often, such tales are the stuff of myth, of stories spun by frightened parents and their playful children. Hardly anything is safe—not even something as innocuously inert as bubble gum.

For example, when Bubble Yum was first introduced in 1976, it was such a success that its manufacturer cut back advertising in order to meet production demands. But by the spring of the following year, sales had slipped noticeably in the New York metropolitan area, for reasons entirely beyond the company's control. People had somehow become afraid that the gum contained a nasty extra ingredient: spider eggs. "One kid came in and said that she heard of a girl who fell asleep chewing it and woke up with spider webs on her face," a Long Island store owner told the *Wall Street Journal*. Another report claimed that nine youngsters had died. The stories were completely fantastical—the product, no doubt, of schoolyard tall tales. The fear, however, was very real. Even after an aggressive and expensive campaign to dispel the fiction, the makers of Bubble Yum had to ac- ◊

it has become a legend of the fried-chicken trade. Children's zest for risky undertakings has also produced its share of food fear. Pop Rocks offers a case in point.

First introduced in test markets in 1975, these fruit-flavored nuggets "fizzled" with a small amount of carbonation when ingested, delighting small consumers with an internal sound some likened to a storm. Although it had been tested extensively and found safe, the combustive candy was so newfangled that it alarmed residents in Seattle. The Food and Drug Administration had to set up a telephone hot line there to assure anxious parents that the fizzing candy would not cause children to choke.

Nevertheless, among children wildly imaginative stories arose about the perils of eating Pop Rocks: Mixing the candy with carbonated drinks would cause the stomach to explode, some whispered with evident satisfaction. According to playground lore, that combination had already killed a little boy known as "Mikey" who appeared in television commercials for a vitamin-enriched breakfast cereal offered by another manufacturer. At the parent company of Pop Rocks, the corporate communications department was flooded with calls from people asking about the exploded tyke, and sales of the effervescent sweet plummeted. Contrary to rumor, the winsome preschooler survived to star in yet another cereal commercial and go to college, from which he graduated in 1991. □

knowledge that customer confidence in the New York area was "never completely restored."

Hardly had the spider-eggs fantasy been quieted than public relations officials at burger-giant McDonald's held a press conference in Atlanta to reassure their anxious customers. They were not, they said emphatically, using any kind of "protein additives" in their beef patties. The company's spokespeople failed to be more specific about the additive in question. The public was less fastidious. Some 75 percent of those surveyed in Atlanta and Cincinnati had heard—and many believed—that earthworms had been added to the hamburgers. After a serious, but temporary, decline in McDonald's sales, the squirmy tale was laid to rest.

Every publicly purveyed product can become the focus of such unjustified contamination fears. In Belgium, beer drinkers switched their allegiances following groundless charges that a certain brand caused headaches and impotence. In 1981, the owner of a British Kentucky Fried Chicken franchise offered a £1,000 reward to anyone who could explain the genesis of a story that a customer had found a fried rat in a bucket of chicken—a tale that has surfaced so often that

Infernal Dialogue

Unhappy with the authoritarian regime of France's emperor Napoleon III, Paris lawyer Maurice Joly wrote a satire in which two posthumous voices from different eras discussed despots. Niccolò di Bernardo Machiavelli, the kingmaking philosopher of the Italian Renaissance, advanced the case for political expediency and sly statesmanship; Charles-Louis de Secondat, baron de La Brède et de Montesquieu, France's clear-thinking eighteenth-century libertarian philosopher, argued the liberal line. *Dialogue aux Enfers entre Montesquieu et Machiavel* (Dialogue in Hell between Montesquieu and Machiavelli) was published in Geneva in 1864, then in Brussels—and confiscated as soon as it trickled into France. Joly was given fifteen months in prison for his thinly veiled criticism, and his life thereafter was a succession of failures that he finally found intolerable. In 1879, he killed himself, not knowing that he had inadvertently achieved a kind of immortality after all. His creation would be revived and widely read, but in a monstrous form. Although it said nothing about races or religions, it would be used to fashion an instrument of insane prejudice, nightmarish persecution, and the murder of millions: the forgery known as *The Protocols of the Elders of Zion.*

Purportedly the confidential minutes of a secret Jewish conclave held in Basel, Switzerland, late in the nineteenth century, the slim pamphlet first appeared in a St. Petersburg newspaper, *Znamya* (Banner), in 1903. The editor, Pavolachi

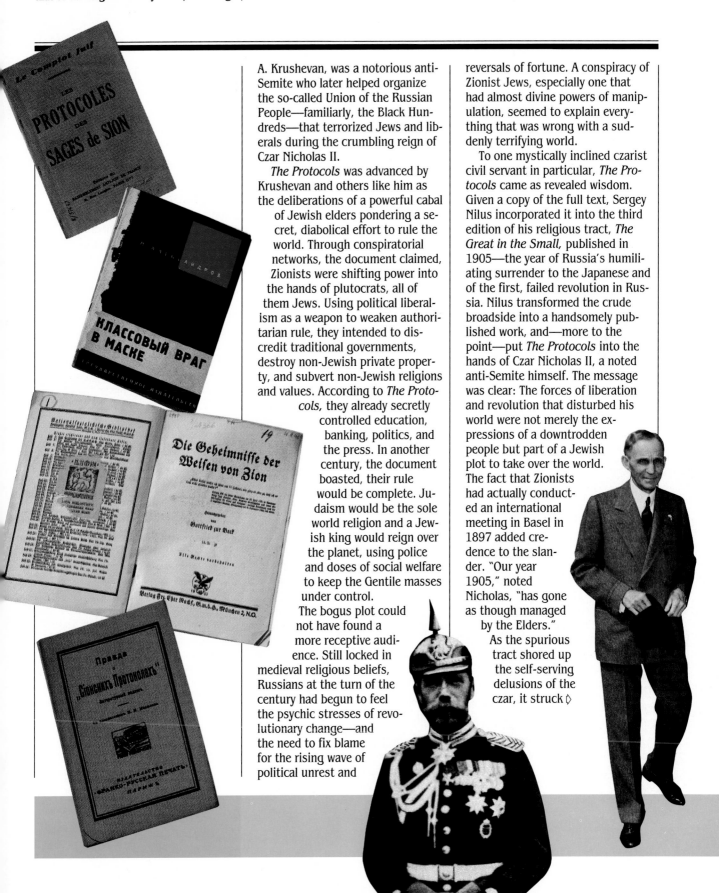

A. Krushevan, was a notorious anti-Semite who later helped organize the so-called Union of the Russian People—familiarly, the Black Hundreds—that terrorized Jews and liberals during the crumbling reign of Czar Nicholas II.

The Protocols was advanced by Krushevan and others like him as the deliberations of a powerful cabal of Jewish elders pondering a secret, diabolical effort to rule the world. Through conspiratorial networks, the document claimed, Zionists were shifting power into the hands of plutocrats, all of them Jews. Using political liberalism as a weapon to weaken authoritarian rule, they intended to discredit traditional governments, destroy non-Jewish private property, and subvert non-Jewish religions and values. According to *The Protocols*, they already secretly controlled education, banking, politics, and the press. In another century, the document boasted, their rule would be complete. Judaism would be the sole world religion and a Jewish king would reign over the planet, using police and doses of social welfare to keep the Gentile masses under control.

The bogus plot could not have found a more receptive audience. Still locked in medieval religious beliefs, Russians at the turn of the century had begun to feel the psychic stresses of revolutionary change—and the need to fix blame for the rising wave of political unrest and

reversals of fortune. A conspiracy of Zionist Jews, especially one that had almost divine powers of manipulation, seemed to explain everything that was wrong with a suddenly terrifying world.

To one mystically inclined czarist civil servant in particular, *The Protocols* came as revealed wisdom. Given a copy of the full text, Sergey Nilus incorporated it into the third edition of his religious tract, *The Great in the Small,* published in 1905—the year of Russia's humiliating surrender to the Japanese and of the first, failed revolution in Russia. Nilus transformed the crude broadside into a handsomely published work, and—more to the point—put *The Protocols* into the hands of Czar Nicholas II, a noted anti-Semite himself. The message was clear: The forces of liberation and revolution that disturbed his world were not merely the expressions of a downtrodden people but part of a Jewish plot to take over the world. The fact that Zionists had actually conducted an international meeting in Basel in 1897 added credence to the slander. "Our year 1905," noted Nicholas, "has gone as though managed by the Elders."

As the spurious tract shored up the self-serving delusions of the czar, it struck ◊

Faked by Russian czarist police, *The Protocols* attracted such clients as *(from left)* Adolf Hitler, Nazi Adolf Eichmann, Joseph Stalin, the Ku Klux Klan, Egypt's Gamal Abdel Nasser, and Soviet president Leonid Brezhnev.

to the very core of Nilus's own disturbed spirit. A visiting Frenchman described Nilus reading to him from *The Protocols* one night in the lay quarters of the monastery at Optina Pustyn. "He read for a long time," the visitor recalled. "I felt a sort of fear. It was nearly midnight. The gaze, the voice, the reflexlike gestures—everything about Nilus gave me the feeling that we were walking on the edge of an abyss and that at any moment his reason might disintegrate into madness."

So strong was Nilus's belief that he ignored the real possibility that the document was fake. "Let us admit that *The Protocols* are spurious," he told a visitor. "But can't God use them to unmask the iniquity that is being prepared?" Accordingly, he reprinted them in the 1911, 1912, and 1917 editions of his popular book. There, but for the

1917 Russian Revolution, the matter might have stayed.

As the Red revolt declined into a punishing civil war, however, émigré czarists—White Russians—took copies of the spurious document to the outside world, using the arguments in *The Protocols* to demonstrate a link between the Bolsheviks and a Jewish conspiracy—and to persuade other countries to aid the disintegrating autocracy. By chance, when the Russian royal family was murdered at Ekaterinburg (later Sverdlovsk) on July 17, 1918, the czarina had only three books with her: volume 1 of Tolstoy's *War & Peace,* a Bible—and a recent copy of *The Great in the Small.* This, and the wave of White Russian refugees driven westward by the new regime, helped make Nilus's volume world-famous.

As they had in Russia, *The Protocols* found an eager readership in a Europe shattered by the First World War. In 1920, German and Polish versions appeared. When a British edition arrived, even the staid *Times* of London was moved. "Have we been struggling these tragic years to blow up and extirpate the secret organization of German world dominion," asked an editorial, "only to find

beneath it another, more dangerous because more secret?"

Then, in 1921, *Times* reporter Philip Graves was given a small weathered volume by a man he did not identify, who had obtained the book from an émigré officer formerly with the Okhrana—the czarist secret police. On the back cover was stamped: *Joli.* It was Maurice Joly's long-lost dialogue, the armature around which *The Protocols* had been fabricated. "I did not believe that Sergey Nilus's *Protocols* were authentic," wrote Graves. "But I could not have believed, had I not seen, that the writer who supplied Nilus with his originals was a careless and shameless plagiarist."

Virtually all of *The Protocols,* he revealed, had been lifted from the Machiavelli role in Joly's satire, then crudely laced with contemporary references to make the text play in Russia. From various clues in the purloined text, scholars have concluded that the first transformation of Joly's booklet may have occurred as early as 1894, three years before the Zionist congress in Basel, and been intended less as an anti-Semitic tract than an attack on Sergey Witte, Russia's

popular, progressive minister of finance. This adaptation has been attributed to a French political journalist, Elie de Cyon—French for Zion—who used Joly's Machiavellian arguments to make Witte seem a tool of Zionist plotters.

In a distinctly Russian gambit, however, de Cyon's version was evidently stolen by Pyotr Ivanovich Rachkovsky, the brilliant, conniving director of the Okhrana's Paris-based foreign branch—acting on Witte's orders. Rachkovsky, recognizing a bombshell when he saw it, appears then to have had someone amplify the anti-Semitic rant in the document and to have passed it to other hard-line conservatives back home—Sergey Nilus among them. Rachkovsky died in 1911, ignorant of the terrible monster he had let loose in the world. Even Nilus, who died on the first day of 1930, never knew that his work had spread around the globe.

Graves's establishing the real provenance of *The Protocols* discredited the vicious document in Great Britain—but nowhere else. The plagiarized lie had acquired a life of its own, nourished by a grow-

ing sense that the turmoil of the times must have a human agent. *The Protocols* was used by Arab nations to fuel opposition to a Jewish state in Palestine. In the United States, auto industrialist Henry Ford published them in his virulently anti-Semitic Dearborn, Michigan, newspaper. (Public pressure finally forced him to apologize for the paper's policies.) Ironically, Soviet dictator Joseph Stalin applied *The Protocols* in his own relentless persecution of the Jews.

Nowhere, however, did *The Protocols* find more favor than in the propaganda and belief of Nazi leader Adolf Hitler, whose delusions were permeated by the idea of a Jewish conspiracy. Christianity itself, Hitler confided to close friends, was part of the fiendish plot. "I have read *The Protocols of the Elders of Zion*," he once told an interviewer. "It simply appalled me. The stealthiness of the enemy, and his ubiquity! I saw at once that we must copy it—in our own way, of course." After Hitler took power in 1933, the fraudulent document became a basic school textbook—and a founding rationale for the Nazis' enduring horror, the virtual extermination of the European Jews. Wherever there have been fears to be played

upon since, *The Protocols* has been trotted out. It was echoed in anti-Zionist attacks by the late Soviet president Leonid Brezhnev, who hinted darkly at a world Zionist plot before his army's 1968 invasion of Czechoslovakia, and it was endorsed by Egyptian president Gamal Abdel Nasser, the late king Faisal of Saudi Arabia, and a host of other Middle Eastern leaders. They have been used to fan anti-Semitism in Japan and Latin America, and they remain a perennial favorite of such American groups as the Ku Klux Klan and Aryan Nation. Even Russia's *glasnost* has helped propagate the lie: In the newly opened society where they began, *The Protocols* is once again available in printed form.

Still, to see the real double-thinking madness illuminated by the forgery, one must go back to Adolf Hitler and his henchmen. "At his trial at Jerusalem in 1961," wrote historian Norman Cohn of Adolf Eichmann, the administrator of the Nazi's so-called Final Solution, he "maintained that Hitler himself was nothing but a pawn and a marionette in the hands of 'the Satanic international high-finance of the western world'—meaning, of course, the mysterious, undiscoverable and omnipotent Elders of Zion." □

Girl Talk

In early May 1969, a tale at once alarming and titillating began to circulate among high-school girls in Orléans, France. In the basement of the Maison Dorphée, a popular boutique catering to chic teenagers, the police had supposedly discovered two drugged and unconscious customers and taken them to the hospital. Regaining consciousness, according to the tale, they reported that as they were trying on clothes in a curtained dressing room, they had been injected by hypodermic needle with a drug. The sinister intent: to smuggle the victims to Caracas, Buenos Aires, and other foreign cities, where they would be forced into prostitution.

The Dorphée was not the only trap for unsuspecting young customers—a network of white slavers was, the girls whispered, operating out of six Orléans boutiques. One was a shoe shop, where drugs were administered by needles hidden in the heels of shoes.

When the white-slave fantasy reached the ears of adults, many of them proved as gullible as the teenagers. Mothers and teachers warned the girls to keep away from the dangerous shops and stay alert to would-be seducers. Yet, given the peril supposedly stalking Orléans's young women, the police were curiously inert.

The first official to get wind of the rumor was a public prosecutor, who had it from several secretaries in his department. Bowing to their wishes, he called the chief of police. The two men agreed that a white-slave operation under their

noses was a ridiculous notion, but the chief made a few discreet inquiries about the shop owners. He then dismissed the affair from his mind, completely satisfied that nothing was amiss. But he was utterly unaware of the rising pitch of anxiety in his town.

Far from allaying people's fears, the silence of officials and the press was given a vicious interpretation: They must have been bought off with Jewish money to keep quiet, for five of the six shops were owned by Jews. The town's chief criminal investigator, for instance, was said to have received some two million dollars for looking the other way. Even the Roman Catholic church was suspected of complicity in the abductions. Absurd elaborations were eagerly lapped up. Tunnels, it was said, linked the basements of the shops and led to the Loire River, where boats waited to whisk the captives away.

A fearsome fantasy's hapless target is often the last to hear it, and so it was in Orléans. Mr. Henri Licht, the Dorphée's owner, had received several anonymous telephone calls that were at once offensive and mystifying; one caller, for instance, asked him for "fresh meat." Not until May 23, weeks af-

ter the evil story's inception, did a friend spell out the alleged white-slavery plot to Licht. The vilified shop owners quickly banded together in order to lodge a complaint with the police.

Their complaint came just as the abduction madness peaked. May 31 was a Saturday, Orléans's traditional market day when people flocked to the city to shop and gossip, and word of the white slavers raced like wildfire through the crowded streets. Shocking new details flew among the alarmed and scandalized shoppers: Sixty women had been abducted, and the white slavers were now using submarines as well as boats to spirit them out of Orléans! Hostile knots of people, some of them muttering anti-Semitic remarks, gathered outside the boutiques, whose usual stream of customers had virtually dried up. The resolute shop owners kept their doors open, though one woman recalled that she was braced for an attack from an angry mob.

Fortunately, no assault materialized, and a controversial election on Sunday shifted people's attention from white slavery to politics. Nevertheless, the market-day pandemonium galvanized public leaders to squash the rumor quickly. On Mon-

Boutique shoppers in this section of Orléans, France, were falsely said to be kidnapped by white slavers.

day, local newspapers pronounced the affair an odious calumny on innocent businessmen. Labor-union officials, the Chamber of Commerce, and the Roman Catholic bishop quickly followed suit, and Orléans's madness was soon being roundly denounced in newspapers and magazines all over the country. A handful of true believers clung stubbornly to the tale, but most of Orléans's citizens regained their senses. Within a week, the six shops had their old customers back, as if nothing had ever happened. Like some nasty fog, the tale of perversion and vice had dissipated.

But not forever. A year later, tales of a cabal of white slavers using clothing stores as a cover swept through the town of Amiens. French sociologist Edgar Morin, head of a six-person team that studied the Orléans panic, discovered that dressing-room disappearances had been the talk of Marseilles in 1959. Even then, the tale had been far from new. Maniacs had supposedly attacked women in a Parisian department store in 1922, and Morin found evidence that the story had made the rounds almost a century earlier. Nor was the Amiens avatar the myth's last appearance. It surfaced in at least twenty French towns during the 1970s and 1980s.

What precipitated the outbreaks was usually a mystery, but in a nice bit of sleuthing Morin pinpointed the immediate inspiration of the Orléans madness. A week before its onset, the newest issue of the pulp magazine *Noir et Blanc* had run what purported to be a news story of a recent dressing-room drugging in Grenoble. In fact, the magazine had lifted the account almost word for word from a sensational collection called *Sex Slavery*. □

That Old Devil Moon

To most people, the emblem of a cheerily anthropomorphized moon and a throw of stars was pleasingly old-fashioned. The crescent man in the moon, drawn in the elegant style that was the fashion a century ago, beamed complacently beneath the glow of stars in the logo of the Procter & Gamble Company, America's largest purveyor of household products. But to some religious fundamentalists, the stylized moon and stars represented the enemy. Certain elements in the logo, the fundamentalists believed, were proof that the thriving company had done a deal with the devil. In the 1980s, they began to express their fears in the form of product boycotts and an energetic whispering campaign, calculated to bring down the demon they discerned in the time-tested design.

In fact, the trademark had begun in the middle of the last century, when Cincinnati dockhands painted Procter & Gamble boxes with a crude cross so that workers who could not read could identify them. Over time, the cross evolved into a circled star, which became a constellation of thirteen, honoring the first American colonies. By 1882, a crescent moon, wearing the benevolent face and swirling beard and hair then in vogue for moon men, had been added to the design, and the emblem had become the

company's corporate signature on almost everything it owned or sold.

But, after a quiet century of branding a host of products, the logo was suddenly perceived as something evil. As though from nowhere, fears began to be expressed that the emblem was not what it seemed. The moon and stars, some people said at first, indicated that the company had been taken over by the Unification Church of the Reverend Sun Myung Moon—a man and church then regarded with dark suspicion by a number of Americans. Two years later, however, the Procter & Gamble insignia had taken on a much more disturbing aspect. The thirteen stars, some religious leaders pointed out, could be connected to create three sixes— 666, the sign, according to the Bible's Revelation 13, of the Beast. Likewise, they said, the stylishly executed curlicues in the man in the moon's beard looked like trios of sixes. Allegations of Satan-worship began in Mississippi, then gained a stronghold in the east as ministers broadcast the frightening news ▷

from their pulpits. Fundamentalist groups distributed flyers in front of schools and stores asking Christians to boycott Procter & Gamble's products, claiming that the company donated ten percent of its profits to devil worshipers. In 1982, followers handed out leaflets claiming the beleaguered giant's president had appeared on several popular television talk shows, where he had admitted his support of Satanism. Although neither he nor anyone else from Procter & Gamble had ever appeared on any of the programs—and could prove it—the company was deluged with telephone calls about its alleged Satanism.

Processing some 15,000 calls a month, Procter & Gamble responded with mailings to 48,000 southern churches. Each packet contained a brief history of the logo and a statement from the Phil Donahue television show that read: "It never happened! Anyone who claims to have seen such a broadcast is lying! Anyone repeating the rumor is bearing false witness!" Religious leader Jerry Falwell was called upon to help dispel the fear. "The only way to stop this is for pastors to inform their congregations that the whole thing is a farce," Falwell told the world. Instead of attacking the company's logo, he said, people "could make better use of their time fighting real and serious problems in our society."

Finally, when even such evangelical help failed to damp the dread of Satan, the company turned to law. Using private investigators to ferret out the sources of the devil-worship stories, Procter & Gamble filed and settled fourteen libel suits against suspected individuals, among them a few small competitors whose interest may not have been entirely religious. After lengthy litigation, Procter & Gamble won $75,000 in a ruling against two door-to-door competitors in Kansas, but it was a small victory in a continuing war. Still plagued with religiously inspired boycotts, the company announced in 1985 that it would phase out the man-in-the-moon logo on packaging but retain it for corporate use. Even that was not enough. Finally, in 1991, Procter & Gamble redesigned its logo—slightly. Now the stars are a bit smaller, and the man in the moon, still smiling, has straight hair that cannot curl into satanic sixes. □

Inside Track

To the very religious, the fearsome voice of evil rises everywhere—a cat may mew of unspeakable things, the sibilant promises of serpents may tempt one to sin. What, then, might one hear in the repetitive, often unintelligible chants of modern rock musicians? To many fundamentalists, the guttural howls and murmurs of such music, speaking as it does of violence, drugs, love, and death, must be a vehicle for Satan. His voice, they maintain, has been injected into the pulsing lyrics. In order to hear the devil, one need only play the music backward—and listen.

Sure enough, when some songs are played backward, something that might be that other, awful voice begins to become audible. Parts of the song "Stairway to Heaven," for example, sound something like "Here's to my sweet Satan." Other reversed lyrics seem to say such things as "Satan, Satan, Satan, he is God," or "I sing because I live with Satan," or "On, Satan, move in our voices." With such slogans, many people fear, rock musicians deliberately lure the young and innocent toward the abyss.

The technique called backward masking mixes reversed phrases into the complex layers of sound tracks that make up modern rock. When the record is played forward, the secret message is mere background noise; played backward, some maintain, it becomes the voice of Satan. Believers in the satanic content of rock music argue that back masking inserts subliminal messages into the music that the subconscious mind can extract and read with ease—without the listener being aware of it. The motive for back masking, they assert, has nothing to do with money, either—the musicians belong to the Church of Satan and have made a pact to do "certain things" on behalf of the devil.

In 1982, the California state legislature heard from assemblymen and various experts aiming to prove that back-masked messages from Satan were part of rock music. The object was to pass a law requiring all "backwardly masked" records to carry a warning label similar to that required on cigarette packages. No one took such fears very seriously, however, especially in the music business. "It's hilarious," said one industry spokesman. "Who is running the state Legislature? Zippy

The British heavy-metal rockers Judas Priest were acquitted in 1990 of charges that self-destructive commands hidden in their lyrics had played a key role in the suicide attempts of two young Nevada men.

the Pin Head?" Most record companies denied back masking anything at all, and one psychologist held that back-masked lyrics, like most subliminal communication, was overrated. "Subliminal stimuli are not powerful," he pointed out, "they are very subtle, even when used directly." He added, "I don't see how they could have any influence" played backward.

"If you took 100 albums, anything from Doris Day to the Police, and played them backward," one record-company representative told the press, "chances are you'll find something because of the way the English language is. The random combination of vowels, syllables, and phonetics will give you certain sounds which you can then interpret as anything you want."

Not everyone agrees. Australian-born David John Oates became convinced in the late 1980s that there was definitely something going on that produced the inverted lyrics heard by religious fundamentalists—but that it had nothing to do with Satan. In Oates's view, there is

such a thing as "naturally occurring backward masking," in which the unconscious mind embellishes what it is saying normally with a concealed, reversed message, inaudible to the conscious mind until played backward. For example, when astronaut Neil Armstrong, the first human on the moon, said, "That's one small step for man," he was also saying backward, according to Oates, "Man will space walk." Oates calls the phenomenon reverse speech and, like the fundamentalists scanning backward-spinning records, finds it everywhere. It is, he maintains, the unconscious, speaking of its own existence.

Whether real or imagined, deliberate or inadvertent, back masking has been perceived as a threat to life as well as character. In 1986, a civil suit was brought against CBS Records and heavy-metal rock's Judas Priest, claiming that two troubled young men in Nevada shot themselves after listening to the group's records. Embedded in the lyrics, the suit claimed, were the exhortations to suicide: "Let's be

dead," and "Do it." The court found that while there were sounds one could interpret as messages on the backward-played record, there was no evidence of deliberate back masking—or destructive intent.

According to Virginia radio personality Cerphe Colwell, called to testify before the U.S. Senate in 1985, such fears have had an odd side effect. "Heavy metal was all but dead," he said. Opposition "helped the recording labels rebuild an industry; it literally breathed life into a dying industry." And the antagonists, he added, "commissioned people to testify about some of the most obscure people that no one had ever heard of"—rendering them instantly famous.

One musical group that nearly everyone *had* heard of took humorous note of all the fuss and added a back-masked bonus for its fans. Played backward, Pink Floyd's "Goodbye Blue Sky" contains this secret signal: "Congratulations, you've just discovered the secret message. Send your answer to Old Pink care of the Funny Farm." □

PHOBIAS

Phobias—highly focused, often irrational fears of certain things—are the world's most common mental disorder. Triggered by the simplest encounter with the feared object or situation, phobias can cripple the afflicted with severe panic, breathing difficulties, rapid heartbeat, a sense of imminent death—even force a lonely, debilitating retreat from society. Their seriousness disguised by the ordinariness of what is feared, phobias number in the hundreds, among them: Fear of . . .

heat	**Thermophobia**
cold	**Frigophobia**
being buried alive	**Taphophobia**
being alone	**Eremophobia**
crossing bridges	**Gephyrophobia**
open spaces	**Agoraphobia**
empty rooms	**Kenophobia**
darkness	**Achluophobia**
daylight	**Phengophobia**
missiles	**Ballistophobia**
gravity	**Barophobia**
eyes	**Ommatophobia**
knees	**Genuphobia**
teeth	**Odontophobia**
itching	**Acarophobia**
being scratched	**Amychophobia**
hair	**Chaëtophobia**
beards	**Pogonophobia**
feathers	**Pteronophobia**
body odors	**Osphresiophobia**
going to bed	**Clinophobia**
standing up	**Stasiphobia**
stooping	**Kyphophobia**
children (or dolls)	**Pediophobia**
robbers	**Harpaxophobia**
rain	**Ombrophobia**
snow	**Chionophobia**
wind	**Anemophobia**
fog	**Homichlophobia**
slime	**Blennophobia**
shadows	**Sciophobia**
trees	**Dendrophobia**
work	**Ergasiophobia**
school	**Scholionophobia**
church	**Ecclesiaphobia**
home	**Domatophobia**
oneself	**Autophobia**
everything	**Panophobia**

Raintakers

Poised eternally between the ruinous extremes of flood and drought, farmers spend a good deal of time watching the sky for hints of what nature intends. Ordinarily, they take rainfall as it comes and do what they can with what they have. In western Maryland, however, farmers have come to the unshakable belief that this gamble has been fixed, and not by nature: They believe that someone is actually stealing their rain.

In Maryland's Frederick and Washington counties—especially a triangle bounded by Hagerstown and Clear Springs, Maryland, and Mercersburg, Pennsylvania—persistent drought has led to the widespread belief that humans, not nature, are the agents. Many area farmers assert that faceless adversaries in small, unmarked aircraft are seeding rain clouds with chemicals that cause the clouds to dissipate without raining. "It rained on one side" of the affected region, reported a Maryland grain farmer in 1983, "and not on the other side, and every time that took place there was unusual aerial activity in the area." Airplanes were seen to fly into cumulus clouds not long before the clouds shredded and disappeared, seeming to confirm the farmers' worst suspicions.

Such reports, which no one has yet been able to confirm, have surfaced since the 1960s—about the time that cloud seeding became familiar to the public. As to the motive for the presumed seeding, some farmers claim that orchard growers are using secret seeders to reduce hail damage to their trees. Others say that government agencies are involved—municipal ones to keep ball games and other events from being rained out, state and federal ones to protect the schedules of major construction projects. There is also a sense that the plot involves powerful, dangerous forces. One Frederick, Maryland, newspaper reporter contends that she was warned not to pursue the story because it was "part of a much bigger problem."

A private investigator hired by the troubled farmers believes he has found proof of weather modification, although his findings have not been publicly disclosed and no one has been charged. In fact, dur-

ing the several decades that such reports have circulated, and despite thousands of dollars in rewards for information and penalties for unreported weather modification, no one has turned up the sinister rain thief. Many believe the sneaky figure is just a dry-weather mirage.

As with most unsubstantiated beliefs in conspiracy, however, this one contains a grain of truth. Weather-modification specialists do fly into growing storm clouds and seed them with such substances as silver iodide and dry ice, with an eye to suppressing some severe effect—hail, for example—or increas-

ing rainfall. According to the National Oceanic and Atmospheric Administration, charged since 1971 with reporting all of the weather-modification efforts in the United States, some thirty to fifty reports are filed annually, almost all for projects west of the Mississippi River, usually in the hope of increasing rainfall or thickening mountain snowpacks. The last known active seeding program in the Maryland area, the agency reports, was in Delaware in the 1970s, and the last one east of the Mississippi was in Illinois in 1989.

One former weather-modification

expert notes that cloud seeding is not the kind of project one can easily conduct in secret. Such programs are expensive and usually funded by an association of local governments or growers. Moreover, weather manipulation is not all that reliable. It cannot yet move rain around in any predictable fashion—target orchards in Pennsylvania, for example, while shutting off rain in a nearby Maryland valley.

Still, people in the cloud-seeding business find the Maryland farmers' allegations to be part of a familiar refrain. "All weather modifiers get this," explains Bruce Boe, director of North Dakota's farmer-funded hail-suppression program. "Anything that goes near a storm is labeled a cloudseeder."

As for airplanes causing clouds to dissipate, Boe notes that normal-looking clouds often lack the strong, sustained updraft needed for development into rainstorms and fall apart for no reason that is apparent from the ground—although an airplane seen flying through such a cloud might seem to cause the coincidental breakup. Weather modifiers also stress that seeding is only practiced when there are abundant clouds around to seed. During drought years, most of the seeders stand down.

Not very surprisingly, the Maryland farmers' suspicions rise and fall with precipitation. The reports of rain rustling began during the severe drought of the 1960s and, more recently, have marched more or less in step with years that were on the dry side, including the severe drought years of 1986 and 1991. In wet periods, no one complains. Like so much in agriculture, the fear of phantom cloud seeders appears to be soluble in water. □

Rumormongerie

Few things inflame irrational human fears more surely than the unverified stories called rumors. They may be utterly false, or reinforced with a grain of truth—or true. Although often innocuous, they can be destructive, racing through a community, spreading terror and confusion as they go. Because they are a serious business, the study of how society handles rumors has become a branch of social science, as specialists examine the wildfire progress of such stories across the world. Preeminent in this field is French sociologist Jean-Noël Kapferer, head of the Foundation for the Study and Information on Rumors.

The Paris-based foundation operates a hot line Allo Rumeur, or "Hello Rumor"—that the public can call to report whatever is current on the French grapevine. On an average day, the hot line rings nine or ten times, although in periods of crisis there may be many more callers. During Operation Desert Storm, for instance, dozens of calls poured in daily concerning perfectly plausible—but unverified—incidents of violence. "Rumors don't have to be true," Kapferer has observed. "They just have to be likely." In fact, tales too tall to be believed are usually short-lived, he says, citing the public's dismissive attitude toward stories about wartime concentration camps as a case in point. Although chillingly real, the whispered horrors were so improbable as to sound like Allied propaganda. But Kapferer is not interested in whether rumors are true. "I am interested in what values rumors express, in how and why they develop."

Aided by the details his on-the-scene informants provide, Kapferer can trace a rumor's genesis and spread, as well as the "facts" that are subtracted or added to produce new versions. He also probes for the hidden emotion that powers a rumor's circulation. Fear—of strangers, of poisoning, of accidents that may befall one's children, of disease—is at the heart of many rumors. Others reflect a common obsession. France, for instance, is rife with stories about food. And when a tale passes from one group or culture to another, it inevitably undergoes a bit of tailoring to improve the fit. For example, when the fiction linking American household-products giant Procter &

Gamble with Satan (*pages 25-26*) crossed the Atlantic to France, the devil dropped out—few Frenchmen believe in him. In Satan's place appeared a more acceptable villain: the so-called Moonies of the Unification Church, a group viewed with considerable suspicion in France.

Kapferer's research confirms what everyone knows, namely, that trying to stop a rumor can be a complicated business. In 1987, the popular French movie star Isabelle Adjani, very much alive, was disconcerted to hear that she was dying, then that she was dead. People were talking about her demise in every quarter of France, and some versions of the story specified the hospital where she was supposed to have been cared for and even the number of her room. Determined to halt the rumor in its tracks, she made a heavily advertised television appearance on the

Despite screen star Isabelle Adjani's widely advertised public appearances, stories of her death swept France during 1987.

national evening news, accompanied by the president of France's Ordre des Medecins (comparable to the American Medical Association) to vouch for her good health. The blitz worked—but not perfectly. According to the poll Kapferer conducted a month after Adjani's appearance, more than two million people remained unshaken in their conviction that she was ill.

In fact, Kapferer notes, official disclaimers are rarely believed entirely. More often than not, government efforts to nip a budding rumor are dismissed as a cover-up. During the uncertain days of Desert Storm, for example, word came of a mysterious paper bag that a Paris police squadron was said to have blown up. After destroying the bag, according to rumor, they then warned neighborhood residents to keep the matter quiet. Immediately, the story raged across Paris. What had been imagined as a single bomb became multiple bombs planted in fashionable neighborhoods, a railway station, and an airport. There had been explosions, even deaths (although there really had been neither), but the press was colluding with the police to suppress the truth.

But here, as in many rumors, fact mixed with fancy. As it happened, a suspicious-looking package *was* found under a bench on Rue Théophile Gautier. Moreover, the police took the precaution of blowing it up. Said one, "We told the residents on Rue Théophile Gautier that the package we exploded turned out to be a thick steak, but no one believed us." Characteristically, the improbable steak story failed to ignite, as Parisians opted for the more plausible possibilities offered by tales of terrorist bombs. □

Excesses of Youth

Knowing evil's hearty appetite for innocence, parents perpetually fear that their offspring will fall into the deadly clutches of monstrous strangers. Often justified by real events, this terror now and then breaks out in the form of ugly, unfounded accusations. Early Christians, for example, were accused of kidnapping the children of Romans. Nobility has been charged with tapping children for their youthful blood, and unspeakable practices have been attributed to kidnappers suspected of providing doctors with small cadavers or the state with pint-size cannon fodder. Almost always, the tales are false, but the profound fear that they engender is very real—for the imaginary child takers invariably rise partly from a cruel truth.

For example, the disappearance of children in eighteenth-century France—where the very poor ones were often simply abandoned to an uncaring world—was rumored to be linked to gruesome medical experiments, dissection, or worse. The missing children, it was said, provided blood for the baths of leprous nobles or the palates of aristocratic vampires, or young limbs to replace the lost ones of princes. Although the ghoulish stories were false, such fears, fueled by the reality of children vanishing into the king's army and French colonies in the New World, helped to spark the Paris riots of 1750. The cruel suppression of the riots—and the massacre of many of the young participants—solidified the people's hatred for the Crown.

In Latin America, where the lot of poor children today is no better than that of the indigent young of eighteenth-century Paris, a brisk, long-established trade in the offspring of the poor has spawned similar tales—but with a grisly, high-tech twist. The young are stolen, frightened citizens whisper, as sources of spare parts for organ transplants. The story first surfaced in Honduras in 1986, after the reported discovery of four secret *casas de engordes*—"fattening houses"—in San Pedro Sula. There, the report said, thirteen children, stolen or purchased from their impoverished mothers, were waiting to be "adopted" by North Americans—but were actually in a kind of juvenile feedlot, from which they would be taken off for slaughter and dismemberment into their various salable parts.

A year later, a similar tale came from Guatemala: Fourteen Honduran children, most of them newborns, were allegedly discovered in a secret foster home, on offer at $20,000 per child. Despite denials by the policemen who reportedly made the discovery, the story, by now involving "thousands" of Honduran children, quickly spread around the world, propelled by the Soviet newspaper *Pravda* and the Soviet news agency Tass.

Soon the sordid stories multiplied in number: Abandoned Haitian children's organs were being sold to a Florida clinic; Venezuelan children's corneas were peddled as transplants for the eyes of the rich; Mexican children's bodies had been found drained of their blood. Most of the lurid tales were circulated by leftist organizations as part of a calculated disinformation campaign, which the Soviet Union ultimately abandoned. ◊

And yet, experts believe the baby-parts story was more than mere disinformation—it arose from a kind of human despair among the planet's very poor, who have little to sell but themselves. In some parts of the world, such as Brazil and Turkey, impoverished donors routinely sell kidneys and corneas to the ailing rich. In a sense, say scholars in the field, the stealing of children for their parts is not a great leap from such disturbing realities. It is also analogous, they say, to exploiting a developing nation's resources to enrich the industrialized ones. Peru's nihilist guerilla force, Sendero Luminoso—"Shining Path"—stokes this age-old fear with fables of the Pistaco, a tall white man who goes abroad at night, using his knife to dismember Indians, whose fat he uses to oil his machines. In 1988, this mythic stranger was paralleled in Lima by the Sacaojos, or "Eye Robbers," machine-gun-wielding foreigners who kidnapped children only to gouge out their eyes. But neither Pistaco nor Sacaojos really exist.

Such imaginary figures are not restricted to Latin America. In the autumn of 1990, a black ambulance reportedly roamed central and southern Italy, its drivers scooping up and murdering children for their negotiable organs. Although no evidence of such a project was ever found, belief in the kidnappers remains strong in some areas, especially where children are known to be at risk from human monsters that are all too real. □

Paraguayan police spokesman Osvaldo Palacios displays photographs of seven Brazilian babies who were allegedly slated for sale in the United States until rescued in Asunción.

Headstrong

Building highways and bridges in the jungle-covered mountains of Borneo—an East Indian island partitioned among Brunei, Malaysia, and Indonesia—has always required sacrifices. But, from time to time, a chilling story has suggested that something more was needed to make such works endure, some further sacrifice—for example, a gross of human heads buried at the site.

Such reports have special force among the native Dayak people of Borneo, for, in the old days, headhunting was both commonplace and deeply feared. The Iban, or Sea Dayak, were said to attack other tribes purely for the glory of taking a few heads, and severed heads were important in various rituals—especially as offerings to the spirits that governed the success of great undertakings. The more serious the sacrifice, the Dayak reasoned, the more successful the project's outcome. Heads were the offering the spirits valued most. Thus, modern reports that headhunters are at large has a credibility that can still kindle terror in the Dayak heart—their headhunting ancestors scare them with whispers of an unspeak-

able practice abandoned long ago.

The Dayak's neighbors on Borneo have no headhunting history with which to frighten themselves, however. Malays sniff that using heads as a sacrifice for a bridge is something the Chinese do; Chinese think it Malaysian. Old-timers claim ◊

Such reminders as these human heads, collected by Borneo's Sea Dayak warriors around 1850, keep modern islanders in superstitious touch with their headhunting ancestors.

that the Japanese occupation soldiers did it. The fact is no one has ever turned up evidence that anyone blessed constructions with human heads. The government of Malaysia believes it is evil to spread such tales in the first place and offers a fine of 2,000 Malaysian dollars and a year in prison for doing so.

Still, every so often, word comes that the headhunters are on the prowl again, and terror moves into the jungle villages called kampongs. Headhunting reports surfaced in 1955 and 1967, and several times in the 1980s. In the fright of 1980, word came that 600 heads would be needed in order to guarantee a gigantic project at Port Dickson, some fifty miles from Kuala Lumpur; but, as the builders already had 400 heads in hand, the rumored hunters were seeking only 200 more for the sacrifice. The streets of Kuala Lumpur became deserted after dark, children were kept home from school, and vigilante patrols roamed the city, hunting the mythical headhunters.

In late 1989, the Malays of the state of Sabah heard that the sultan of Brunei, following a fortuneteller's advice on how to keep his oil fields from drying up, had sent out Land Rovers full of headhunters. The general fear deepened when three headless bodies were discovered near Kota Kinabalu, Sabah's capital, despite police assertions that they were just murders in ritual disguise. A number of heads seen floating off Sabah's east coast turned out to be coconuts.

The road builders of Borneo scoff at the scares. "I assure you we don't need human heads to build bridges," says Zaini Amran, whose company, Bumu Hiway, has raised many bridges there. "We need steel piles." Government engineer Teoh Lye snorts, apparently intending no pun, "There is absolutely no foundation to the story." Still, it is said that out in the kampongs, at least, a project nearing completion needs its *doa selamat*—prayer for safety—and possibly some less heady sacrifice—a chicken, perhaps. □

FEVERS OF WAR

Truth is often said to be the first casualty of war; sanity must be the second. In the blink of an ideological eye, the world can become a febrile landscape of political mirages—the figurative flags with which a society wraps excessive sacrifice and aberrant behavior. Loyal citizens are cruelly interred, erstwhile allies caricatured as vermin, and the most unspeakable acts attributed—sometimes accurately, but often not—to the enemy of the moment. In the throes of this high fever, great cities are razed to rubble; fathers kill their offspring and are slain by their sons. Rumor fills the skies with imaginary bombers, the seas with illusory submarines, and the land with mythic columns, inexorably advancing or in confused retreat. This transient madness provides a fertile soil for the cultivation of wars by the people who wish to see them fought; it persuades those whose lives will be most shattered to give their unflagging support and inspires hatred and some fleeting expectation of glory in the men and women who must do the killing and dying. Indeed, without some abandonment of reason, few wars could be fought—not even the long, ruinous cold wars that enfever the multitudes with the chronic possibility of a final, catastrophic conflict that, providentially, never comes.

Greek Tragedy

In 427 BC, civil strife broke out in Corcyra, on what is now the Ionian island of Corfu off the northwestern corner of Greece. Linked to a larger conflict—the Peloponnesian War, which raged from 431 to 404 BC with only one fragile seven-year-long truce—events at Corcyra presaged the moral and military erosion that would give Sparta victory and bring defeat and ruin to the once-powerful city-state of Athens. But Corcyra also achieved lasting fame as a cautionary model for how wrong things can go when conflict becomes civil war.

This enduring example might have been lost had the larger war not had a fine historian: Thucydides, a young Athenian aristocrat and budding soldier when the conflict began in 431 BC. Sensing that it would be an important struggle,

Thucydides decided to be its scribe. His *History* is the only extant first-hand account of the Peloponnesian War and a masterpiece of military reporting. The dispassionate voice of the disciplined historian prevails throughout—even when recounting the horrors of Corcyra.

The seeds of the doomed island-city's downfall had been sown several years earlier, in about 433 BC. Then, in a dispute with Corinth—later, an ally of Sparta—over the nearby port of Epidamnus, the nautically adroit Corcyraeans won a stunning victory at sea. The angry Corinthians struck back with an overwhelming naval force but fled at the approach of a fleet from Athens, Corcyra's powerful ally. When the Peloponnesian War began, neutral

Corcyra was divided, as many Greek city-states were, into two political parties: the oligarchs and the democrats. The oligarchs, representing the wealthy and privileged, supported Sparta. The more plentiful democrats used their majority to tilt the city's support toward the Athenian cause.

But Corinth had other plans. It now returned some 250 Corcyraean prisoners taken six years earlier at Epidamnus. "The story was," Thucydides wrote, "that these prisoners had been released by the Corinthians on the security of 800 talents put down by their official agents in Corinth; in fact they had undertaken to win Corcyra over to the Corinthian side, and they went about their business by approaching the citizens individually with the aim of detaching the city from Athens." Despite the returnees' efforts to persuade, however, the people of

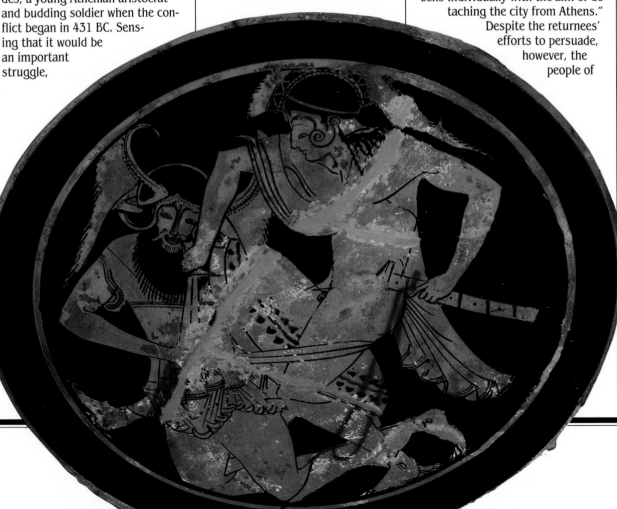

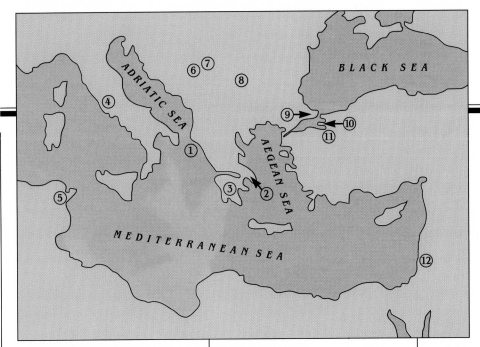

Civil strife in Corcyra (1) marked the Peloponnesian War between Athens (2) and Sparta (3). Rome (4) destroyed Carthage (5) in the third Punic War, described on the following pages. Semlin (6), Belgrade (7), Sofia (8), Constantinople (9), Helenopolis (10), Nicaea (11), and Jerusalem (12) all figured in the People's Crusade (pages 39-41).

Corcyra voted again to continue as Athens's ally. The disappointed oligarchs went after the leader of the democrats, a citizen-representative named Peithias, accusing him of selling out Corcyra to Athens. Acquitted, Peithias struck back by bringing the five richest oligarchs to trial for violating sacred vineyards. Condemned, heavily fined, and humiliated, the five took a final, desperate vengeance. Rallying the rest of their party around them, they burst into a Council meeting and with their daggers killed Peithias and sixty of his supporters, then boasted that they had saved Corcyra from Athenian slavery—a claim few believed.

Fighting between the two factions quickly spread across the city. Initially disadvantaged, the retreating democrats moved to fortify the acropolis—a fortified citadel overlooking the city—and the higher ground. From their new vantage point, they turned the tide of battle. The oligarchs fled, setting fire to their own stores and property to slow the advance of the democrats. In the middle of the melee, the Athenian general Nicostratus arrived with twelve ships, intending

to arbitrate a peace. But matters had by then gone too far to be affected by reason.

When a thwarted Nicostratus prepared to sail for home soon afterward, Corcyra became paralyzed by fear of an approaching fleet of Spartan vessels, which easily won a naval skirmish against the disorganized Corcyraeans. Then, as word spread throughout the city that relief, in the form of a large Athenian fleet, was on the way—the killing began in earnest. The democrats, now out of danger, began to slaughter their helpless enemies. Oligarchs who had sought refuge in the temple of Hera killed one another and themselves rather than wait for the savagery of the victors. "There was death in every shape and form," wrote Thucydides. "There were fathers who killed their sons; men were dragged from the temples or butchered on the very altars; some were actually walled up in the temple of Dionysus and died there."

But Corcyra was just the beginning: A revolutionary madness swept through the Hellenic world. In this fevered atmosphere, even words lost their true meaning,

Thucydides reported. "What used to be described as a thoughtless act of aggression was now regarded as the courage one would expect to find in a party member; to think of the future and wait was merely another way of saying one was a coward; any idea of moderation was just an attempt to disguise one's unmanly character; ability to understand a question from all sides meant that one was totally unfitted for action. Fanatical enthusiasm was the mark of a real man." Political ambition and greed quickly destroyed the fabric of daily life. Promises meant nothing; trust was ridiculed; hostility was the norm. A voice of diplomacy and understanding was interpreted as indecisiveness. Superior cunning was the mark of the greater intelligence.

Morality in Corcyra was never fully restored. Instead, the city became a paradigm of democracy driven mad by fear and anger—a vile pattern that has been studied for two dozen centuries, although to little effect. Despite the dire warnings of an ancient Greek historian, Corcyra's ruinous strife has been more often imitated than avoided, right up to the present day. □

Suggestive of the civil war that once raged at Corcyra, a young Greek warrior mortally wounds an older, bearded countryman in this detail from a decorated cup fashioned about 410 BC.

The Empire Strikes Back

Before Rome became Europe's great imperial power, the city-state of Carthage dominated the western Mediterranean. Situated on the North African coast where Tunisia is today, Carthage was a success story that galled the emerging, expanding empire just across the narrow sea. Inevitably, the two drifted into a series of conflicts—the three Punic Wars, named for the Punic, or Phoenician, ancestors of Carthage. The first was ignited by a disturbance in Sicily, lasted from 264 to 241 BC, and broke the Carthaginian grip on the region. The second, which erupted after Carthage had been forced to cede Sicily and Sardinia to Rome and had extended itself into Spain, began in 218 BC. After seventeen years of war, despite the near-legendary trek and early victories of Carthage's great general Hannibal, Rome triumphed in 201. Carthage's sphere of influence was reduced to a fraction of its former size—but the city somehow endured and even prospered. Having survived the Roman legions, however, Carthage could not escape the implacable hatred of one bitter old man—the Roman senator Marcus Porcius Cato.

As a young officer, Cato had fought against Hannibal, whose ghost still stalked Rome. Even after the peace of 201, Roman children were warned that Hannibal and his elephants would come and get them if they misbehaved, and politicians stampeded at the faintest whiff of danger from Carthage—a situation Cato would use to good effect.

In 157 BC, then in his seventies, Cato joined an embassy dispatched to arbitrate a dispute between Carthage and the king of neighboring Numidia, an ally of Rome that had been nibbling away at the remaining Punic territories. When Cato saw that the city from which Hannibal had come was once more prospering—and that it had armed against the encroachments of the Numidians—he smelled disaster. Returning to Rome, he warned the Senate that Carthage, their great enemy, was on the rise again. According to some historians, Cato let a few still-fresh Carthaginian figs spill from his toga—to remind the Senate how swiftly figs, or troops, could cross the sea to Rome. At first few in the Senate shared his apprehensions: Carthage posed no threat to the empire.

But Cato was not to be deflected. Year after year, to every speech he gave he added: *"Delenda est Carthago"*—"Carthage must be destroyed." "The Carthaginians are already our enemies," he declared, fanning his colleagues' fears, "for he who prepares everything against me, so that he can make war at whatever time he wishes, is already my enemy even though he is not yet using weapons." Then the inevitable chorus: "Carthage must be destroyed."

Cato's unrelenting arguments eventually prevailed. In 150 BC, Carthage gave them an excuse to act by attacking the seasoned forces of Numidia. Although the rash act destroyed the Punic army, Carthage's warlike behavior gave Cato further oratorical ammunition. Finally, convinced by his accusations that Carthage had broken the peace, the Roman Senate declared war on the weakened city.

Seeing no hope of victory, Carthage swiftly offered to surrender, submitting to increasingly humiliating demands to avoid further warfare. But when Rome ordered that Carthage be obliterated and its citizens exiled from their sea, the Carthaginians mounted a heroic defense, which a Roman siege failed to break for more than two years. Then, in 146, soldiers breached the city's walls and raged through the streets for a week until the city surrendered. The 50,000 Carthaginian survivors were sold into slavery. Their city was razed, and—according to legend, at least—the land sown with salt so that nothing would ever grow there again.

But the old man whose memories of war had instigated the fatal, final phase of the Punic Wars was not there to see it. Cato had died in 149 BC, aged eighty-five, never able to gloat, *"Deleta est Carthago"*— "Carthage has been destroyed." □

Urban Renewal

Christianity, it seemed to French priest Odo de Lagery, was suspended fragilely between the ruinous feudalism of medieval Europe and the rising tide of Islam in the east. When, in AD 1088, the tall, bearded forty-six-year-old was elected Pope Urban II, he began to think of ways to unite his church against the non-Christian enemy.

Returning to his homeland in the summer of 1095, Urban appears to have taken the political temperature among the Norman aristocracy. Then, in November, he had the papal throne set up on a platform in an open field at Clermont and summoned the multitudes to hear him. Islam, he said, had defiled Christian shrines and made access to the holy places more difficult for religious pilgrims. The factional differences of Christians should be put aside and sinners forgiven; all, rich and poor alike, should join forces in an armed pilgrimage to reclaim the Holy Land for the Cross—a crusade.

The response to his words was immediate and universal. *"Dieu le veut!"* they cried—"God wills it!" Men and women, tears streaming down their faces, pledged their lives and their property to God. They would save Jerusalem, save Christianity, and save themselves, too. Nobles swore to undertake the long trek to fight Islam in the Holy Land, promising to set out in August 1096, after the harvest was in. But, hoping to move the knights and bishops, the pope had greatly agitated the pawns as well. Word of his holy summons to action sped across France, relayed by commoners and evangelists—and by one man in particular: Peter the Hermit.

No one knows if Peter, a middle-aged wanderer born near Amiens, had heard the actual words of Urban II. But no one played them back to the populace—embellished with a personal, charismatic mysticism—to greater effect. People said that he had made the pilgrimage to Jerusalem some time earlier and had been appalled by the treatment the Turks accorded Christians. Word spread of Peter's visions, in which Jesus Christ had visited the hermit to urge the liberation of Jerusalem and had even given him a letter. Slight, ascetic, and plain, Peter the Hermit became a magnet for the men, women, and children of the People's Crusade. "Whatever he said or did," said one acquaintance of the persuasive preacher, "it seemed like something half-divine." Part of his perceived divinity, historians believe, arose from the state of northern Europe at the time. Peter's followers were not just going to Jerusalem—they were abandoning a wasteland of pestilence, endless strife, famine, and poverty to find a better life in the biblical realm of milk and honey.

Peter began preaching the Crusade late in 1095, riding his donkey from one town to the next, urging the martial pilgrimage and attracting such disciples as Gautier Sans Avoir—"Walter Without Possessions." By the time Peter and his ◊

In this miniature from a thirteenth-century French manuscript, Peter the Hermit preaches the Crusade to a gathering of armored knights.

retinue reached Cologne in April 1096, four months before the "official" Crusade was to begin, 15,000 people followed him. Devout though they might have been, the disorganized, undisciplined marchers were not much better than a mob.

Impatient to get under way, Walter and a few thousand crusaders left Cologne just after Easter, setting out for Hungary, which his party crossed uneventfully. At Semlin (now Zemun), they forded the river Sava to Belgrade. The unheralded arrival of thousands of civilian crusaders startled the commander there, who was unable to feed them. Soon the hungry marchers were pillaging the neighborhood, provoking Belgrade's soldiers to attack them. Several pilgrims died in the fighting, including some burned alive in a church. But Walter persevered, and he and his tattered army reached Constantinople in mid-July.

Meanwhile, Peter was only two weeks behind with his much larger horde of impromptu soldiers, along with a cohort of German knights who had joined up in Cologne. Peter's marchers maintained a rough kind of discipline until they reached Semlin in late June—and there the People's Crusade began to rip apart. Nervous at having

20,000 uncontrolled crusaders in his city, the town's governor tightened security. The marchers, for their part, had begun to hear how Walter's followers had fared in Belgrade. Tensions erupted into a riot, which quickly became a siege of the city's citadel. The crusaders stormed the stronghold, capturing provisions and killing some 4,000 Hungarian Christians in the process. Now outlaws, the pilgrims fled across the river and started on the road to Sofia.

But their discipline had been shattered. Continued looting and burning brought the local militia

down upon them, cutting away perhaps a fourth of their swollen ranks. Finally, in mid-July, the ragged, volatile mob reached Sofia, where an escort from Constantinople took them the rest of the way. So touched were people by the hardships the pilgrims had endured that they contributed food and money, and word came that their crimes would be pardoned by the Byzantine emperor Alexius. Peter the Hermit, it is said, wept for joy.

They reached Constantinople in August 1096—the month when the true knights of the Cross were scheduled to begin their march

Nineteenth-century French artist Jules Rigo's engraving shows Gautier Sans Avoir (right) with Peter the Hermit in the background.

from France toward the Holy Land. Peter the Hermit's crusaders rejoined those who had followed Walter. In August, all crossed the Bosporus in what is now Turkey and pillaged their rude way along the coast to a well-provisioned camp near the port of Helenopolis. Emperor Alexius, who had long experience fighting the Turks, pressed them to wait there for more seasoned knights before going into battle. But the unruly mob ignored him and began ranging farther and farther into the Turk-controlled countryside, slaughtering eastern Christians and infidels alike. On one sortie, a German-led party of several thousand people came upon a castle called Xerigordon and managed to hold it against attacking Turks— but not its external supply of water, which the Turks seized. After a week without water, the crusaders surrendered the castle, their leader experienced a sudden conversion to Islamic belief, and the other survivors were sent into slavery or used as archery targets.

Back in the crusaders' camp, however, Turkish spies spread quite a different story: The Christians had overrun the key city of Nicaea and kept the spoils for themselves. Immediately, the soldiers began to agitate to join their fortunate comrades at Nicaea—until they learned what had really happened at Xerigordon. Their excitement disintegrated into panic. Peter was in Constantinople at the time, and Walter could scarcely control the jittery army, which wanted to avenge Xerigordon. When Peter did not return on schedule, however, and reports trickled in of a large Turkish force advancing on the camp, Walter lost his purchase on the situation. At dawn on October 21, the impro-

vised army straggled out, some 20,000 strong, to meet the enemy.

But the Turks were not advancing: They awaited the Christians in a carefully prepared ambush only a few miles away. When the crusaders entered the narrow, wooded defile of the trap, the Turks struck, drove them into blind retreat, and followed them back to their undefended bivouac. Several thousand Christians managed to hole up in an abandoned castle and resist the siege until help arrived from Constantinople. But most of the faithful

were massacred. The Turks celebrated with a fitting monument, described by a Greek chronicler as a "mountain of bones, most conspicuous in height and breadth and depth." That was about all that remained of the 40,000 enfevered faithful who surrendered their sanity—and their lives—to save their souls. As for the knights summoned to the Cross by Urban II, their Crusade had only just begun—they were still months from Constantinople, where the indestructible Peter the Hermit would join them. □

Revolting Rounds

After a century of British colonial rule, India by the mid-nineteenth century had become a tinderbox of injured feelings and religious resentments. In that volatile setting, the rebellion of the sepoys—native troops in British forces—seemed apocalyptic when it came in 1857, raging across much of India for a bloody year and a half. Historians would describe the mutiny and its suppression by British troops as one of the most horrific wars of the nineteenth century and discover subtle plots and conspiracies behind it. In fact, the tinderbox seems to have been ignited not by design but by accident—and not by a match but by a rifle.

At the time, the armies of the world were trading in their muskets, which fired balls out of

smooth gun barrels, for rifles, whose bores were grooved to give the ball spin, stability, and greater accuracy. But the rifling grooves caused a problem: The expanding gases that expelled the bullet leaked out through the grooves, weakening the discharge.

In 1853, Britain's royal small-arms factory at Enfield had perfected an improved rifle round in which the ball was enclosed in the same cartridge as the powder and heavily greased at one end for a good gas seal. To test the shelf life of the new cartridge, a batch was sent out to India, where the grease—a tallow that was made from beef and pork fat—held up admirably in the harsh climate. The native soldiers never fired the test cartridges, and the rounds were returned to Enfield in 1855.

On January 1, 1857, the British began issuing the new rifle and cartridge, fabricated at army arse- ◊

To use the greased .577-caliber Enfield cartridge *(above)*, soldiers bit open the powder-containing end of the round *(left)*, poured the powder down the rifle barrel, then rammed in the rest of the cartridge, which contained the bullet.

nals in Ambala, Sialkot, and Dum Dum (later famous for developing the expanding bullet, or dumdum). For any muzzle-loaded weapon of the time, soldiers had an elaborately choreographed loading procedure that used both hands and, often, teeth as well. Ordinarily, they would rip open the end of the cartridge that contained the gunpowder, spill the powder down the barrel of the gun and then ram down the ball. The trouble was that most soldiers ripped open the cartridge by using their teeth. Barely three weeks had passed before the rumor spread that the new Enfield cartridge was a vile thing for a Hindu or a Muslim to touch with his mouth.

It began when a low-caste laborer at the Dum Dum arsenal asked a high-caste Brahman sepoy for a drink from his water pot. The Brahman refused, saying that he would lose caste if he shared with the man. According to legend, the laborer's reply was something like, "So what? You will soon lose your caste anyway when you bite cartridges covered with the fat of pigs and cows"—anathema to Hindus and Muslims alike. Although the Enfield cartridges, like all rounds produced at Dum Dum, were apparently covered with dietarily acceptable mutton-based tallow, the fear of caste contamination spread like wildfire among the sepoys. The British, some whispered angrily, were using the unspeakable cartridge to pollute Muslims and Hindus as a prelude to converting them to Christianity. Sepoys and their families drew the taunts of civilian compatriots, who accused them of selling out their religion to the colonial intruders.

Smelling trouble ahead—but blind to the real magnitude of the problem—the English took steps to smooth the ruffled sensibilities of their soldiers. Some officers urged that the sepoys be allowed to grease their own cartridges, but they were ignored; the factory greasing was continued, with the proviso that nothing but mutton tallow be used for the purpose. As a further stopgap, the British changed the loading drill for the new rifles, specifying that the cartridges be ripped open with fingers instead of teeth. But their efforts were too little, too late; the fuse of rebellion had been lit.

The explosion came on April 24, 1857, at the military station at Meerut, where eighty-five of ninety sepoys in the Third Native Cavalry refused to touch the new cartridges on the parade ground. Court-martialed, the men were sentenced to ten years' hard labor. On Saturday, May 9, in front of hundreds of their fellows, they were stripped of their uniforms and shackled as felons. "It was a piteous spectacle and many there were moved with a great compassion, when they saw the despairing gestures of those wretched men," wrote John William Kaye, a leading historian of the rebellion. "Lifting up their hands and lifting up their voices, the prisoners implored the General to have mercy upon them, and not to consign them to so ignominious a doom.

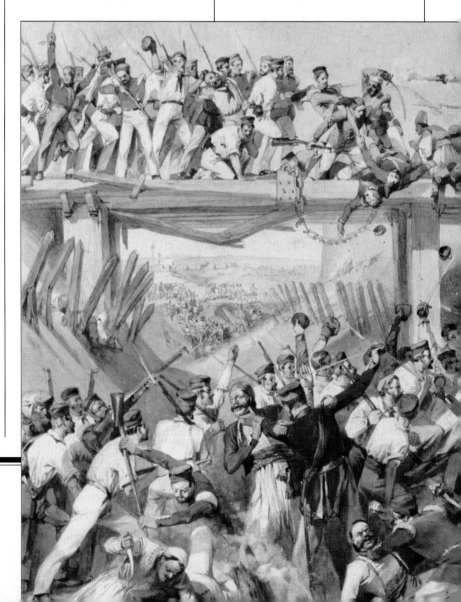

Then, seeing that there was no other hope, they turned to their comrades and reproached them for quietly suffering this disgrace to descend upon them. There was not a Sepoy present who did not feel the rising indignation in his throat."

A day later, indignation had boiled into murderous rage. At five the next evening, when the British were at church, hundreds of sepoys charged into the compound, freed their comrades and the other prisoners, and went on a rampage of murder and arson that set the tone for the mutiny and its suppression. "The sepoys had sown the wind," wrote one scholar, "and the Indians reaped the whirlwind."

Having taken the irretrievable step of mutiny, the sepoys made for Delhi, forty miles away, where they quickly overran the city. For reasons no one fully understands, the British made no effort to pursue them, and the military mutiny took on the characteristic of a national revolt. Rebellion swept uncontrolled across northern India, with spontaneous, uncontrolled episodes of violence, murder, and arson flaring up from one English settlement to another, all marked by a terrible brutality. Europeans were slain on sight, women and children included, English property was burned, all criminals were freed and treasuries looted. In early June, a mutineer

named Nana Sahib led an infamous massacre of British troops and their families at Kanpur, a commercial center 245 miles southeast of Delhi. At nearby Lucknow, the British were besieged from June until November and finally forced to abandon the city.

Most students of the rebellion believe that if the sepoys—who outnumbered European troops five to one—had been truly insurgent and had begun with a plan and widespread support, they could have beaten the British. But the princes supported the British, who allowed them their local sovereignty, and the Sikhs, eternal enemies of the Hindus, were only too glad to take the European side.

Slowly, the English and their native allies suppressed the revolt, using a matching cruelty. Prisoners were summarily executed, and some, it is said, were made to lick away the blood that they had spilled before their own execution. Delhi was retaken in September 1857, as were the other rebel enclaves. In July 1858, Charles Canning, first viceroy of India, declared victory official. Parliament then passed the Government of India Act, by which the East India Company relinquished its hold on the giant colony and power over India was given to the Crown. To prevent subsequent sepoy uprisings, the army reorganized: Instead of one British battalion to every five Indian ones, there was now one to every two.

The incendiary matter of the Enfield rifle cartridges—the presumed trigger of the mutiny—had long since passed into irrelevance. In fact, it appears that the rebel sepoys, quickly overcoming their repugnance, used their new Enfields to good effect. □

English artist M. S. Morgan painted *Storming of the Kashmire Gate* only months after British troops had stormed the bridge leading into Delhi, which was then being held by sepoy mutineers, on September 14, 1857.

Bulletproof Chests

During the summer of 1900, a wave of terror gripped foreigners living in the northern provinces of China. In a frightening revival of the country's medieval past, a band of young, utterly committed men had begun to rid China of its Western taint by killing the "foreign devils" and Chinese who had converted to Christianity. Surfacing under the name *Yi he tuan*—the Righteous Harmony Fists—the secret society of youthful warriors practiced an ancient form of calisthenic fighting, whose resemblance to fisticuffs earned the group an occidental nickname: Boxers.

The so-called Boxer Rebellion tapped into a widespread panic among the peasants of China's industrially backward north. Although the central government supported a limited form of westernization, the peasants had felt increasingly threatened by rising foreign influence, the intrusion of missionaries, and such artifacts of alien invasion as railroads and telegraph lines. When a series of natural disasters struck—two failed harvests, the flooding of the Yellow River, and a plague of locusts—the foreigners were blamed. In this climate of xenophobic hatred, the Boxers began to attack Christians in 1898, and by 1900, they were ready to embark on what would be their final killing spree.

Appealing to the superstitious elements in the provinces and promising to wipe out the foreigners, the Boxers swarmed out of control. On June 13 and 14, they entered Beijing, killing and looting. Six foreign children and seventy-six foreign troops were killed along with several hundred Chinese Christians. But the real slaughter came in the provinces, where 32,000 Chinese Christians were massacred.

For all its cruel fury, the Boxer Rebellion was quickly and ruthlessly subdued by foreign armies; by mid-August, it was over. But the rebels had been doomed by their own delusions. Mostly teenaged peasant boys, drawn to the rituals and camaraderie of a secret society, they had passwords and hand signals, wore colorful turbans and sashes, and believed that they could become possessed by deities, who would protect them from death. "Cannon cannot injure, water cannot drown," was one of their incantations. For the unconvinced, demonstrations were staged in which a rifle was loaded with blanks and a Boxer was "shot" to demonstrate their invulnerability. In the event, however, belief proved no match for real bullets, and the Righteous Harmony Fists were mowed down by foreign guns. □

After the retaking of the city of Tianjin, American and British cavalry captured these prisoners, said to be Boxer rebels.

Mountain of Youth

"O Jesus, make it stop!" wrote British poet Siegfried Sassoon of the First World War, England's bloodiest and most terrible conflict. Whole brigades were lost within hours. In one day of fighting, Britain lost more men than it had in the Crimean and Boer wars combined. To feed a killing machine of such efficiency, the British needed a much larger force than the small professional army in existence when the war began. For that, the government had turned to the newly named secretary of state for war, Lord Horatio Herbert Kitchener, whose military and diplomatic exploits in the Middle East, southern Africa, and India had made him into a national hero.

On August 5, 1914, Kitchener was put in charge of building the huge army of civilian enlistees that the coming campaigns in Belgium and France would require. He was to do this without instituting conscription, however, which Parliament feared would sit poorly with the public. The next day, Kitchener received approval to expand the army by half a million men and a day later issued his renowned "Call to Arms." Advertisements went out in the name of the king, declaring that 100,000 men were needed "in the present grave National Emergency," adding, "Lord Kitchener is confident that this appeal will be at once responded to by all those who have the safety of our Empire at heart." The enlistments would be "for the period of the war only," and one had to be between nineteen and thirty, fit, and at least five-foot-three-inches tall with a thirty-four-inch chest to qualify.

The response was overwhelming. On the first day, the number of volunteers was so great that mounted police were needed for crowd control. Kitchener had read the national mood precisely. The first increment of 100,000 men was raised quickly. By the end of August, Kitchener had his second 100,000 with no end in ◊

Eager to fight the enemy, young British volunteers queue up in the rain outside the Central London Recruiting Depot, Great Scotland Yard, in August 1914.

BRITONS "WANTS" "YOU" JOIN YOUR COUNTRY'S ARMY! GOD SAVE THE KING

Reproduced by permission of LONDON OPINION

Originally painted by Alfred Leete as a cover for the weekly *London Opinion,* the First World War's best-known recruiting poster featured Lord Kitchener.

the army, now committed to a constant supply of new men, stepped up their campaign with slogans and advertisements: "Is Your Conscience Clear?" "Is Anyone Proud Of You?" "It Is More Blessed To Go Than Be Pushed." The exempt clergy were attacked. Why, wondered the head of the dockers trade union, "should men so fond of talking about Heaven be so afraid to pass through its gates?" Mothers learned that it might be a punishable offense to "harbour" a son wanted by the army. There were roundups at underground stations and at music halls. By mid-1915, nearly three million young men had volunteered for what was being called Kitchener's New Armies.

Ill-equipped and poured into the trench war of attrition with minimal training, the enlistees were cut down like wheat. The Pals who had signed up to fight together died together—and robbed entire cities of a generation of young men. Summed up one historian: "The Kitchener armies were never demobilized, they died." □

sight—on a single day in September, 35,000 men signed on. Private recruiting efforts created what were called Pals battalions—units with such names as the Hull Commercials, composed of clerks and young professionals from the city of Hull; the Tramways Battalion, made up of Glasgow transit-system workers; and such units as Bristol's Own and the Liverpool Pals—ensuring that friends who signed up together would also fight together. In less than six months, nearly 2 million men volunteered to go overseas. A kind of rabid patriotic fervor gripped the land.

In November, a member of Parliament, James H. Thomas, said that any young man who had not enlisted was either a coward or a traitor. Recruiters stormed to soccer matches to solicit the crowds. A group of women armed with white feathers—a symbol of cowardice—accosted any out-of-uniform young man they encountered in the street. To shame its male employees into enlisting, one firm promised it would not hire any single men who were eligible for enlistment.

When recruitment began to flag,

The Shining

World War I's first major contact between British and German troops came on the bleak, flat fields near the Belgian city of Mons, August 23, 1914. Almost immediately, the overwhelming German force— whose size Allied intelligence had underestimated by some 50 percent—buckled the French flanks and drove the English units into an exhausting retreat. For thirteen days they marched, with little food or rest, their rear guard hectored by the advancing Boche. Then, on September 4, the battle-worn, weary British troops and their French allies turned in a counterattack that became the First Battle of the Marne. It stopped the German advance and reclaimed some German gains. To the worn-out Allied troops, both the retreat and the victory seemed nothing short of a miracle. Soon, soldiers were swearing that heavenly intervention, as well as their own force of arms, had saved them. Among the many chimeras they had seen along their fevered retreat were phantom knights in golden armor, celestial archers, luminous free forms—collectively, the Angels of Mons.

"I could see quite plainly in midair a strange light," reported one lance corporal, adding that, as the light increased, he had discerned three shapes "having what looked like outspread wings," draped in what appeared to be "a long loose-hanging garment of a golden tint, and they were above the German line facing us." He and his comrades watched the vision, he said, for some forty-five minutes. Another soldier vouched that he and his fellows had been followed by squadrons of "ghostly horsemen." Wounded French soldiers claimed to have seen Joan of Arc and their knight Saint Michael; English soldiers saw Saint George. Some merely confessed to having seen a luminous cloud that had concealed them from the enemy. A Weymouth clergyman read a letter from a soldier who reported that, as the Germans were about to shoot members of his regiment who had taken refuge in a quarry, "the whole top edge of the quarry was lined with angels, who were seen by all the soldiers and the Germans as well. The Germans suddenly stopped and galloped away at top speed."

One of the most popular testimonials came from a woman named Phyllis Campbell, who had been a nurse at the front and who had repeatedly been told by wounded soldiers of the miracle at Mons. "First there was a sort of yellow mist," she quoted one witness to the *Occult Review*, "sort of risin' before the Germans as they come on to the top of the hill, come on like a solid wall they did—springing out of the earth just solid—no end to 'em. I just give up. No use fighting the whole German race, thinks I; it's all up with us. The next minute comes this funny cloud of light, and when it clears off there's a tall man with yellow hair, in golden armour, on a white horse, holding his sword up, and his mouth open as if he was saying, 'Come on, boys!' " The German troops immediately turned tail and fled, the British pursuing them, "fighting like ninety." Stories circulated that German corpses had been found on the battlefield with fatal arrow wounds—evidence of supernatural archers.

Most historians believe that fatigue must have produced at least some of these saving visions. "I had the most amazing hallucinations marching at night," wrote one young officer who was killed soon after the retreat, "so I was fast asleep, I think. Every one was reeling about the road and seeing things," he continued, adding, "I saw all sorts of things, enormous men walking towards me and lights

and chairs and things in the road."

But the Angels of Mons evidently came not from the experience of the retreat but from the pen of an obscure English writer of fables, Arthur Machen. He had read of the retreat in the *Weekly Dispatch* just before he left for church one hot Sunday toward the end of August. His mind drifting from the sermon, he suddenly had a vision of death and terror and the British troops, who had, as he remembered imagining, "a great shining about them."

In church with the altar, and the priest, and the flames, and the heat of the day, he said later, he became inspired with a story of a soldier going to heaven and finding out that it was a fine pub, which he calls The Soldier's Rest—the title of Machen's fantasy. Still reeling from the vision, another story came to him, which he called "The Bowmen." There, a thousand British soldiers are about to meet their end when suddenly the air is filled with "a long line of shapes, with a ▷

Inspired by tales of the Angels of Mons, British artist Alfred Pearse painted heavenly warriors fighting on the Allied side, as in this illustration, which is entitled *Heaven's Knight Aid Us*.

shining about them. They were like men who drew the bow, and with another shout their cloud of arrows flew singing and tingling through the air towards the German hosts." The enemy is decimated, "the grey men were falling by the thousands." As the awful bowmen did their work, "the singing arrows fled so swift and thick that they darkened the air; the heathen horde melted before them."

As Machen's romances were repeated, they evidently began to be the reality of the Retreat from Mons, as remembered by the men who had actually been there. They began to tell of the angels they had seen on the battlefront. Soon Machen was being scolded for calling his fiction fiction.

"The Bowmen" was first published in the *Evening News* of London on September 29, 1914. A few days later, the editor of the *Occult Review* wrote Machen to ask if the story were true; Machen said it was not. Then the editor of *Light*, another occult journal, called; he, too, was informed that the story was entirely a romance. Two months later, parish magazines began to reprint the story—and quickly sold out. Ministers built sermons around the tale, which was particularly popular around Easter time. By April 1915, Arthur Machen was being told that his story simply could not be construed as fiction. The writer was furious. "Some ass," he complained, "wrote me a solemn letter charging me to walk humbly and to give thanks for having been made the vessel and channel of this new revelation," adding, "I cannot conceive of anyone being foolish enough to take pride in begetting some of the silliest tales that have ever

disgraced the English tongue."

Machen blamed the clergy for having spread this romance in an irresponsible attempt to drum up faith. In an essay that implored readers not to believe the story, he ended in a diatribe against British ecclesiastics. What more could be expected, Machen wondered, from a people who spent their time "changing the Wine of Angels and the Bread of Heaven into gingerbeer and mixed biscuits."

Still, despite the author's bitter disclaimers, the visions during the Retreat of the Eighty Thousand retained some of their mystery. For example, a diary entry by one of the Great War's historians, British brigadier general John Charteris, reported the phenomenon. "Then there is the story of the 'Angel of Mons,' " he wrote in his detailed account of the retreat, "going strong through the 2nd Corps of how the angel of the Lord on the traditional white horse, and clad all in white with flaming sword, faced the advancing Germans at Mons and forbade their furthest progress. Men's nerves and imagination play weird pranks in these strenuous times. All the same the angel at Mons interests me. I cannot find out how the legend arose." The entry was dated September 5—three and a half weeks before the first appearance of Machen's fantasy. □

In September 1914, Britain was swept by rumors that Russians were going to join the fighting on the western front. Suddenly, burly cossacks were imagined everywhere. The British government saw nothing wrong with letting people believe that help was on the way and made no disclaimer until the first Allied victories in the Marne.

Running Scared

Although the Cold War between Western democracies and the East's Communist regimes was a legacy of the post-World War II era, its first chilling gusts blew through America after the First World War, causing the flame of liberty to gutter ominously. To guarantee public support for United States involvement in World War I, the government had enacted laws banning not only subversive acts but also expressions of objectionable opinion and routinely censored the press and the mails. When the war ended in November 1918, however, American civil rights did not immediately resume, for a new enemy had arisen on the ashes of Europe: the Red Menace.

This fresh foe was not entirely imaginary but occasionally surfaced in the form of anarchist attacks. On April 29, 1919, a letter bomb severely injured the wife and the maid of former Georgia senator Thomas Hardwick, an advocate of stricter immigration controls. Hearing of the Atlanta bomb, a postal official in New York remembered sixteen other small packages he had temporarily shelved only days before. Also bombs, the packages had been addressed to the nation's powerful and wealthy, from tycoons J. P. Morgan and John D. Rockefeller to Supreme Court Justice Oliver Wendell Holmes. One of the addressees, Alexander Mitchell Palmer, would eventually give his name—and, in a sense, his career—to the events set in motion by this flurry of anarchist terror.

The times had been tailor-made for Palmer. Russia's Bolshevik Revolution of 1917 had shaken demo-

cratic governments with the fear that the insurgency would spread, borne on the revolutionaries' cry to the workers of the world to rise against their oppressors. Indeed, at the end of 1918, American troops were in Russia helping czarist forces against the Red Army. But at home, where labor unions had suspended strikes in time of war, workers seemed to have heard the Bolshevik message all too clearly. As postwar inflation drove prices skyward, employees began to walk off their jobs, striking for better wages and working conditions. On January 9, 1919, the first major walkout hit New York harbor and was soon followed by a strike by some 35,000 dressmakers. In February, a general work stoppage paralyzed Seattle. Elsewhere,

railroaders struck, as did coal miners and steelworkers—and even the police. In one year, more than four million workers went on 3,600 separate strikes.

Such behavior, people began to believe, could not have arisen spontaneously: Clearly, the strikers were the agents of a sinister foreign power. Ironically, the radicals' bombs seemed to confirm the existence of conspiracy, suggesting that there was a legion of secret enemies rather than a few lathered dynamiters on the political fringe.

The bombs also made Palmer the man of the hour. A liberal Quaker from Pennsylvania, he had served in the House of Representatives from 1909 to 1915. In 1917, he became the oddly titled "alien property custodian," charged with managing German holdings in the United States during the war. When Attorney General Thomas Watt Gregory resigned in the spring of 1919, President Woodrow Wilson named Palmer to succeed him. The new attorney general was further anointed by the bombers: On June 2, a terrorist explosive destroyed part of his home, narrowly missing Palmer but reinforcing his reactionary hand.

Palmer quickly mounted a government attack against what he perceived as the ◊

Hyman Kaplan *(right)* broods in a freezing cell near Boston after being arrested in one of the Palmer Raids. Other presumed Reds *(above)* caught in the net await deportation at New York's Ellis Island.

dangerously radical element of American society, using a blitzkrieg of suppression that still bears his name: the Palmer Raids. One of his early moves as head of the Justice Department was to establish an antiradical division in the Federal Bureau of Investigation led by a young man named J. Edgar Hoover, then twenty-four. Under Palmer's mentorship, Hoover compiled a list of 60,000 "dangerous radicals" residing in America—most of them loyal immigrant aliens. Palmer planned to use the Deportation Act of 1918 to ship such people out of the country; one could be deported without the time-consuming formality of a trial.

His first series of arrests, over the weekend of November 7 and 8, 1919—perhaps not coincidentally, the second anniversary of the Bolshevik Revolution—targeted members of the Union of Russian Workers. Though many people had joined the union simply for its English language classes, Palmer's raiders herded 249 captives aboard the ship *Buford,* nicknamed *The Soviet Ark,* set to sail from New York Harbor in late December. Overnight, Palmer became a national hero, his stature inadvertently aided by the radicals themselves. During an Armistice Day parade in Centralia, Washington, snipers in the Industrial Workers of the World hall gunned down several marching veterans; one of the gunmen was later hanged from a bridge by a lynch mob. In New York, police discovered what the press called a Red Bomb Lab hidden behind a false wall. Such incidents seemed to justify Palmer's heavy-handed methods.

More Palmer Raids followed, culminating in further arrests of "foreign trouble-makers," who joined other deportees aboard the *Buford.* Although some officials winced at the ease with which Palmer's Justice Department sliced through civil liberties, there was no one to brake him. That September, President Woodrow Wilson had suffered a nervous collapse and a stroke from which he never recovered. In fact, Palmer had become a leading contender to succeed Wilson in the 1920 presidential election.

The election year began with Palmer's masterpiece—what some called the night of terror. The FBI had carefully infiltrated various radical organizations in the late summer of 1919. Beginning on the evening of January 2, 1920, more than 4,000 suspected radicals were rounded up in thirty-three major cities in twenty-three states. Rooms were searched without warrants. Agents, instructed to arrest first and find evidence later, burst into restaurants, pool halls, bowling alleys, and school classrooms, rounding up everyone in sight.

Those arrested in Palmer's big raid spent months in jail without being charged, unable to tell friends and families where they were and without recourse to counsel. But Palmer had overlooked a key detail: Deportations had to be approved by the Department of Labor. In the absence of the secretary of labor, who was ill at the time, the acting secretary Louis Post, who was appalled by the raiders' tactics, began to undo Palmer's creation. He canceled more than 2,000 warrants for deportation on the grounds that they were totally illegal. By the time Post was through, only 550 of the detainees were found legally deportable. The raids had not only failed, they had been an embarrassment—and the public knew it.

During the massive Palmer Raids of January 1920, federal agents look for evidence in the Brooklyn office of *Laisve,* a Lithuanian newspaper considered radical by the government.

The discredited Palmer Raids soon ceased altogether, along with the presidential aspirations of erstwhile front runner A. Mitchell Palmer. In the course of his party's national convention that summer, he came to be regarded as a hopeless choice. The dynamiters also went out, but not with a whimper.

Around noon on September 16, 1920, a bomb concealed in a horse-drawn wagon exploded outside Wall Street's House of Morgan, killing thirty-three of the lunchtime crowd, blowing out windows for blocks around, and pockmarking the granite facades of New York's financial heart. So benumbed was the public

by Palmer's suppression of dissent, however, that the bombing spurred no cry for vengeance. As it had materialized in the acrid fumes of a letter bomb some seventeen months earlier, the Red Menace went up in smoke on Wall Street, flickering intermittently until revived at the end of yet another world war. □

A terrorist bomb concealed in a horse-drawn wagon killed thirty-three Wall Streeters and injured hundreds more when it exploded during the lunch hour on September 16, 1920.

Pet Cemetery

In the tense, "Phoney War" atmosphere of London in September 1939, the road to good intentions was paved with pets. As the city waited for the Blitz to begin, the Royal Society for the Prevention of Cruelty to Animals warned pet owners that their familiars would not be allowed in air-raid shelters. Further, families that had to be evacuated would have to abandon their pets—or have them destroyed.

The RSPCA's caution triggered a gruesome panic among the English, known for their affection for animals. A call by certain dog lovers to kill mongrels, but preserve the pedigreed, was blasted as a sentiment worthy of the Nazis. Twenty-two pet-euthanasia centers were set up by the government. Overly protective owners, fearing that a delay would cause their pets to be lost in a raid or left to starve, swarmed animal clinics to have their beloved cats and dogs "put to sleep." Animal welfare shelters were so overcome they could merely stack the dead, and heaps of small four-legged corpses began to appear across the city. In one night, some 80,000 pets were interred at an unofficial, impromptu burial mound.

Fortunately, not all pet owners joined in this grisly stampede. Many cats and dogs, like London children, were sent to the country, where special boarding homes cropped up. One Donegal farm sheltered gun dogs for one pound a week; lesser breeds had a weekly rate of just ten shillings. Other owners, unable to euthanize or transport their animals, did what they could by buying gas-proof kennels, antihysteria tablets, and nerve foods for their dogs. Canine gas masks were popular but not recommended—the dogs wearing them lost all sense of smell and direction.

Cats and dogs were not the only pets to suffer. In a nation devoted to rearing racing pigeons, the homing birds were suddenly perceived as potential message bearers for the enemy. Police clambered over roofs to raid dovecotes and clip the wings of long-distance flyers; sometimes the whole flock was ordered destroyed. Pigeon owners were constantly required to show their permits, and birds found dead or alive with an identification tag or message attached were to be delivered to the police, no questions asked—under no circumstances was the finder to try to decode the message.

But pigeons also served. Many were conscripted into the National Pigeon Service to fly with the Royal Air Force, whose Falcon Control Unit was in charge of mobilizing feathered fighters. To protect its messengers, a Falcon Interceptor Unit trained birds of prey to attack and destroy airborne pigeons deemed unfriendly.

Curiously, beekeepers were allowed to keep their bees, even though the Japanese had reportedly trained the insects to carry messages. But bees could fly for only four or five miles and thus were not, the government concluded, a significant security risk. □

IMPORTANT!

NO. OF PERSONS SLEEPING IN THIS HOUSE

DOG / CAT

(Cross out whichever is inapplicable)

ALSO **IN HOUSE HIS BED IS**

(State location of bed as exactly as possible.)

Issued by

The National Canine Defence League, Victoria Station House, S.W.1.

The Royal Society for the Prevention of Cruelty to Animals, 105, Jermyn Street, S.W.1.

Subversion

British prime minister Winston Churchill wrote in his memoirs that the only thing that really frightened him during World War II was Adolf Hitler's fleet of submarines—and with good reason. The U-boats (from *Unterseeboot)* had transformed the lifelines of the Atlantic Ocean into a dangerous gauntlet that every supply-bearing convoy had to run en route to or from Britain. By the end of the war, 2,800 Allied seamen had been killed by the undersea wolf pack and 175 Allied ships had been sunk. The lurking submarines exerted almost as much power on the imagination as they did on shipping.

So pervasive were the U-boats to Americans, in fact, that people saw them everywhere they looked, from Miami Beach to the Mississippi River, from Boston to Galveston, Texas. But the German submarines were not merely stalking Allied shipping—they were making secret landfalls. According to rumor, men aboard a German submarine that was washed ashore in Massachusetts had ticket stubs from a movie theater in Gloucester, dated just the previous night. In Norfolk, Virginia, home of the largest U.S. Navy base, German sailors were reportedly seen at the movies.

A Boston bakery was said to have a German U-boat crew as its best customers, buying hundreds of loaves at a time at a designated coastal rendezvous. Legend held that bread from that bakery was found aboard a beached sub. Farther south, the same story was told about a bakery in Portsmouth, Virginia, and in Florida, a captured U-boat was reported to have bought its milk and bread in Miami. Local Italian Americans had supposedly fed spaghetti and information to the crew of an Italian submarine found off Long Island.

The Germans paid dearly for their toll on Allied shipping and for these mythical snacks and movie dates along the American coast. From 1941 through 1945, about 28,000 German seamen lost their lives, and only 63 of a fleet of 842 U-boats made it home. From this arose yet another legend. So many submarines had been destroyed offshore, it was said, that seamen used the many exposed periscopes as navigation markers. □

Enemy Within

In 1936, as General Emilio Mola Vidal *(below)* assembled his rebel troops outside Madrid for one of the first sieges of the Spanish Civil War, journalists asked him which of his four army columns would take the city. None of them, he is said to have replied—victory would come from a fifth column of secret supporters inside the capital. Mola was wrong about victory. His assault failed, and he died the following year in an airplane crash. If the legend is true, however, General Mola's response gave the world its contemporary equivalent of the Trojan Horse: the fifth column.

The term swiftly entered the language of warfare, conjuring secret legions of the enemy, doing their sinister work disguised as ordinary citizens. In July 1940, for example, some 71 percent of Americans surveyed believed the Nazis had a fifth column operating in the United States. In Los Angeles, an Erase-the-Fifth-Column, Inc., was formed. Kindergarten teachers, volunteer firemen, and even hobos banded together and publicly pledged themselves to fight against the fifth column. *Life* magazine called the worldwide secret infiltrations a hydra-headed menace, adding that

Americans were "fed up with such Fifth Column monkeyshines." Hitler denied the existence of this enemy within, but no one listened—at that time, the U.S. Senate had just passed a bill requiring that three and a half million resident aliens put their fingerprints on file.

Citizens began turning in their neighbors as spies and Nazi sympathizers—one even murdered a fifth-column suspect. At one point, there were so many leads pouring into the Department of Justice—3,000 a day—that Attorney General Robert Jackson warned people to calm down and let the FBI do the investigating. One New York politician thought he had found members of a fifth column concealed among teachers and police. Conservatives thought that fifth columnists had been parachuting into America for decades—and were liberals. Socialists thought the fifth column must be America's rich capitalists. Congressman J. Parnell Thomas *(pages 62 and 64)* told a radio audience that "the surest way of removing the Fifth Column from our shores is to remove the New Deal from the seat of government." To qualify as a fifth columnist then, one had only to disagree with someone else.

One reason the idea of a secret enemy had such power to produce hysteria in the United States was that it was a real and pervasive force in wartime Europe. Nazi agents actually had been introduced into Great Britain (and, for that matter, into the United States as well), and secret internal enemies were employed by Germany against Western democracies. In fact, perhaps the greatest fifth columnist of them all was a man who, like General Mola, added to the language. Norwegian defense minister Vidkun Quisling so deftly betrayed his nation to the Nazis that his surname became a synonym for traitor. □

A Stamp for Little Alf

One day in 1918, according to legend, a man in England received a letter from his son, an inmate in a German prisoner-of-war camp. The boy wrote cheerfully of his life in captivity but added a mystifying reference. The stamp on the envelope was rare, he said, and would make a nice addition to Little Alf's collection. As no one knew who Little Alf could be, the puzzled family duly steamed the stamp off the envelope. To their horror, written where the stamp had been was: "They have torn off my tongue." This shocking anecdote, which spread rapidly across Great Britain, was not the barbarity it seemed, however. It was merely the latest appearance of a wartime perennial: the Little Alf atrocity story.

At about the same time, a few hundred miles to the east, a Munich woman was said to have received a letter from *her* son, a prisoner of the Russians. He also called attention to his letter's unusual stamp, which his mother steamed off to find the chilling confidence: "They have cut off both my feet so that I cannot escape."

These were neither the first nor the last Little Alf stories. In 1866, a captured Confederate soldier's letter home reportedly carried this message under its stamp: "My God!

They've cut out my tongue!" Not quite a century later, during the Second World War, an American mother was said to have received a letter from her son, who was in a Japanese prison camp, saying he was doing well and that she should not worry. The rare stamp on the envelope, he added, should go to a friend for his collection. But when she removed the interesting collectible she, like so many mythical mothers before her, found written: "They have cut out my tongue."

Credible only in time of war—but evidently always credible then—the deathless saga of Little Alf's stamp enjoys a life of its own. No one ever seems to note that mail from prisoners of war is franked, not stamped, and always has been. After all, someone might use stamps to conceal a secret message. □

A pair of World War I vintage German stamps *(below, center)* are flanked by two Second World War Japanese issues.

DENIGRATION AND RIDICULE are time-honored tools for rendering fearsome enemies less so. A powerful war machine designed and operated by rodents, bugs, and other nasty little vermin must be inferior to one's own. Thus, Cold War cartoonists in the former Soviet Union portrayed Uncle Sam as a sunglass-masked Texas spider, with nuclear warheads for boots, creeping across Spain and Europe *(left)*. During World War II, an earlier generation of Russian illustrators made German dictator Adolf Hitler a mustached rat *(below, right)*, while, in the United States, *Colliers* magazine scorned the Japanese enemy as a bomb-toting Samurai bat *(below, left)*.

Dislocations

Early in World War II, one of the combatant governments transported more than 100,000 of its residents to remote, guarded compounds fenced with barbed wire, where the detainees remained until an Allied victory was assured. The camps were not in Europe or Asia, however, but in the western United States; and most of their inmates were Japanese Americans, born and reared in California.

In a sense, the forced evacuation was not a great surprise. Tensions between Californians and immigrants from Japan had simmered for half a century before the war. Having banned further Chinese immigration in 1882, Californians viewed the rising influx of Japanese with hostility, fear, and suspicion. In 1900, for example, the mayor of San Francisco had quarantined Oriental neighborhoods for an alleged bubonic plague outbreak—intended, the victims claimed, to drive them out of business. The *San Francisco Chronicle* in 1905 favored such headlines as "Crime and Poverty Go Hand in Hand with Asiatic Labor" and "Brown Asiatics Steal Brains of Whites." "Every one of these immigrants," cautioned the newspaper, "is a Japanese spy." By 1913, the xenophobic climate in America had produced an act forbidding Japanese to acquire further property in California—and had created an atmosphere between the two nations that many observers thought would soon end in war. A 1920 propaganda film depicted Japanese farmers secretly regulating California produce prices, to the detriment of native growers. The same film depicted two American girls abducted by Japanese men—but rescued by American Legionnaires. In 1921, mobs began to force Japanese off their remarkably productive farmlands. Rumors circulated that the emperor had ordered every Japanese woman in America to have a new baby annually. "At this rate," warned the controller of California, John Chambers, ignoring mathematics, "by 1949 they will outnumber white people."

The Immigration Act of 1924 reinforced the notion that a Japanese, not being "a free, white person," was ineligible for citizenship. For immigrants who had been promised citizenship for fighting in World War I, it was a broken vow. Protested an Osaka newspaper: "Americans are as spiteful as snakes and vipers—we do not hesitate to call that government a studied deceiver." As Japan grew into a major economic and military power across the Pacific Ocean, the racial strife in California argued against continuing friendship with the United States. By 1941, that long friendship had ended. On December 7, the Japanese launched a surprise air attack on Pearl Harbor in Hawaii, crippling the Pacific fleet and American morale—but also mobilizing a searing wave of hatred in the United States.

To many, the attack could not have succeeded without the aid of an effective fifth column *(page 54)*. Rumor held that Japanese farmers had cut their Oahu cane fields into arrows legible only from the air, to direct overflying planes to the anchored fleet. Japanese truck drivers supposedly drove wildly on military roads to Honolulu to delay American pilots trying to reach their fighter planes. A dog found barking on the beach was suspected of sending messages to Japanese ◊

submarines listening offshore. In California, it was noted that many Japanese lived near airfields, railroads, gas and water mains, and power lines, all "within a grenade throw of coast defense guns." In peacetime, these were such undesirable locations that they were the least expensive for poor immigrants to acquire. The electric company, for example, rented land beneath its power lines for only fifteen dollars an acre. It was said that the Japanese plotted with Mexico to attack the United States, that they had secretly charted California waters, and that they had formed a military alliance with American Indians. According to some accounts, one diabolical farmer had plowed messages for invading aircraft into his farm in the California hills.

On the night of the Pearl Harbor strike, the Federal Bureau of Investigation rounded up suspected nationals of enemy countries: 147 from Italy, 857 Germans—and 1,291 Japanese. The next night brought reports of enemy aircraft over San Francisco—planes that no one ever saw—followed two days later by word that 20,000 Japanese Americans there were about to revolt. On December 13, word came that Los Angeles was about to be invaded. As such baseless stories swept California, Pearl Harbor's senior admiral and general were stripped of their commands. Perhaps taking note of those wrecked careers, jittery Lieutenant General John L. DeWitt, commander of the army district comprising California, began to lobby for evacuation of all ethnic Japanese from coastal and other prohibited areas. Ridiculed by FBI director J. Edgar Hoover and rigorously opposed by Attorney General Francis Biddle, the general

pleaded military necessity and ultimately had his way.

His cause was greatly aided by the public outcry. Grocers would not sell the Japanese any food, milkmen would not leave milk at their doors, banks would not cash their checks, and all were tainted with the treachery of the suprise attack on Hawaii. "A viper is nonetheless a viper wherever the egg is hatched," cried the *Los Angeles Times,* echoing the national anger expressed even by such noted liberals as columnist Walter Lippman. On February 19, 1942, President Franklin D. Roosevelt signed Executive Order Number 9066, which set in motion the forced removal of en-

emy nationals from certain prohibited areas. Curiously overlooking Italian and German Americans, the order was aimed at the Japanese. Soon, more than 100,000, taking with them only what possessions they could carry, were on their way to assembly centers. From there the military dispersed them to inland concentration camps—generously labeled Relocation Centers. The relocated left their former lives in shards. Many had been bought out at scandalously low prices—homes were sold for a few hundred dollars, trucks for twenty-five dollars, businesses for less than the value of their inventories.

None of the Japanese was found

A government eviction notice nailed to their steps, this Japanese-American family waits in wartime San Francisco to be shipped to an internment camp.

to be a spy, but many served with distinction during the war. The Japanese American 442d Combat Regimental Team was one of the army's most decorated units. Nor was there any trace of sabotage—or hardly any. According to author John Hersey, one strawberry farmer, told he would not be permitted to harvest his crop before reporting for relocation, angrily plowed it under. He was jailed for sabotage.

Finally, late in 1944, the government began to empty the camps—those inmates who met loyalty requirements were allowed to go home. Given only a train ticket and $25, the dispossessed discovered that their world had been shattered in their absence. Tenants had expropriated their property, land had been seized for unpaid taxes, and they found the old prejudices very much in place, if more virulently open. Some neighborhoods were posted: *No Japs Wanted.* It took thirty-three years for the American government to acknowledge that the wartime confinement of loyal residents had been a travesty and illegal. As compensation, each survivor received $20,000—about $7,000 for each year spent in America's concentration camps. □

*E*arly during World War I, Britons read of a Belgian child whose hands had been amputated by the Germans. Editorial cartoons soon depicted the kaiser surrounded by piles of hands, while other cartoons showed German soldiers eating them. Only when offers to adopt the child poured in to British newspapers did it become clear that the Belgian baby had been the creation of journalists who were hard-pressed for news.

A Man for One Season

Joseph Raymond McCarthy, the Republican junior senator from Wisconsin, appropriated Communism in 1950, following a post-World War II interval that had seen the imposition of loyalty oaths and the first convulsions of the infamous Hollywood blacklist *(pages 62-64).* Cynically grandstanding as the leader who would scour Communism from every corner of American life, he became a hero to some and a fraudulent scourge to others. In fact, the man whose surname gave history the term McCarthyism was not much of an ideologue at all. Rather, he had sniffed an atmosphere of fright and discovered opportunity.

Late in 1949, after a lackluster three years in the Senate, McCarthy began casting about for an issue with "sex appeal" that would assure him reelection. No one is quite sure how he settled on Communist infiltration. Some biographers have written that, at a dinner on January 7, 1950, Father Edmund Walsh, dean of Georgetown University's foreign service school in Washington, D.C., suggested that McCarthy go after Communists in the government. According to another account, however, the Wisconsin senator had by then received a stolen FBI report on Communist subver-

sion, which inspired his campaign. But there is consensus on his cynical acceptance of this new mission. "Joe McCarthy bought communism in much the same way as other people purchase a new automobile,"

Window-shopping New Yorkers pause in 1954 to watch Senator Joseph McCarthy in televised hearings on alleged Communist infiltration of the army.

wrote McCarthy aide Roy Cohn later. "It was as cold as that."

McCarthy opened his crusade with a speech in Wheeling, West Virginia, on February 9, horrifying his audience with the accusation that the State Department was "thoroughly infested with Communists." He said he had a list that was 205 names long. A second speech in Salt Lake City modified that number: Of the 205 bad risks, 57 were "card-carrying Communists." Although his figures were contrived, ◊

his bluff gave them authority; the further from the truth he ranged, the greater his assurance.

A Wisconsin farm boy who had helped finance college and a law degree by playing poker, the forty-one-year-old senator was used to bluffing. He had turned to politics in 1939, after less than a decade of practicing law. In his race for circuit judge against sixty-six-year-old Judge Edgar Werner, the thirty-year-old McCarthy made age the campaign issue, saying he was twenty-nine and his opponent seventy-three—or was it eighty-nine? The judge protested, but the damage was done. Using a lie like a blackjack, McCarthy had won.

When he ran for the Senate in 1944, his campaign literature dubbed him Tailgunner Joe and featured photographs of McCarthy manning the rear-seat machine gun in a marine dive bomber. Stationed in the Pacific as a marine intelligence officer, he had never flown in combat; the limp that he attributed to "ten pounds of shrapnel" actually came from a broken leg sustained at a shipboard party. Although men in uniform were not allowed to speak on political issues, the slippery McCarthy managed to evade the rules by prefacing his remarks with: "If I were able to speak, here's what I'd say." When he lost, he ran for reelection as circuit judge and won handily. His second try for the Senate in 1946 succeeded. As with so many of his dealings, however, his victory was tainted: In Wisconsin, circuit judges were not supposed to run for political office. The state supreme court ruled that he had violated the law and his oath as a judge and an attorney; then, curiously, it dismissed the case, noting that he was not likely to repeat the

offense. Four years later, in 1950, the Republican from Wisconsin and Communism discovered each other.

Smelling the pervasive fear of the Red Menace everywhere around him, McCarthy quickly found that he could say anything, about anyone, with impunity. Portraying himself as a man of deep convictions, he came to dominate the issue of government subversion with his tactics of bold attack, villification, and false accusation. As in earlier Red Scares, the Communists themselves strengthened the accuser's hand: Word of Russia's atomic spies and American reversals in the Korean conflict seemed to confirm what McCarthy and his minions purveyed. Careers and reputations were shattered. Soon, as McCarthy's early victims went down before the nation's febrile anti-Communism, no one dared to cross him. Even a Senate inquiry into financial irregularities was stymied by the bluff McCarthy.

Tailgunner Joe made headlines

for seeking out—or seeming to seek out—Communist subversives and sympathizers in government. He alleged that distinguished soldier-statesman George C. Marshall had been the architect of "a conspiracy so immense and an infamy so black as to dwarf any previous such venture in the history of man." Subversion, he claimed, stifled the anti-Communist message of the Voice of America. He battled constantly with the two presidents of his career: Harry S. Truman and Dwight D. Eisenhower. Every newspaper that criticized him he branded a Communist publication. Often, mere accusations were enough to bring an enemy down. By 1953, his witch hunt in full swing, he had threatened investigations of the military, the Atomic Energy Commission, the Central Intelligence Agency, and the Government Printing Office. He even went after the Protestant clergy, which an aide called "the largest single group

supporting the Communist apparatus in the United States today."

Finally, McCarthy went too far. In February of 1954, he hauled in Army Brigadier General Ralph Zwicker and savaged the bemedaled war hero over an honorable discharge awarded a suspect dentist. When Secretary of the Army Robert Stevens tried to intervene, McCarthy brutally subdued him, later boasting to the press that Stevens could not have capitulated "more abjectly if he had got down on his knees." But the world the senator had dominated had begun to change. On March 9, Edward R. Murrow, America's preeminent broadcast journalist, televised an entire half-hour of Joseph McCarthy in action on his "See It Now" program.

Two days later, the army counterattacked McCarthy. The senator, it charged, had tried to blackmail the military to obtain preferential treatment for a particular serviceman, former McCarthy staffer G. David Schine. In April, McCarthy's fight with the army became a fixture on live national television—and gave an enormous audience another look at McCarthyism in the raw. Then, on June 11, six days before the ruinous hearings ended, an aging Republican senator from Vermont applied the *coup de grâce.* Seventy-three-year-old Ralph Flanders introduced a resolution that revived earlier questions that concerned McCarthy's financial dealings. By December, the man from Wisconsin had been censured by his colleagues.

Although he continued to rant against Communism, McCarthy never regained his former audience or power. Instead, he spiraled toward obscurity, doomed by failed investments and alcohol, and tormented by imaginary enemies. "They're murdering me," he reportedly said in 1957, "they're killing me." He died on May 2 of that same year, when his exhausted liver failed. One right-wing writer and resolute McCarthyite claimed that the great man had been murdered, not by Communists, but by a secret group called the Illuminati *(pages 10-12).* Even in death, Joe McCarthy could evoke impossible conspiracies. □

Moments after Senator Joseph McCarthy finished berating army counsel Joseph Welch (left), the distinguished attorney opened the counterattack that helped expose the Wisconsin Republican as a calculating bully to millions of surprised American television viewers.

Movie Heroes

The Cold-War chills and fevers of the early post-World War II era came to be characterized by the tactics of one man, Wisconsin Senator Joseph McCarthy *(pages 59-61)*. Before McCarthy even reached the Senate, the House Committee on Un-American Activities—HCUA—had opened a Red hunt of its own. Its search for Communists in the motion-picture industry was one of the longest-running political events of its kind in American history and one of the most damaging. Among other things, it demonstrated that heroes of the silver screen were not always heroes on the witness stand.

A collection of anti-New Deal conservative congressmen, the committee had not targeted Hollywood idly. Following World War II, many of the film industry's workers were in unions perceived as radical organizations, and there were several ugly strikes against studios. The Los Angeles chapter of the Communist Party, with 4,000 members, was a magnet for congressional investigation, as well as the rancor of industry conservatives. So were studios that, in such films as *Mission to Moscow, Song of Russia,* and *Days of Glory,* had seemed infatu-

Writer: Dalton Trumbo

ated with the Soviet Union. Crowd pleasers while the Soviets were wartime allies, in peacetime the films seemed to glorify the enemy.

In March 1947, the committee declared that the motion-picture industry must be cleansed of Communists. Six months later, forty-three witnesses were subpoenaed, including what came to be known as the Nineteen—an assemblage of writers, producers, directors, and actors believed to have been linked to the Communist Party. On October 20, the first day of hearings, HCUA chairman J. Parnell Thomas began to call his galaxy of friendly witnesses. Actor Robert Taylor told of his chagrin at being cast in *Song of Russia* and promised that he would never again work with any left-leaning colleagues. "I would love nothing better than to fire every last one of them," he declared, "and never let them work in a studio or in Hollywood again." Shy superstar Gary Cooper testified that he had been put off by Communist ideas he found in film scripts. Ronald Reagan, then president of the Screen Actors Guild, music-man George Murphy, and dapper actor Adolphe Menjou also testified. Walt Disney claimed the Screen Cartoonists Guild was seething with Communists who had tried to put party

propaganda in Mickey Mouse's mouth. Studio boss Jack Warner swore he would not know a Communist if he saw one but nevertheless he identified sixteen writers and directors as Communists or sympathizers. Producer Louis B. Mayer corroborrated Warner's testimony and later cautioned Katharine Hepburn against speaking up for actors who had come under suspicion. The parade seemed endless—until, abruptly, the hearings ceased.

Of the Nineteen unfriendly witnesses, only eleven testified, and one of them, German-born writer Bertolt Brecht, arrived at the Washington hearings with an airline tick-

Actor: Adolphe Menjou

et to Europe already in his pocket. The remaining ten—famous as the Hollywood Ten—had placed their hopes in the free-speech guarantees of the Bill of Rights and refused to answer the committee's definitive question: Were they now, or had they ever been, members of the Communist Party? Despite the support of such industry titans as di-

Writer: Ring Lardner, Jr.

Supporting writers and directors charged with Communist ties, stars *(from left)* Danny Kaye, June Havoc, Humphrey Bogart, and Lauren Bacall appeared at 1947 hearings of the House Committee on Un-American Activities.

rectors John Huston and William Wyler and actors Humphrey Bogart and Gene Kelly, the Ten were indicted in December for contempt of Congress. Those who still had their jobs were quickly dropped by the studios. After the Supreme Court refused to hear their case in 1950, the Ten lost their freedom as well: Two were sentenced to prison for six months, eight for a year.

But the modern-day inquisition had barely begun. After a jittery three-and-a-half-year lull, the committee once again turned toward Hollywood in 1951. Under the leadership of Congressman John S. Wood, the committee subpoenaed forty-five unfriendly witnesses, with an eye to forcing them to provide names of colleagues with Communist ties. The committee had already obtained this information, which the unfortunate witnesses were expected to corroborate—as penitent informers against former friends and fellow workers. The collective nerve of the industry, already weakened by the destruction of the Ten, now shattered. The industry established a blacklist: Those who did not cooperate and recant took a long—usually a permanent—vacation from work.

The Screen Writers Guild at first merely refused to protect members who were Communists and then finally barred them altogether. The Screen Actors Guild required members to take a loyalty oath, as did the Directors Guild. As president of the Motion Picture Alliance for the Preservation of American Ideals, screen hero John Wayne waxed enthusiastic about ridding filmland of Communists. The American Legion warned that fellow travelers were still hidden in the woodwork of filmmaking. In 1951, a group called the Wage Earners Committee did its patriotic duty and published a list of ninety-two movies which employed "commies" and contained "subversive matter designed to defame ◊

Actor: Sterling Hayden

America throughout the world." Among them: *Death of a Salesman*, based on Arthur Miller's play.

Even those who had been brave in 1947 scrambled to save themselves. Actor Edward G. Robinson, appearing before HCUA in 1952 for the third time, admitted, "I was duped and used. I was lied to." Bandleader Artie Shaw wept, recounting how the Communists had tricked him. Director Elia Kazan named eleven former Communists and renounced his earlier support for the Ten. Writer Abe Burrows lamented his stupidity in joining the party, and playwright Clifford Odets, named by Kazan, named the director in turn, among others. Actors José Ferrer and Larry Parks expressed regret, some thought too mildly. Lucille Ball said she had registered as a Communist only as a favor to her grandfather. Lloyd

Playwright: Lillian Hellman

Bridges arranged to testify in secret. He-man actor Sterling Hayden captured the taint of the time in his 1963 autobiography: "I was a real daddy longlegs of a worm when it came to crawling."

The committee returned to Hollywood in 1953, 1955, 1956, and 1958. All in all, seventy-two witnesses cooperated with the HCUA and named some 325 industry workers as past or present Communists. But more than 200 others took another path. Dashiell Hammett, the creator of *The Maltese Falcon* and *The Thin Man*, went to

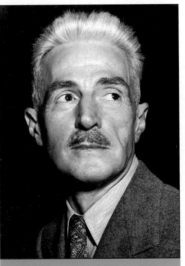

Writer: Dashiell Hammett

jail. Playwright Lillian Hellman graciously declined to inform upon others. Lionel Stander was offered $150,000 a year and his own television show if he would go before the committee and swear he was not a Communist—but defied the congressmen. Asked about former party membership, Stander declined to answer, not wanting to join "a whole stable of informers, stoolpigeons, and psychopaths." Comedian

Actor: Lionel Stander

Charlie Chaplin left the country for Europe and did not return until 1972, to pick up a special Academy Award. Actor John Garfield, singer Canada Lee, and actor J. Edward Bromberg, among others, died under the pressures of the hearings.

Many writers went into exile or worked under a pseudonym. Of approximately 250 blacklistees, a few managed to salvage their careers. A handful of actors and directors survived by moving into legitimate theater. In 1960, producer-director Otto Preminger said he would give writer Dalton Trumbo, one of the jailed Hollywood Ten, screen credit for *Exodus*, and Kirk Douglas said he would acknowledge Trumbo's authorship of *Spartacus*. Blacklisted writers Carl Foreman and Michael Wilson wrote 1957's distinguished *Bridge on the River Kwai*, and, as the pall of fear lifted, other authors resumed distinguished careers. Ring Lardner, Jr., another of the Ten, created the 1970 classic *M*A*S*H*. Coincidentally, Lardner was also witness to one of the era's oddest counterpoints. Back in 1950, serving his time in Danbury prison, he had run into a short, plump, red-faced fellow inmate in the exercise yard: former HCUA chairman J. Parnell Thomas, jailed for payroll padding. □

CURIOUS CULTS

From the outside, a cult may seem a dangerous construct of falsehood, distortion, delusion, even madness institutionalized—a collective of unreality. But from within there must seem to be method and logic, rich interaction between like-minded people, and the glow of an elusive, unlikely truth finally revealed.

No soil is infertile. Cults thrive on the secular, exposing the hitherto concealed roots of social evils and prescribing a remedy—often one that is worse than what it purports to cure. For religious cultists, revelation sets them at the deity's right hand, on the path to salvation and paradise. And some sects are evidently bound by the gruesome gravitation of death.

Almost always, these crusaders are led by a single individual, a visionary commander and conduit to truth, and his or her compelling web of dogma. Disciples may attribute to such figures powers verging on the messianic—or concur in the belief of a mortal claiming to be God. It is here that cults, overtaken by delusion, spiral toward madness, confirming the outsiders' most terrible fears.

Barthélemy Enfantin's vest reads "Le Père"—The Father; his pendant honors the cult mother.

Arrested Development

A great weekend amusement for Parisians in 1832 was a trip to the suburb of Ménilmontant to enjoy the ritual parades, singing, and recitations staged at a peculiar sort of monastery. Its residents were the self-declared father, strikingly handsome Barthélemy Prosper Enfantin, and his forty followers. Committing themselves to celibacy, these well-educated young men had recently come to live in a grand house. Their aim was lofty: to found a new socialist society.

Instead of drab monks' habits, however, the residents wore a symbolically colorful outfit designed by Enfantin. It consisted of white trousers representing love, a blue tunic for faith, and a white vest with red trim for labor that had the wearer's name emblazoned on the front. Enfantin's vest read Le Père— "the Father." The vest closed in back to make the point that everyone in this world is dependent on others, even for help in dressing.

Enfantin and his crew were admirers of the late philosopher Henri de Saint-Simon, who had advocated a social religion—a new, more utilitarian brand of Christianity that would incorporate science and industrialism. Enfantin had studied engineering at the elite École Polytechnique, but instead of building bridges and canals like his fellow graduates, he had set about engineering a kind of religion. Highly ethical but secular in spirit, the plan Enfantin es-

poused turned the teachings of Saint-Simon into a more outright socialism, calling for public ownership of industry and banking and the abolition of property inheritance. Enfantin also advocated great freedom, including enfranchisement, for women. He envisioned a future where individuals would both work and love according to their capacity—one in which people would be free to fall in love, marry, even divorce, according

to what their hearts told them—a radical idea in Catholic Europe.

Enfantin tested his secular religion in Ménilmontant. He and his followers rose at 5:00 a.m. sharp, helped one another into their vests, and began the day's work—cooking, washing, cleaning, and gardening. There were no servants. The group preached sermons to one another, composed and sang mirthless hymns, and professed mutual love.

Before long, the more stolid middle class grew concerned. Enfantin's radical ideas, officials feared, invited moral corruption. Along with several followers, he was arrested and charged with offending public morality. During the trial in Paris in August 1832, Enfantin expounded on his theory of love. He blasted his accusers as the true corrupters of youth, charging that by defending the social order they encouraged

In this nineteenth-century French caricature, Barthélemy Enfantin waves a jester-topped scepter and makes eyes at his idealized "free woman."

promiscuity, prostitution, and other unseemliness. The judge brushed Enfantin's philosophizing aside. The accused were found guilty and sentenced to a year in prison, but they were released after serving only seven months.

Free again, Enfantin went off with some of his followers to North Africa and the Middle East to search for the perfect "mother" who would serve as his female counterpart. He had tried but failed to secure one previously—it was said that Lucile Dudevant (author George Sand) had declined the offer of the position. Enfantin was once again unsuccessful at winning a consort. His engineer's instincts resurfacing, he played briefly with the idea of building a canal across Egypt to connect the Mediterranean and Red seas. Some years later, the Suez Canal was built by Ferdinand de Lesseps, a lapsed follower of Saint-Simon. But Enfantin did not live to see the canal open in 1869. His entourage dispersed, and he became more conventional. When he died in 1864, the one-time monastic had become the successful chief of the Paris-Lyon-Méditerranée railway line. □

The onionists of France reportedly looked to the vegetable for a lesson in achieving perfection and immortality. According to their *Little Book of the Lord,* if the onion's stem was cut before the plant went to seed, the eunuch bulb would live on to sprout anew—offering an example for those who were pure enough to follow it.

The Bride of the Lamb

Joanna Southcott (*overleaf*) was a humble forty-two-year-old domestic servant in the town of Exeter, England, when a mysterious but distinctly audible voice suddenly began speaking to her one day in 1792. In waking hours and in dreams, a stream of prophesies reached Southcott's attentive ear. Even her sister's declaration that she must be mad did not shake Southcott's conviction that it was God's voice that spoke to her.

Southcott was quick to share with her neighbors the messages purported to have come from God. Many dealt with mundane matters—dying cattle, a family's change of fortune, the local harvest—and were on target often enough that people were convinced she indeed must have some uncanny power. Especially impressive was her foreshadowing of the fate of the bishop of Exeter. He appeared to be perfectly healthy when a letter from Southcott reached a local vicar, who followed her instructions not to read it for a year. He finally opened the letter to discover that it had foretold a recent unexpected event—the death of the bishop. The pinpoint prophecy added to Joanna Southcott's prestige, as well as providing fodder for detractors who suspected her of witchcraft and called for her hanging.

But the petty affairs of yeomen and shopkeepers were not the focus of Southcott's dreams and visions. It was, instead, the end of history—the second coming of Christ and the Day of Judgment. In 1796, the voice brought her an astounding message: Her own life had been foretold in the New Testament's Book of Revelation. She embodied two of the book's figures—"the woman clothed with the sun, and the moon under her feet, and upon her head a crown of twelve stars," and "the bride of the Lamb." Southcott's role, the voice explained, was a momentous one indeed—someday she was to deliver humanity from the burden of Eve's sin in the Garden of Eden.

When Southcott solicited support from various Exeter ministers for her unorthodox notions, she had little success. One reviled her as the mouthpiece of the devil; others ignored her letters or returned them with derogatory remarks. She was, however, determined to win a wider audience, and in 1801, she used her savings to publish *The Strange Effects of Faith.* The pamphlet, which recorded Southcott's prophecies, did the trick: Seven educated and influential readers came calling on her to learn more about the voice and its messages. Convinced that Southcott was a genuine prophet, these new converts, who included three Anglican clergymen, enthusiastically took up her cause. The gratified Southcott called the group the seven stars of her movement, which, with their material and moral support, spread quickly.

Southcott added what became a potent talisman among her followers. On small scraps of paper she wrote: "The Sealed of the Lord, the Elect precious. Man's Redemption to inherit the Tree of Life. To be made Heirs of God and Joint-Heirs with Jesus Christ." Adding her signature, she folded the paper and affixed a seal bearing two stars and the letters *I.C.,* which she took to be Jesus Christ's initials.

For true believers, these bits of ◊

paper were regarded as shields against evil. By 1804, more than 8,000 of the seals had been distributed to followers. The total number of sealed followers eventually climbed to the tens of thousands, though never to the much-desired 144,000—the number of the elect guaranteed salvation in the Book of Revelation.

Over the years, Southcott wrote or dictated hundreds and hundreds of communications from the voice she came to call her Spirit. In 1814, she received the climactic message of her career, with tragic results. Nearly two decades after first hearing of her supposed role in human redemption, Southcott shared the voice's newest revelation: Age sixty-four and a virgin still, she was to give birth to Shiloh, a new messiah. The birth date was predicted to be October 19, 1814.

Sure enough, Southcott miraculously began to look pregnant. For the sake of propriety, she arranged to marry an old friend, John Smith, so the child would not be born a bastard. Followers donated expensive gifts: a silver cup and salver, a Bible bound in red Morocco, a £200 satinwood cradle lined in blue cloth with the name Shiloh embroidered in Hebrew letters of gold.

As word got around, Southcottians were subjected to ridicule, and families divided over what to make of these extraordinary events. The expectant prophet got the stamp of approval from seventeen of the

twenty-one eminent physicians invited to examine her—but only externally. They reported that the pregnancy appeared genuine to them. As the birth approached, however, Southcott seemed to grow weaker and weaker, and became wracked with self-doubt. On December 27, she died. Physicians performed an autopsy and discovered that there had been no pregnancy—Southcott's increased girth was attributed to obesity and glandular enlargement. There was no obvious cause of death. The faithful kept the body warm with hot-water bottles for four days, as Southcott had instructed, in the hope of a resurrection. When none came, the remains were buried secretly in St. John's Wood Cemetery on January 2, 1815.

The Southcott legend lived on, and a century and a half later her society still claimed a following of some 100,000 in England and the United States. Today, the focus of their interest is a box that Southcott filled with unpublished writings said to contain the panacea for the world's ills. The box has supposedly passed from one guardian to another over the years. In 1916, a group of Southcottians organized the Panacea Society. It claimed to have the box but would not open it until twenty-four Anglican bishops would agree to attend an opening ceremony and validate the contents. To put pressure on the bishops, the Panacea Society began placing an advertisement in newspapers warning that "Crime and Banditry, Distress of Nations, and Perplexity will continue to increase until the bishops open Joanna Southcott's Box of sealed writings."

The bishops were—and continue to be—uncooperative. One of their number did appear at an event unsanctioned by the Panacea Society. In 1927, an English psychic researcher named Harry Price claimed to have come into possession of the box. With the press and the aged bishop in attendance, Price opened it to reveal a peculiar assortment of items, including a horse pistol, a lottery ticket, a 1773 French diary, a pair of earrings, a nightcap, and a book entitled *The Surprises of Love.*

The Panacea Society declared the Price box a hoax and still awaits a quorum of bishops to step forward. For some Southcottians, time is growing short—they expect the world to end in the year 2000. □

Native Dancer

To some, he was known as plain Jack Wilson, but to many Indians of the American West he was Wovoka, the messiah whose Ghost Dance would hasten the coming of a glorious millennium. Born into the Northern Paiute tribe, the young Indian established close contact with a family of Presbyterian ranchers, from whom he took his English name. During the years he spent with the Wilsons, Wovoka absorbed the Christian notions that later reappeared in the hopeful—and desperate—message he

spread from Oregon to Oklahoma.

Like his fellow Indians, Wovoka looked to visions for religious insight and guidance. On January 1, 1889, he had a vision of the future as he lay deliriously ill with what may have been scarlet fever. The Great Spirit revealed to him a rich and happy land where the ghosts of all Indian ancestors enjoyed eternal youth. If his people would do as the Great Spirit instructed, Wovoka learned, they would escape suffering and death and live in bliss with the ghosts. The Indians must avoid quarreling, lying, and fighting, and live in peace with white people. Most important, Wovoka's people must practice the dance that would summon their ancestral ghosts.

Wovoka's potent vision came at a time when all hope of resisting the white settlers had been crushed. His message quickly spread from tribe to tribe, and Indians all over the West began to perform the Ghost Dance. Each tribe, however, had its own variation on Wovoka's

central theme. The prairie tribes abandoned the old funeral practices, in which horses were slaughtered and relatives of the dead cut themselves with knives, believing that they would soon be reunited with lost loved ones. The Sioux interpreted Wovoka's doctrine to mean that vanished herds of buffalo and ponies would return to the reborn land and the whites would be swept away bloodlessly.

The dancers in some tribes—men, women, and children—preferred to dress in traditional buckskin clothing, shunning everything that they had received from the white man, such as metal ornaments. Moving in a slow, shuffling circle, the Indians danced for several nights in a row. Many of them fell into trances and had visions that they would recount later. On the last night, the dancing continued until the morning.

Some Indians believed their consecrated Ghost Dance shirts could even stop bullets—a delusion ◊

Wovoka, also known as Jack Wilson, conceived the Ghost Dance, photographed (top) during an 1893 performance of the ritual.

that proved tragic in South Dakota during the latter part of 1890. Tensions had been mounting between the dancing Sioux and U.S. government Indian agents. By November, 3,000 soldiers had been called in to quell the disturbance, and the Sioux began to flee in large numbers into the Badlands. Sitting Bull, the Sioux chief at the Standing Rock reservation, was fingered as a "hostile" by the agents, who sent a band of Indian police to arrest him. On December 15, Sitting Bull was shot dead during the attempt, and his followers fled to join the Indians converging on the Badlands. About two weeks later, the band of Indians— by this point tired and hungry—surrendered to cavalry troops at an encampment on Wounded Knee Creek. But the following morning, a scuffle broke out, and the soldiers opened fire on the Indians, who believed they would be protected by their ghost shirts. Some 200 or 300 Indians were massacred, many of them killed after being pursued for miles. The catastrophe at Wounded Knee ended the Ghost Dance—by 1893, the ceremony was rapidly disappearing. The dance's creator lived on until 1932, dying in Yerington, Nevada. His original headstone was a simple marker noting the resting place of Jack Wilson, but in 1980, a new plaque was put in place, memorializing him as "Wovoka, Founder of the Ghost Dance." □

The painted buckskin shirt that the Arapaho donned for the Ghost Dance was, some Indians believed, impervious to the white man's bullets.

Bizarre Baptism

When Catherine the Great learned of a Christian sect in the province of Tambov that was secretly practicing a grisly ritual, she ordered the police to root it out. The founder of the sect, Kondratii Selivanov, managed to elude arrest and for two years more continued to recruit new members. In 1774, he was finally caught and exiled to Siberia. But many Russians, from peasants such as Selivanov to aristocrats, embraced the sect, and it continued to flourish during Selivanov's twenty-year absence.

Selivanov's followers were the Skoptsy—the "Castrated Ones." They were impelled by a literal interpretation of a line in the Gospel of Matthew: "And there are eunuchs who have made themselves eunuchs for the sake of the kingdom of heaven." The Skoptsy believed that Jesus, his apostles, and the early saints had castrated themselves to be free of lust, the original sin of Adam and Eve.

The preferred instrument of their principal rite, the "baptism of fire," was a red-hot poker. Male converts used it to destroy their own testicles (the "lesser seal" of faith) and their penises (the "great seal"); women mutilated their breasts and sometimes their genitals. In consideration of human frailty, instruments other than the poker were permitted for the rite. The faint of heart most commonly chose a knife, but razors, hatchets, scythes, and sharp pieces of glass were also used. At their ceremonies, the Skoptsy sang hymns and performed a heavy rhythmic dance, working themselves up into a frenzy of

twitching and speaking in tongues.

The faithful came to regard the exiled Selivanov as a divine figure, perhaps even the reincarnation of Jesus Christ. When he had 144,000 followers, they believed, the Day of Judgment would take place, initiating the millennium prophesied in the Bible. Anxious to fill the ranks of their sect, the Skoptsy proselytized energetically. Not all of their converts, it seems, were voluntary, for there were reports of men who were kidnapped and forced to endure castration.

Selivanov returned from Siberia in 1795, asserting in Moscow that he was in fact the emperor Peter III, who had been assassinated in 1762. But in 1797, after an audience with Peter's son Paul in St. Petersburg, Selivanov was promptly locked up in a madhouse. His fortunes improved when Alexander I became czar in 1801. A mystic himself, Alexander freed Selivanov. For some years, the sect leader was maintained in luxury by worshipful members of the St. Petersburg aristocracy. When Selivanov eventually fell from royal favor, he was confined to a monastery until his death in 1832.

During Selivanov's years in St. Petersburg and after, the sect developed into an elaborate institution with a powerful hierarchy. But the czar who came to the throne in 1825, Nicholas I, was determined to destroy the Skoptsy, and the persecution that began then continued into the twentieth century. The sect nevertheless survived, and there may have been as many as 100,000 members in 1917, when the Russian Revolution took place. What their fate was under a regime that vigorously suppressed religion is uncertain. Some say that the Skoptsy fled to Romania and may still be there. Others report that the sect, though reduced in numbers, survived World War II and subsequently underwent a resurgence—without their former seals of faith. Today, according to current legend, the Skoptsy still shun sex but have abandoned the poker and the knife; a purely symbolic, spiritual castration initiates the faithful into a life of celibacy. □

For Whom the Bell Tolls

In the gloomy depths of the Depression, California businessman Arthur Bell turned his nightmare vision of the world into a movement that he peddled with evangelical fervor. His manner and appearance belied his dark outlook, for he was suave, well-spoken, handsome, and always exquisitely dressed. When he was thirty-three, Bell married a wealthy widow in her sixties and with her money published *Mankind United* in 1934 to warn humanity of the vicious conspiracy he had discovered and to rally his readers to defeat it.

According to his tract, the world had been dominated for centuries by a handful of very wealthy families. They had conspired to thwart moral and economic development around the globe, sowing war and famine in every quarter. In order to seize property and increase their profits, for example, they had deliberately created the worldwide depression. These Hidden Rulers, as Bell called them, kept themselves abreast of the most intimate details of peoples' lives through a network of 10,000 spies and retained henchmen to exterminate the forces of good. The ultimate aim of the conspiracy was to build what Bell called a World Slave State. Each of the Hidden Rulers families would live at the top of a twenty-five-story apartment building large enough to house 25,000 servants and serfs. Among the prerogatives of the head of the household would be choosing women for his harem.

It was a grim scenario but not an inevitable one. The Hidden Rulers, Bell reassured his readers, were not invulnerable. A group of enlightened but anonymous people who called themselves the Sponsors had come together on Christmas Day, 1875, to devise a plan for saving the world. They created a self-perpetuating institution—Mankind United—that remained a closely held secret until the publication of his book. Already, Bell reported, the Sponsors had destroyed a horrible machine the conspirators had invented to "cause the eyes of millions of people to be vibrated out of their sockets." Other dangers still lay ahead, however, and the Hidden Rulers could be defeated only if 200 million people agreed to take up the fight. Once the 200-million mark had been reached, Bell promised, the Sponsors would put into action a "30-day program" that would make public their incredible findings. Everyone who signed up with Bell would be given a special radio attachment that would allow them to tune in directly to the latest reports from Mankind United.

Bell's message found a large audience. During the 1930s, he

registered about 250,000 followers and boasted that his organization possessed a vast network of "bureaus"—Los Angeles alone was said to have twenty-five. Overseeing the organization was no problem for Bell, who laid claim to occult powers. Mankind United followers were informed that he had created seven perfect doubles of himself, in order to help handle his enormous responsibilities.

But the zip went out of the movement when World War II broke out. Bell denounced the war as the Hidden Rulers' newest attempt to achieve world dictatorship. Although devotees of the cult may have agreed, Bell's position put him at odds with the federal government. In 1942, he was arrested under the Wartime Sedition Act for conspiring to interfere with the war effort. He was convicted and sentenced to five years in prison, but the verdict was later overturned on appeal.

While he was doing battle with the government, Bell began transforming Mankind Unit-

ed, which in 1944 became Christ's Church of the Golden Rule. Loyal disciples hoped that the establishment of the new church meant that the illuminating thirty-day program was about to begin. But Bell had moved on to other, more practical things. The primary purpose of the remade movement, he said, was to bring about the adoption of what he called Christ Jesus' Golden Rule of absolute economic equality. To this end, he urged the 850 or so followers who had stuck with him to donate at least 50 percent of their wealth; by 1945, the net worth of the organization was estimated to be $3.5 million.

In his new role as a religious leader, Bell variously called himself the Voice of the Right Idea, the Speaker, or the Prophet. Unfortunately for Bell, however, he seemed to have lost his touch. His following declined, eroded by ongoing legal troubles. In 1951, he notified his flock that he had been called upon by the Sponsors to fulfill other duties in the "International League of Vigilantes." His exit was not without hope, however, for he assured the faithful that they would one day colonize a paradise in outer space, on one of the planets whose inhabitants lived in utopian bliss, free of suffering and death. They would make the journey one by one, with each colonist taking off moments from his or her "so-called death," to be propelled across the galaxy by a machine manipulating the body's "vibrational rate and atomic structure." The traveler would arrive rejuvenated and ready to enjoy eternal happiness.

Bell passed his mantle on to one of his trusted lieutenants. She did no better, and within five years the cult was virtually dead. □

California Dreaming

On Northern California's Mount Shasta, a mining engineer named Guy Ballard had an extraordinary encounter that inspired the great I AM movement that flourished in the 1930s. In his book *Unveiled Mysteries,* Ballard reported that in September 1930, he was hiking up the mountain when he happened to encounter a young man at a spring. As Ballard was about to fill his cup, the stranger offered him "a much more refreshing drink than spring water." Ballard swallowed the creamy liquid and was suddenly filled with an electric feeling of health and vigor.

Declaring that the drink was a

taste of Omnipotent Life itself, the stranger introduced himself as the comte de Saint-Germain. The name had been familiar to occultists since the eighteenth century—in that era, a self-styled French count won notoriety for claiming to have lived for centuries. Saint-Germain said that he was one of the Ascended Masters of Light, a group that included Jesus Christ, among others. Through self-discipline and meditation on something called the I AM presence, the masters had escaped the coils of mortality.

Ballard wrote that in several meetings on Mount Shasta, Saint-Germain took him on tours of the past and future. In one scene, Ballard saw himself officiating as a priest in ancient Egypt, alongside a vestal virgin called Lotus—who ◊

turned out to be the same person as his Iowa-born wife, Edna Wheeler. Nearby was another priest—their son Donald. This was just the beginning. On subsequent excursions, Ballard said he witnessed a 70,000-year-old civilization in the Sahara, the lost continent of Mu submerged in the Pacific, buried Amazon cities, and a future golden age whose guiding light would be North America.

Edna Ballard, an accomplished harpist and devoted mystic, had been editing *The American Occultist* in Chicago since the 1920s. With the publication of *Unveiled Mysteries* in 1934, the Ballards began to spread the faith they called I AM, whose basic tenet is that the I AM presence can be used to improve one's life. Its name is derived from the biblical conversation between Moses and the burning bush. When Moses inquired of the bush who was speaking, God's voice answered: "I am that I am." The faith caught on like wildfire. Ten proselytes attended the Ballards' first ten-day class in 1934. By August 1935, they filled the Shrine Auditorium in Los Angeles with several thousand ecstatic followers.

I AM had a pronounced puritanical streak: To be counted among the deeply faithful "hundred percenters," a person must shun any form of sex along with alcohol, tobacco, drugs, and meat. Eating garlic and onions was also on the long list of I AM vices.

The colorful rites featured a huge representation of the Magic Presence—a painting of the sacred Mount Shasta and the "Royal Tetons," another holy locale, against a background of deep blue. Superimposed on this image was a human figure surrounded by a transparent lavender cylinder. Over the head was a halo and a series of bright rays descending from a second figure in the sky above. On either side were portraits of Jesus and Saint-Germain, rendered in romantic style by artist Charles Sindelar, an I AM follower who claimed the two subjects had sat for their portraits. From the dais various leaders would read telegrams and I AM hymns were sung. The Ballards arrived toward the end to deliver messages from the Ascended Masters and make stirring speeches.

As their flock grew, the Ballards earned an estimated $1,000 a day for I AM and took to driving around in a cream-colored limousine with a harp mounted on the trunk. They produced a vast literature to support their movement, including scores of textbooks and numerous photos. In 1939, the I AM faith reached its crest, then went into a rapid decline in the face of litigation and mounting criticism in the press. Ballard died suddenly in December, his mortality a bewildering shock to the faithful. Then came the indictments. On July 24, 1940, Edna Ballard, her son Donald, and a score of church leaders were charged with violating federal mail-fraud laws. Mother and son were the only ones convicted. In 1946, the U.S. Supreme Court overturned their convictions, citing improper selection of a grand jury.

Over the years, the I AM movement has shrunk, but true believers carry on even though there is no Ballard at the helm—Edna died in 1971, Donald in 1973. Every year, several thousand I-AMers and curious onlookers gather on Mount Shasta for a pageant celebrating the accession of Jesus to the rank of Ascended Master. □

Love's Old Sweet Throng

The Reverend Henry James Prince, a Victorian churchman of great charm and eloquence with a notable fondness for women, became a notorious prophet of "free love." In his early days as an ecclesiastic, Prince had seemed conventional enough. A devout student when he was attending a seminary, in 1840 he became curate of a small parish called Charlinch in southern England, at the age of twenty-nine. But, hearing rumors of scandalous behavior, the bishop of Bath and Wells removed Prince from his curacy. Not long after, the censured pastor began to make extravagant religious claims. He told his brother-in-law that the Holy Ghost had taken over his body, and he announced to the world in his book, *Great Declaration*, that God had made him a "perfect man," incapable of sin. He declared himself immortal and promised followers that they, too, could live forever.

Ousted from the Anglican church, Prince kept up his preaching, sometimes in barns, sometimes out in the open. He attracted wealthy followers and with their financial backing secured a church building—Adullam Chapel—in the resort town of Brighton. Prince's flock grew and prospered there, and he was soon able to purchase a large estate near Spaxton in Somerset. He named it Agapemone, Greek for "Abode of Love." After extensive renovations paid for by his generous backers, Prince and sixty disciples settled into the new quarters in the great house. The more a donor had contributed, the more spacious the accommodations to which he—or more often she, since Prince's

group was predominantly female—was entitled. Agapemone's center of activity was a large hall that served as both chapel and salon, housing a high altar, an organ, easy chairs, sofas, and a billiard table. Here the faithful could say their prayers, play a game of billiards, or enjoy a glass of sherry from Prince's impressively stocked wine cellar.

Prince assumed the title of the Beloved, while his aides were called Anointed Ones, Angel of the Last Trumpet, and the Seven Witnesses. At the peak of his career, Prince rode in a four-horse carriage that had been purchased from the royal family. An old villager recalled later how Prince had gone through town attended by a footman who let loose trumpet blasts and cries of: "All hail! All hail! The Messiah!"

In his writings, Prince proclaimed the innocence of sexual intercourse, absolving from sin all those who followed him in the true religion. Prince had a wife, but his matrimonial state did not deter him from taking several other "spiritual brides." His proclivity for polygamy, however, provoked controversy. Some members of the flock were shocked when Prince, dressed in a handsome silk robe, staged a ceremony that culminated in his seduction of Zoe Paterson, a sixteen-year-

old orphan who had been entrusted to his care by her widowed mother. He insisted to his followers that no child could be born of the spiritual union, despite Paterson's obvious signs of pregnancy. The son she bore was kept out of sight when visitors came to Agapemone.

Prince was later hauled into court to answer a lawsuit filed by former disciples Louise Jane Nottidge and her two sisters. The trial in 1860 revealed some of the strange goings-on at Spaxton, and the court found that Prince had deprived the Nottidge sisters of £5,728 of property. He was ordered to return it—a financial blow to the sect. Soon afterward, Agapemone began a slow decline, and little was heard of it for many years. Predictably, Prince failed to live up to his claim of immortality, dying in 1899 at the age of eighty-seven. He was buried under the lawn, in a vertical posture.

But the saga of Agapemone did not end with the death of its founder. His mantle was assumed by another eccentric Anglican minister, the Reverend J. H. Smyth-Pigott, a former Salvation Army evangelist who had been a devotee of the late leader for some years. Like his mentor, Smyth-Pigott was no slouch at creating a stir. On Sunday, September 7, 1902, he made a startling revelation from the pulpit

of his Ark of the Covenant Chapel in nearby Clapton: He was God. His words caused a great celebration among the Agapemonites, but on the following Sunday a mob showed up at the Ark of the Covenant and pelted Smyth-Pigott with stones and umbrellas. The self-styled Supreme Being retreated to Spaxton.

Smyth-Pigott carried on at Agapemone with his wife and his largely female following, which at its peak numbered about 100. From among the devoted women he chose Ruth Preece as his spiritual bride, and in due time she gave birth to a boy who was given the name Glory. Later arrivals included second son Power and Comet, a daughter whose name was later changed to Life.

But even one spiritual bride proved to be one too many for the Anglican church, which expelled Smyth-Pigott from the priesthood in 1909. Although he and his followers shrugged off the ruling, he was unable to match his predecessor's success in recruiting the wealthy, and Agapemone once more declined. Smyth-Pigott died in 1927, leaving a modest—and inadequate—trust fund to support his movement. As the Agapemonites found it more and more difficult to make ends meet, they were forced to rent the outbuildings dotting the estate's grounds. During World War II, the hall of the great house served as an air-raid center. By the mid-fifties, Agapemone had shrunk from 100 or so followers to just a few. Ruth Preece, Smyth-Pigott's spiritual bride, died in 1956, and his heirs lost interest in the sect. In 1962, the big house was sold and converted into small dwellings. The Abode of Love was no more. □

Cargo Hold

During a visit to the Papuan village of Vailala in 1919, a visitor witnessed adults and children behaving very oddly. "The natives," he reported, "were taking a few quick steps in front of them, and would then stand, jabber and gesticulate, at the same time swaying the head from side to side; also bending the body from side to side from the hips." These "automaniacs," as one British anthropologist labeled them, were in the grip of a new religious cult.

Called the Vailala Madness, the faith is believed to have begun when a villager named Evara experienced a powerful vision as he lay in a trance: A great steamship, he said, would soon bring all of Papua's dead ancestors home, their dark skin now faded to white. In its hold, the steamer would carry a cargo of consumer goods in crates marked for each village: rifles, flour, rice, and tobacco. In the past, such cargoes had been reserved for the island's ruling European colonials, but now the Papuans would take possession of the goods that Evara had envisioned—provided they had first driven the white people away from the island.

The Vailala movement combined elements of earlier native faiths with the Christian teachings brought to the island by missionaries. Evara's followers called themselves "Jesus Christ men" and threw their traditional religious paraphernalia into bonfires.

At the peak of the Vailala Madness, Papuans stopped working on their gardens and refused to engage in trade, believing it was just a matter of time before the great ship arrived with its booty. Devotions were practiced in small, specially erected European-style buildings that the cultists called offices. They also installed religious flagpoles and aerials mimicking those used by colonial officials. The movement was so fixated on the material side of European culture that one member of the sect who had a vision of God was able to describe in fine detail the coat, shirt, and trousers in which the divine figure was dressed.

During the 1920s, the cult spread enormously and sparked widespread crackdowns by the colonial administration. The islanders responded by going underground, insisting to officials that the movement had disintegrated. Although the appearance of the first airplane in the region caused some cultists to renew their devotions, the general enthusiasm dimmed as the years passed without the arrival of the paradisiacal steamship. By the 1930s, the madness had virtually

disappeared. Even the ceremonial furniture was broken up and used for firewood.

More disruptive was a sect that spread among the inhabitants of the island of Espíritu Santo, in the New Hebrides. In 1923, Rongofuro, or Runovoro, who had attended the local Presbyterian mission school, began prophesying about the return of the dead. Rongofuro told islanders that their home would soon be wracked by a mighty deluge akin to the Christian Day of Judgment. Afterwards a great white ship laden with a rich cargo for the islanders would arrive.

The movement that sprang up around Rongofuro, often called the Naked Cult, was far more hostile to whites than the Vailala Madness. Rongofuro believed that a local British planter named Clapcott, whose relations with the islanders had been tense, was responsible for the death of Rongofuro's wife. Clapcott's presence, he preached, was hampering the arrival of the spirits of the dead and he ordered the planter murdered. By one account, Clapcott's body was cut into pieces and scattered through the coastal ◊

villages. In response, the British shelled Espírutu Santo from a gunboat, arrested the leaders of the group, and condemned several of them to death. Rongofuro faced execution without fear because he believed that he had the power to return from the dead.

The cult continued without Rongofuro, and in the 1940s, its members built a dock at the seaside site where Clapcott had been killed because they believed that the great steamer would tie up there. It would, the islanders said, be manned by Americans—a notion inspired by the presence of American troops and equipment in the South Pacific. In short order, colonial officials had the pier burned down.

Salvation by Americans was also a tenet of the cargo cult that evolved on the island of Tana in the New Hebrides around 1940. Its focal figure was the mystical John Frum. Described by believers as a little man with bleached hair and a high-pitched voice, Frum wore a coat with shining buttons. He was, it was said, an avatar of the god of the island's highest mountain.

As in other cargo cults, the whites would have to be removed before John Frum could shower his followers with riches and usher in a reign of bliss. The first step, cult leaders said, was to get rid of European money; if there were no money left on the island, they reasoned, the whites would have no motive to stay. So the people of Tana went on a binge, buying goods willy-nilly in European stores and throwing extravagant feasts. Some even threw their cash into the sea.

The cultists abandoned the mission churches and devoted themselves instead to John Frum, who some now believed was the king of America. The sight of several airplanes flying over the island gave rise to the story that John Frum's three sons were arriving to become the kings of the island. When black American troops landed on Tana, the dark-skinned islanders were thunderstruck. Some of them declared that the troops had come to fight for John Frum, while others prophesied that they were only the first of the black Americans coming to rule over Tana. Finally, one islander declared that he was John Frum, and his followers built a landing strip for cargo planes complete with magical markers and gates. Then, like their predecessors, they waited in vain for cargo to arrive from . . . somewhere.

Despite years of repression and the failure of treasure-laden steamers and airplanes to arrive, the cargo cults of Melanesia never entirely lost their appeal. When British film producer David Attenborough was working on a documentary in Tana in 1960, he saw a John Frum chapel that contained a life-size wooden figure with a white face and scarlet clothing. Before it stood a scarlet cross, and at one side was a scarlet model of a four-engine cargo plane.

And in 1964, reports trickled out of the island of New Hanover that cultists had tried to vote for American president Lyndon Johnson in their local elections. When their attempts failed, a large sum of money was raised in hopes of "buying" Johnson—pidgin English for paying him to come to the island. The Johnson draft soon evolved into a more legitimate and sophisticated political movement—a fate shared by many of the cargo cults. Even so, there may be some Melanesians who continue to believe that one day their ship will come in. □

Many Are Called

The charismatic and protean Alfred Lawson—professional baseball player and promoter, aviation pioneer, writer, economic visionary, philosopher—died in 1954, but his memory and faithful disciples linger on. Every year, many of them gather from all over the United States for a long weekend devoted to discussing the philosophy of Lawsonomy and its late founder in reverent tones. They raise their voices in hymns of praise to the commander, "God's great eternal gift to man." If the sound of the choristers is a little thin and quavering, it is because so many of them are old. Since the commander's death, there have been few converts to Lawsonomy. It is up to the faithful old-timers, some of whom are approaching their hundredth birthdays, to celebrate the self-styled Man of Destiny. Lawson was a man with a mission, and he proclaimed it with unqualified confidence: He had been created to improve mankind, and he was satisfied that Lawsonomy's all-embracing scientific and moral principles were precisely those that God had intended.

Born in 1869, Lawson spent most of his youth in Detroit, Michigan. When he was eighteen, he became a pitcher for the Frankfort, Indiana, baseball team; he spent the next twenty years playing (including three weeks in the major leagues), managing minor-league teams, and promoting the sport. But something besides baseball was on his mind during those years. In a novel that was drawn from his life and budding philosophy, Lawson described how his protagonist, John

Convert, discovered that degrading habits such as smoking and drinking conflicted with "Natural Law" and tried to persuade the world to adopt a healthy way of life.

In 1908, Lawson left baseball for aviation. He edited two widely read magazines in the new field, then went on to found the Lawson Aircraft Corporation. In 1919, his company built the first passenger airplane in the United States, a huge vehicle for its day that called at cities between Milwaukee and Washington. His company received the first government contract for delivering airmail. Un-

fortunately, a crash and a series of financial setbacks forced Lawson out of the airplane business. There was, however, the consolation of having won national recognition.

In 1931, as the Great Depression settled upon the nation, Lawson created the Direct Credits Society to promote his radical economic ideas. Financiers, he claimed, had triggered the Depression by preying on the poor and middle classes. As a consequence, the victims were losing their farms, their businesses, and their homes to the scheming bankers. Lawson railed against usury and the gold standard and made alarming predictions: If the citizenry did not wake up, democracy would collapse and dictatorship would follow. Part of the solution, Lawson argued, was that banks should be government-owned and provide interest-free loans direct- ◊

In 1952, an irate Alfred Lawson faced a U.S. Senate committee investigating his business practices.

ly to individuals—a system that he called Direct Credits.

Tens of thousands heard Lawson's message and rallied to his cause. Members enjoyed "commissions" as lieutenants, captains, majors, and generals; Lawson was, of course, the commander-in-chief. In city after city, there were huge public meetings preceded by festive parades with floats, marching bands, and platoons of white-uniformed men and women. Lawson could hold his adoring followers spellbound for hours—to many of his listeners, he alone explained the tribulations of the United States with crystal clarity. His Direct Credits Society disciples adored him. At many rallies, when he appeared on the speakers' platform, the throng cheered for fifteen minutes without stopping. They sang songs that were composed by impassioned followers whose lyrics styled Lawson as the "mastermind" appointed by God to save humanity. To some, Lawson had qualities approaching the superhuman; they felt that he could divine their thoughts.

Mesmerizing though he was, his Direct Credits movement began losing steam when the economy began to improve later in the decade. Once again, Lawson, now seventy-four years old, changed course. In 1943, to further his pursuit of "the knowledge of life and everything pertaining thereto," he bought a defunct university in Des Moines, Iowa. Students were expected to enroll for at least ten years, but to complete the program required thirty years. The founder insisted that it would degrade his ideas to mix them with anything base, such as those "infinitesimal grains of knowledge" produced by Copernicus, Galileo, and Newton. Therefore, the only

texts to be read and the only ideas discussed were those produced by Lawson—an indefatigable writer, he had more than fifty books to his credit. This fountain of Lawsonomy was his crowning achievement.

For decades, Lawson had been revising western science. In his habitual way of referring to himself in the third person, he declared, "Lawson lifted the entire science of physics out of the quick-sands of theory and mysticism and placed it upon the solid foundation of absolute fact and reality." He first got a glimmer of his law of Penetrability when he was only four years old and down with a case of the measles. The law stated that pressure and suction govern physical processes throughout the universe, modulated by, among other things, the principles of Equaeverpoise and Zig-Zag-and-Swirl. Equaeverpoise represented equilibrium between suction and pressure. Zig-Zag-and-Swirl derived from the fact that nothing in the universe moves in a straight line.

According to Lawson, earth was a great pump, pulling gaseous substances into one end of a tube opening at the North Pole and expelling the substance through the tube's other end, at the South Pole. Pores covering the planet's surface also sucked these substances in, and volcanoes expelled them. Gravity, in Lawson's scheme, was merely a by-product of suction.

The human body was a bundle of suction and pressure pumps, according to Lawsonomy, while the brain was controlled by two opposing kinds of microscopic creatures, the Menorgs, or mental organizers, and the Disorgs, or disorganizers. When the Menorgs were in good condition, they promoted the traits of the ideal society—simplicity,

sharing, cooperation, and classlessness. Movies, dancing, rich foods, meat, beards, kissing, cocktails, and tobacco products harmed the Menorgs and strengthened the Disorgs. Lawson prescribed a regimen for his followers that included sprinkling a bit of fresh cut grass on salads and dunking the head at least twice a day in cold water.

As many as a hundred students at a time immersed themselves in Lawsonomy on the Des Moines campus. Their little community aspired to be a utopia, with a five-foot fence built around the grounds to keep the unconverted at bay. However, Alfred Lawson's university produced controversy and lawsuits long before it produced any graduates. In 1952, the U.S. Congress investigated the university's tax-exempt status, noting that it had sold for a profit some machinery obtained under a government education program. Lawson cut his losses by selling the campus to a businessman who planned to replace it with a shopping mall.

The commander died in 1954, and two years later, the University of Lawsonomy was reestablished on a Wisconsin farm. There, his followers installed a virtually sacred object—the urn containing his ashes.

The farm campus today has fewer than a half-dozen resident students but claims a much larger body of correspondence scholars—all hitting books written, as the founder decreed, by Alfred Lawson. In 1979, thirty-six years after it began, the University of Lawsonomy held its first graduation ceremony. Nine people, most in their eighties and nineties, earned their sheepskins and the honorific that until then only their master had enjoyed: Knowledgian of Lawsonomy. □

Heart of Darkness

James Warren Jones had two passions when he was growing up in Lynn, Indiana, in the 1930s, according to those who knew him: He loved animals, and he adored religious ceremonies. One friend recalled an elaborate funeral that handsome, dark-haired, thirteen-year-old "Jonesie" performed in a candle-lit barn for a dead mouse. In his later teenage years, he enjoyed preaching sermons to any congregation that would listen, and with his gift for public speaking, he soon was appointed a student pastor in the Methodist church. But Jones found traditional groups such as the Methodists stiff and confining. With money made from importing monkeys and selling them door to door as pets, he founded his own church, Community Unity, in Indianapolis. By 1956, he had moved to an old church building, which he named Wings of Deliverance. This soon became the Peoples Temple, and it was as pastor of this congregation that the Reverend Jim Jones entered the history of madness.

Jones wanted to create a paradise on earth—a socialist community without racial hatred or private property. In 1961, he became obsessed with nuclear war. After reading an article about towns that might survive a holocaust, he moved with his wife and children to Belo Horizonte, Brazil. But the move was unsuccessful, and Jones and his family returned to Indianapolis for a time, only to move across the country in 1965. His destination was the town of Redwood Valley in Mendocino County, north of San Francisco—another area Jones believed safe in the event of war. A hundred faithful members of his Indianapolis flock went with Jones, and he set about winning more.

The message of Jones's sermons was a peculiar mixture of Christian evangelism, socialism, hopeful sentiment, and paranoia: Sinister organizations were out to destroy the church. The supposed healing rites Jones practiced were even odder than his words. Claiming that he had Christlike stigmata, he would invite the sick to touch a finger to his blood-covered palms, promising that the fluid would cure them. In fact, the blood was not his—his aides extracted it from their arms for his use. Crippled old people who rose from their wheelchairs, suddenly able to walk again, were in fact healthy young followers who at Jones's insistence had donned convincing disguises for their role in the ceremony.

However strange his services and confusing his ideas, Jones's magnetic style inspired blind, impassioned devotion; his following swelled and his coffers filled. Jones established temples in San Francisco and Los Angeles; all told, his congregations numbered in the thousands. And he was apparently achieving the racial harmony he sought—most of the white preacher's followers were black. Ignoring the oddities of Jones's ministry—or perhaps unaware of them—prominent politicians praised the activism of the Peoples Temple; it provided many volunteers for community medical clinics, soup kitchens, and day-care centers for the poor. As a result, Jones could create an illusion of warmth between himself and California governor Jerry Brown, Jr., First Lady Rosalynn Carter, and George Moscone, mayor of San Francisco, who helped ◊

In the wake of the mass suicide Jim Jones decreed, a lone man surveys the grisly carpet of dead bodies.

Jones become chairman of the city's housing authority.

But the facade of respectability had begun to crack. By the late 1970s, Jones had become aware that several journalists were investigating the Peoples Temple, gathering accounts from former members of Jones's paranoid rantings, his practice of humiliating church members in public, and his improper use of funds. Jones decided to pull up stakes. Several years earlier, with the idea of founding a commune, he had leased a several-thousand-acre plot of land in the jungles of Guyana, on South America's northeast coast. Late in the summer of 1977, Jones abandoned California and, with hundreds of his disciples, headed for his Guyana paradise: Jonestown.

Far from civilization's constraints, the leader seemed to lose all self-control. As he prepared promotional brochures describing a beatific community, survivors were painting a picture of evil, suffering, and insanity. Jones insisted that everyone call him Dad or Father. Indeed, he laid claim to total power over the commune. Anyone committing a minor infraction of one of Jones's laws was publicly flogged; errant children received a terrifying nighttime dunking in a well. Women were required to acquiesce to his sexual advances, and he flaunted sex to humiliate men who had incurred his wrath.

Living conditions at Jonestown were far from paradisiacal. Old people were crowded into barnlike quarters where they lay, survivors reported, like cordwood. The communards worked like slaves for twelve hours a day in the 120-degree sun. At night they were frequently required to attend Jones's

lengthy harangues, which sometimes lasted until two or three in the morning. The most extreme demonstration of obedience was the White Night—trial runs of group "revolutionary suicide." Even the children of Jonestown took part in the dreadful rehearsals.

On November 17, 1978, Jonestown received unwelcome guests. They were led by Congressman Leo Ryan of California, who was trying to help constituents worried about relations said to be captives of Jones's church. Ryan, along with the searching relatives and some journalists, spent a day touring the commune with their friendly host. In the course of the visit, several members asked to return with the visitors—with Jones's apparent acquiescence. The following evening, as the congressional party and defectors were about to board their planes, Jones's henchmen opened fire on them. Ryan and four others were killed. One plane managed to take off with a few survivors; the others fled into the jungle.

Meanwhile, Jones ordered that the White Night ritual at last be carried out—and not as another grim rehearsal. Prodded by guards armed with guns and bows and arrows, the Jonestown medical staff filled a large tub with a purple fruit drink called Flavour-aide and mixed it with sedatives and cyanide. The youngest were the first to drink the poison, aided by their parents.

Because the airstrip near Jonestown had no runway lights, it took a day for Guyanese troops to reach the Peoples Temple. At Jonestown, they found 914 bodies, including Jones's. He had died of a gunshot wound to the head; whether he killed himself or asked an aide to pull the trigger is unknown. □

King of the Cosmos

One morning in May 1954, George King was washing the dishes in his small London flat when, from out of the blue, an invisible presence boomed, "Prepare yourself. You are to become the voice of the Interplanetary Parliament." That was the sum total of King's first notification of a special mission, but eight days later, a white-robed yoga master mysteriously entered King's home and clarified it: There was a galaxy-wide struggle between good and evil, and he had been chosen to alert earth dwellers to their responsibilities in the conflicts that lay ahead. Through him, the so-called Cosmic Masters of the Saturn-based Interplanetary Parliament would relay important news. Thus began one of the most enduring and energetic of flying-saucer cults.

After months of careful prepara-

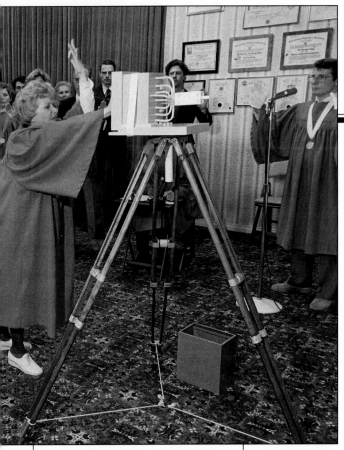

At an Aetherian Prayer Power session designed to charge the "spiritual battery" perched on the tripod, a woman prays energetically while others line up behind her for a turn.

tion, King had established contact with his chief instructor: Cosmic Master Aetherius, an inhabitant of Venus some 3,000 years old. In January 1955, an audience gathered in London's Caxton Hall to hear Aetherius address them via the entranced King's vocal chords. Other cosmic personalities heard in this manner included Lord Buddha, Jesus Christ, Saint Peter, the obscure Saint Goo-Ling, and a scientist known as Mars Sector 6. King soon organized his enthused followers into the Aetherius Society and began to reach out for others with a mimeographed newsletter called *Aetherius Speaks to Earth* and a full-fledged journal called *Cosmic Voice*. In 1960, after a successful visit to the United States, King moved the society's headquarters to Los Angeles.

At times, the Aetherius Society has encountered considerable hostility. In 1955, for instance, it went through a rough period after King was supposed to have served as a channel for Jesus Christ. According to the message King relayed, Jesus, a Venusian by birth, had visited Earth twenty centuries earlier on a spaceship described in the Bible as the Star of Bethlehem. The British press reacted to this startling statement by accusing King of blasphemy, and one newspaper suggested that he was a Communist dupe. The fuss soon died down, but several years later there was another flap over a purported message from Christ revising the Lord's Prayer to include a Buddhist-inspired line, "Om Shanti Shanti Shanti."

The Aetherius Society's journal became the target of hoaxers in the late 1950s when it published some phony items that seemed to back King's revelations. Among them was an article by the learned Dr. Dominic Fidler entitled "Mescaline and Flying Saucers." Other pieces cited obscure scientists whose names should have been red flags to the editors—R. T. Fischall, L. Puller, and N. Ormuss. These embarrassments have since been edited out of *Cosmic Voice* reprints.

In the judgment of Aetherius Society members, their most important activities have been what they call their Missions—military-style operations aimed at ameliorating specific global problems. One such maneuver, Operation Starlight, was executed from July of 1958 to August of 1961. Its aim was to charge eighteen holy mountaintops with spiritual energy. Beginning on Holdstone Down in England, the campaign had King and his crew climbing peaks over much of the globe—the American West, Australia, New Zealand, and Switzerland. Other Missions followed, including Operation Karmalight and Operation Bluewater—the last one involving boat trips into the Pacific Ocean, the society asserted, to lay spiritual charges in various deepsea locations.

One of the society's ongoing Missions is Operation Prayer Power, in which members chant and pack mental energy into "spiritual batteries" for use in future crises. The group claims that their emergency discharges have been responsible for major world events, including the cease-fire in the 1974 Cyprus War and the temporary lifting of curfews and other restrictions in strife-torn Poland in 1982.

The aging King no longer transmits what his followers take to be transmissions of news from outer space, but the society remains active—especially during the periods designated as "spiritual pushes," when "unselfish Spiritual action" by earth dwellers is greatly magnified by the presence of a huge spacecraft in earth's neighborhood. The Aetherians proudly describe what they characterize as their contribution to the galactic conflict—their efforts, they say, have continually helped to thwart the armies of evil. It is this heroic record which, the *Cosmic Voice* reports, sets them apart from "so-called 'spiritual workers' sitting around the feet of a flower-carrying yogi." □

Of Cabbages and Things

At an old monastery on a hill north of Rome, not far from the ancient Etruscan town of Sutri, the monks have been replaced by a small band of technological mystics. The objects in the monastery, which is named Sapientia, or "Wisdom," hint at the group's eclectic outlook. There are ancient frescoes representing Jesus and many saints, statues of Buddha, stuffed animals, and masks with monstrous faces. The modern monastics celebrate the New Year on April 16, the birthday of their leader, Marcello Creti. Part mystic philosopher and part technologist, and a messiah-like figure to his disciples, he is said to have given the world 118 potentially revolutionary "scientific revelations" over a lifetime of invention.

Creti has also evolved the principles of his movement Ergos, an acronym derived from *energia radiante governante ogni scienza*—literally, "radiant energy governing all science." The Ergonians strive to free themselves from the "mud of convention" through creativity and knowledge. Their ultimate goal is to progress from a vegetative existence—life as a cabbage, as Creti calls this condition—to the mystic state of "subjective serenity."

Despite his interest in technological innovation, Creti is scornful of modern life. "Worm colonies are better organized than mankind nowadays," he chides. He traces the Ergonian lineage to the men of great vision who ruled the world during a prehistoric time that he calls Antalidei. Creti says that he is able to detect the lingering spirit of these enlightened people in the archaeological sites around Sapientia. His power of divination, he asserts, has also let him locate quite effortlessly many rare minerals hidden underground. The large collection is on view in a museum that was once the monastery's dungeon.

In the opinion of Sapientia's dozen or so residents, who share a dual bent toward science and the occult, Creti is a new Leonardo da Vinci whose inventive powers will bring about a better way of life. They assist him with developing his ideas, for which he declines to take all the credit: Some unknown being, he explains, dictates to him when he is in a trancelike sleep. Upon awakening, he jots down the formulas, diagrams, and drawings that were communicated to him. Creti also comes out of his trances with thoughts on religion, philosophy, science, and ethics that now fill a large number of volumes.

Creti's devices and ideas for machines are remarkably wide-ranging. His first, which dates to 1929, when he was only seven, is simple but quite useful—a pair of scissors for clipping hairs inside the nose. By the time he was thirty, he had marketed an electric car and a multi-track telephone amplifier. Among the more sophisticated advances revealed to the entranced Creti are a device for electroshock treatment, a cure for cancer, a skateboard equipped with a sail, a pocket typewriter, a meter for registering energy intentionally radiated by plants, and an underwater spotlight for fishing.

In addition to their technological labors for Creti, Sapientia's Ergonians continue the restoration of

Silhouetted before his monastery north of Rome, Ergonian leader Marcello Creti wears a double cross he calls a symbol of the law of equilibrium.

its buildings, which they say once housed a tribunal of the Inquisition. They also have the care of the grounds and a variety of live animals in residence, including dogs, five types of monkeys, and goldfish that grow to enormous size in a pond fed by a thermal spring.

Although they have retreated from the world, Ergonians are not total recluses. The Ergonian Cultural Association offers lectures and seminars to the public in the monastery chapel and also welcomes friendly outsiders to hear Creti hold forth at Sunday lunch on his technological discoveries, his philosophy, and the mistakes made by contemporary civilization. If outsiders find Creti's inventive projects and devices odd, the faithful are unruffled. In each Ergonian's personal odyssey, the goal is serenity, not objects—not even objects from the hand of the new Leonardo. □

Douks of Hazard

On the morning after her husband's trial in 1953 for his involvement in a bombing in British Columbia, a young woman got out of bed at 3:00 a.m. She doused her furniture with coal oil, set the place ablaze, and removed all her clothes. With her small son in tow, she stepped out stark naked into the chilly air and watched the house burn down. A journalist, seeing that the woman was pleased with what she had done, asked for an explanation. The answer: "I knew I had to do it, just as I have seen my mother do it when I was young."

Like her mother, the woman belonged to the Svobodniki, or "Sons of Freedom," a radical splinter group of a pacifist religious sect known as the Doukhobors. Among the Svobodniki, nudity and arson are time-honored means of registering scorn for material wealth and government authority. Their creed, which earned practitioners the nickname Mad Douks in Canada, traces its roots back to eighteenth-century czarist Russia. The first Doukhobors—literally, "Spirit Wrestlers"—were Ukrainian peasants who rejected the authority of the priests of the Orthodox Church, replacing it with the authority of the "inner light" of the individual spirit. Like Quakers, the Doukhobors were resolute pacifists who refused military service. In time, they adopted more prohibitions: no meat, no liquor, no tobacco, and, out of consideration for animals, no leather. Some conservative Doukhobors were even known to let their wives pull their plows to spare the oxen.

In 1895, the Russian government sought to break the Doukhobors' resistance to military service by persecuting them ruthlessly. Leo Tolstoy and a group of British and American Quakers organized a rescue, and in 1899, about 7,500 Doukhobors were resettled in present-day Saskatchewan, Canada.

Although the Canadian government was far more tolerant of the Doukhobors than the czar—for example, it enacted an exemption from military service—some of the transplanted Doukhobors still found it oppressive. By 1902, an extremist wing calling themselves the Sons of Freedom had begun to coalesce around the notion that any type of assimilation was sinful. And in 1906, after the Canadian government rescinded its offer to allow the Doukhobors to own communal land, the group became increasingly belligerent, refusing to cooperate with the government. Although the genesis of the practice is unclear, the Sons also began to disrobe en masse to demonstrate their dissatisfaction. As their anger continued to overflow, the extremists resorted to acts of violence and destruction. In April 1937 alone, for instance, eleven public schools and halls were torched; in May, sections of track on a major railway line in British Columbia were destroyed. In the crackdown that followed the outburst, leaders of the Sons of Freedom were imprisoned for incendiarism and nude parades, and some children of sect members were taken away from their parents.

The Sons of Freedom have been known to direct their anger at fellow Doukhobors as well. Although it has never been proven, many believe the Sons responsible for the 1924 explosion that killed Doukhobor leader Peter Verigin and several oth- ◊

ers. Automobile ownership among moderate Doukhobors has provoked more than one nude march by the Svobodniki, and all the inhabitants of one town saw their cars go up in flames together. By one estimate, the Svobodniki were responsible for an average of 100 public rampages a year during the 1950s and 1960s, including two dozen deaths.

Despite some mellowing, the Sons continue their occasional agitations. In 1981, for instance, sixty-eight-year-old Mary Astaforoff entered a moderate Doukhobor's British Columbia restaurant, where she stripped to the waist and announced that she had just set fire to the building. Even in prison, Astaforoff and two other Freedomite matriarchs managed to set fires. "They burnt their panties and their pyjamas," a prison official reported. After Astaforoff died in 1985 following a hunger strike, her compatriots—Tima Jmaeff and Mary Braun—kept up the fight. In May of 1991, they sat naked in the courtroom while being convicted of setting two fires in August of the previous year. Jmaeff and Braun, however, appear to be the last ardent Freedomites, whose membership has declined to fewer than 100. The days of the Mad Douks appear to be numbered. □

Star Struck

Frederick von Mierers (*right*) was the perfect oracle for money-crazed Manhattanites of the 1980s. In his apartment on chic East Fifty-fourth Street, the one-time model turned astrologer advised a rich and beautiful coterie of Ivy Leaguers, lawyers, executives, yuppies, and fashion models how to live their lives—and spend their money. The members of his group, called Eternal Values, accepted without demur von Mierers's instructions, for they believed he was what he claimed to be: a creature of supernatural powers who was visiting Earth from the star Arcturus.

Von Mierers's rise to fame and fortune as a self-proclaimed alien astrologer began in the 1970s, according to journalist Marie Brenner, who profiled von Mierers for the magazine *Vanity Fair*. Reportedly born plain but ambitious Freddy Meyer of Brooklyn, von Mierers adopted his noble-sounding name and a clipped aristocratic accent to match it. His new persona as scion of an illustrious old New York family was so convincing that in 1976 he won a listing in the exclusive New York *Social Register*.

Classed as one of the "Playboys of the Eastern Coast" by *Harper's Bazaar*, von Mierers had already made a name for himself as the companion of wealthy dime-store widow Helen Kress Williams, with whom he dabbled in astrology. But when she had an accident in 1977, followed by an incapacitating stroke, her son stepped in to block her financial support of von Mierers.

Following the loss of his "grandmother-godmother," von Mierers turned seriously to astrology and laid claim to former, long-

In June 1962, a female member of the Sons of Freedom stolidly watches a house burn—one of a hundred or so buildings set on fire by cultists in an outburst of antimaterialist protest.

forgotten lives. He told his friends he recalled being a mathematician and astrologer in ancient Egypt and, still more remarkable, a contemporary of the Buddha of India. But before his stint on Earth, of course, he had been a resident of the distant star Arcturus. One day in 1979, von Mierers was browsing in an astrology book shop when he met John Andreadis, a clever sixteen-year-old. They became friends, and Andreadis began helping von Mierers prepare astrological charts for clients.

Von Mierers's stellar venture flourished. In 1984, with Andreadis's assistance, he won an audience with famous New Age author Ruth Montgomery. The two hit it off, and Montgomery gave von Mierers a lavish write-up in her 1984 book, *Aliens among Us.* She said that her mystic sources, the Guides, confirmed that von Mierers had come from Arcturus. She described von Mierers as "a remarkable soul who has experienced every type of life on earth and on numerous planetary systems." His present mission, Montgomery wrote, was driven by the "urgent need to reach the young people who will be founding the new society after the shift of the Earth on its axis."

The resulting publicity brought thousands of letters and a flood of disciples. Von Mierers was providing so many $350 "life readings" and astrological charts that he had trouble keeping up with the demand for the merchandise. Within this galaxy of disciples, von Mierers created an exclusive inner cluster of 100 or so devotees, among them such top models as Jacki Adams and Hoyt Richards. Von Mierers steered these special souls to selected doctors, chiropractors, and nutritionists, and to a rigorous dietary regime called "food-combining." New members were reportedly subjected to a sex initiation rite.

When it was in full flower in 1987, the inner circle met on Wednesday nights for "family dinner." Von Mierers referred to his flock as the duchesses and lords of New York, in conversation that was a mixture of flattery, bullying, grand prophecies, anti-Semitic gibes, and specific fashion advice. One visitor recalls von Mierers comment on the proper choice of luggage: "Don't ever carry a Vuitton bag! Vuitton is too Jewish. Only Hermès."

To the chosen few, von Mierers also sold jewels—sapphires, topaz, cat's-eye, emeralds, and rubies. They were his unique prescription for curing various inadequacies. Jacki Adams reported that she gave von Mierers more than $100,000 in cash over four months in return for some magical gems and help in decorating her apartment. The stones were supposed to heal ailments and make her think more clearly. Von Mierers told clients that he was providing jewels at a tremendous discount, but in fact, according to *Vanity Fair,* his appraisers routinely inflated their value—they received a percentage commission based on the purchase price. Von Mierers always demanded payment in cash; when clients tried to get refunds, the guru bullied them into keeping the jewels.

The Eternal Values group began to ravel in late 1987, when Andreadis and Adams announced plans to marry and leave their companions. They were berated by the other acolytes—von Mierers reportedly beat Andreadis—but nevertheless abandoned the cult. Their departure greatly weakened the internal structure of Eternal Values, whose troubles soon included an investigation by Manhattan District Attorney Robert Morgenthau. Two years later, von Mierers himself was gone. He died on February 4, 1990, at his palatial marble house near Asheville, North Carolina, of pneumonia brought on by AIDS. □

Godfather

Adolfo de Jesus Constanzo had been disappointed by his most recent sacrificial victim, a tough drug dealer who had borne the pain of the fatal ritual in obstinate silence. For his next sacrifice, Constanzo wanted a man less steely. He also needed a well-educated brain to increase the potency of his black-magic medicine. It was mid-March of 1989, and the nearby town of Matamoros, just across the border from Brownsville, Texas, was crowded with American college students on spring break. Constanzo ordered his followers to capture one for him.

On March 14, in the early morning hours, several dutiful disciples left their ranch headquarters and drove into Matamoros, where they dragged Mark Kilroy, a junior at the University of Texas, into their truck when he was momentarily alone. His friends searched for him that night, but it seemed that he had vanished into thin air.

Bound, gagged, and delivered to the waiting Constanzo, Kilroy was dead within hours. Watched by a dozen or so disciples, Constanzo beat and tortured his victim, then lopped off the top half of his skull with a machete. The brain was added to the foul-smelling stew of human and animal remains that bobbed in a squat black pot called an *nganga*—an implement of his occult art. Whatever their scruples might have been, Constanzo's followers had become eager converts to his cult of black magic. His foul sorcery, Constanzo told them, would make them invulnerable to bullets and knives and render them invisible to police.

The bloodthirsty yet charismatic Constanzo was a twenty-six-year-old Cuban-American who had grown up in a Miami neighborhood where both benign white magic called Santería and the more sinister Afro-Caribbean religion known as Palo Mayombe were commonplace. Thought to have originated in the Congo centuries ago, Palo Mayombe practices rituals requiring animal sacrifice and human body parts stolen from graves; its adherents believe that they thereby capture the power of the spirits of the dead. Introduced to these dark arts by his mother, Constanzo sought to capture the same power—and created a monstrous distortion of Palo Mayombe. His brand of black magic demanded that the ritual parts be fresh—from the living and not from the dead. Constanzo borrowed the nganga from the old religion and chose as his patron spirit Kadiempembe, a traditional African figure representing profound evil.

In 1984, Constanzo moved to Mexico City, where his cult found its first members—and may have sacrificed its first victims. Constanzo's disciples called their leader *padrino,* or "godfather," and fell under the spell of his seemingly enormous potency. Constanzo made his living as

a practitioner of spirit medicine and a minor figure in the drug trade. When he met the head of a Matamoros narcotics operation whose fortunes had been declining, Constanzo proposed a deal: He would supply magical power and invulnerability in exchange for half the trafficker's profits. Like the Mexico City cultists, the Matamoros drug gang was mesmerized by Constanzo.

It was the Matamoros drug chief's nephew, Serafin Hernandez Garcia, who unwittingly betrayed Constanzo's grisly cult just weeks after Mark Kilroy's disappearance. On April 1, the Matamoros police set up a roadblock to screen travelers for drugs. Certain that his padrino's magic shielded him from detection, Hernandez drove past the roadblock as if it did not exist. The police tailed Hernandez to the dirt road leading to the ranch and waited until their quarry reappeared and

drove away. Following the road, they came upon a parked car with a weird cement statue with shells for eyes in the back seat, which the squad leader immediately identified the object as the paraphernalia of magic. After tailing the drug ring for several days, the police arrested Hernandez and three others. Proceeding with their drug bust, police interrogated a caretaker at the ranch, who identified Kilroy's photograph as that of a young man he had seen bound in the back of a truck there.

Serafin Hernandez Garcia soon confessed to how worshipfully he and the others had done Constanzo's bidding. Hernandez led the police to the place where Kilroy and several others had been sacrificed: an innocuous-looking wooden shed that they had overlooked in previous searches. Inside, they found blood-spattered walls and telltale

signs of black-magic rituals—including the gruesome nganga. He also showed them where Mark Kilroy and twelve others had been buried. A wire protruded above the earth covering the American's body; the other end was attached to his spine. Constanzo had planned to retrieve the spine once the body had decomposed and make a magical necklace of the vertebrae.

The Mexican police brought in a practitioner of white magic to exorcise the evil spirits, then burned down the sacrificial shed. In a nationwide manhunt, Constanzo was finally tracked to an apartment in Mexico City. But the bloody cult's high priest escaped justice. Before the police could reach him, Constanzo ordered an assistant to shoot him and his male lover with a machine gun—to which, despite the padrino's gory magic, they were not immune. □

Minders

Therapists at the Sullivan Institute for Research in Psychoanalysis conducted their practice in a peculiar setting—a commune in New York City. In several Manhattan buildings therapists, patients, spouses, and children lived together, following the psychological tenets of the patriarchal Saul Newton. He had named his creation after his one-time mentor, the highly respected psychiatrist Harry Stack Sullivan, who died in 1949. Everything was not sweet harmony in the Sullivan Institute, however. Gradually, former Sullivanians began to reveal what life was like in the big, unhap-

py family that Saul Newton controlled with an iron hand.

According to ex-Sullivanians Paul Sprecher and Michael Bray, Newton's ostensible goal was to create better people who would make the world better. In fact, the defectors insisted, institute therapists used their power to destroy normal family ties and to rearrange totally the members' personal relationships. Newton called Sprecher and Bray "liars and crooks."

Newcomers to what critics have called the psychotherapeutic cult were often recruited at a time of crisis in their lives—Bray, for instance, came seeking help with his troubled marriage. Sprecher, howev-

er, entered by a completely different route. Fresh out of college, he was looking for an apartment and answered an advertisement for group housing that members had posted on a college bulletin board.

Those who joined the commune were forbidden to contact their parents except to ask for money, according to former members and their relatives. One woman reported that after her son became involved with the Sullivanians, he returned a Christmas present she sent him and threatened to call a lawyer if she sent another gift. Newton imposed many other restrictions on patients—planning love affairs, arranging marriages, ordering di- ◊

During a ritual exorcism of the shed where Adolfo de Jesus Constanzo (inset) sacrificed victims, flames leap from the nganga in which he stewed some of their body parts.

Communal apartments occupied by groups of Sullivanians are denoted in this New York building directory by the Latin *Et Al.*—and others.

vorces, even directing whether and when a couple could have a child. Newton headed a policy council consisting of his wife, Helen Moses; his ex-wife, Joan Harvey; and her husband, Ralph Klein. The regimen that they prescribed for a patient was passed on to the junior therapist handling him or her.

Members of the group were required to carry "date books" in which they recorded meetings with one another. To avoid becoming "too focused" on one person, they were required to have numerous sexual partners. Spending more than two nights a week with the same individual was frowned on, and policy dictated that husbands and wives sleep together only rarely. Several therapists, including Newton, had sex with their patients. Sprecher told a reporter from *News-*

day that Newton "started dating my wife while he was my analyst and she was his cook. I told him I was feeling jealous. He told me to read [Freidrich] Engels on women and private property."

Children were kept at arms' length, often cared for by babysitters or sent to boarding school starting as early as age three. On orders from the policy council, parents were sometimes "taken off" their children, who were then assigned to other commune members for parenting.

Heavy fines that sometimes mounted to thousands of dollars were imposed on patients who broke the rules. Sullivanian therapy was an expensive proposition, requiring fees for the therapy, commune dues, and occasional special assessments; some members had

to take more than one job in order to pay for their treatment. The top therapists prospered, earning salaries of around $100,000 each, as the commune population soared to a peak of some 400 members in the 1970s. The Sullivan Institute accrued enough money to purchase two Manhattan apartment buildings, a retreat in the Catskills, a theater in Greenwich Village, and other valuable real estate.

As they shared everything else, the Sullivanians also joined in group fears. Following the 1979 nuclear reactor breakdown at Three Mile Island in Pennsylvania, for example, many of them fled in a panic to Orlando, Florida. They returned a week later but began taking radiation readings around Harrisburg, Pennsylvania, with Geiger counters, monitoring levels of radioactive strontium in milk, and buying escape vehicles to be used in the next nuclear emergency. During the 1980s, the group also followed strict rules for preventing AIDS: Members were to avoid eating in restaurants within a fifty-mile radius of New York and to shun sexual encounters with anyone outside the commune. Moreover, Sullivanian dogs were to have their paws washed after every walk, presumably to prevent their tracking the AIDS virus home.

But by then the institute had begun to collapse from within. Relatives of members and disaffected former communards started a group called PACT, for People Against Cult Therapy, to help other Sullivanians break free. The final blow came when Saul Newton died in 1991 after a long illness, leaving his policy-council lieutenants to squabble over the remains of the disintegrating commune. □

Three times a day chanting devotees of Brazil's Vale do Amanhecer gather to communicate with friendly extraterrestrials they call Jaguares.

Brazil Nuts

It takes less than an hour to drive from Brazil's ultramodern capital city of Brasília to the Vale do Amanhecer—the "Valley of Enlightment." Still, a stranger arriving for his first visit to the community may feel he has stepped into a time warp.

Founded in 1969 by a truck driver called Tia (Aunt) Neiva, the 600-family community resembles a medieval village, focusing always on the heavens and ordering its daily routines by the tenets of a mystical creed. The hierarchy of the Valley is organized as a pyramid, with four elite ministers at the apex, and male and female mediums making up the middle. Twenty-one groups of women, called nymphs, compose the pyramid's base.

The faithful of Amanhecer dress in long, brightly colored robes decorated with stars, moons, and other mystical symbols. Three times a day, everyone gathers in pairs around a large, star-shaped yellow and blue pool with a triangular island covered with arcane images at its center. The worshipers seek to communicate with a superior race of aliens known as Jaguares, who are said to whirl overhead perpetually in their spaceships. Songs and chants are employed to enable the high-voltage energy the aliens emit to penetrate an invisible barrier known as the neutron layer and reach the faithful. The Jaguares are said to be the successors to the Equitumãs, an earlier race that first came to Earth from the planet Capela 32,000 years ago to prepare the way for present events.

Such is the creed of Tia Neiva. When she died in 1985, she passed her mantle on to her husband, Mario Sassi, who became one of the four governing ministers. They say that the Jaguares are instructing them on how to weather the calamities prophesied by Tia Neiva, which are expected to wipe out two-thirds of the world's population by the year 2001. The Valley dwellers believe it is their mission to care for the survivors and to rebuild human civilization in the third millennium.

Eccentric they may be, but the people of Amanhecer are not a lone band of believers. There are some 100,000 followers of Tia Neiva in Brazil, and they have established more than 100 outpost temples. Moreover, the world is beating a path to the Vale do Amanhecer: Each month about 10,000 people make a pilgrimage there, not to join the cult, but in hopes of tapping into a mysterious cure for disease—the energy of the Jaguares. □

Ruth Redux

The Unarius Academy of Science may be the only religious group in the United States that has constructed a landing pad for visitors from outer space. It was Ruth Norman's idea to prepare the touchdown site, situated on a sixty-seven-acre tract near San Diego. She bought the land because of her conviction that the Space Brothers of the Intergalactic Confederation would soon touch down.

PLANET VULNA

PLANET VIDUS

Born in 1900, Norman founded Unarius with her husband, Ernest, in 1954. According to his wife, his earthly life ended in 1971 when he "slipped from out the body in so-called death." Now based on Mars, she asserts, he is in regular contact with the Unarius headquarters in El Cajon, a San Diego suburb. Ruth Norman says that, like her husband, she has had more than one life: She is currently the incarnation of the archangel Uriel, only one of scores of identities that her spirit has assumed over time. Her list includes Buddha, King Arthur, a fourteenth-century Dalai Lama, Elizabeth I of

Unarius Academy of Science head Ruth Norman (left) lays claim to numerous incarnations going back to 800,000 BC. At a Unarian gathering (above), a family displays the banners of planets where they believe they once lived.

England, and Peter the Great. According to Unarian belief, Ernest and Ruth Norman knew one another some 2,000 years ago, when he was Jesus Christ and she was Mary Magdalene. A major activity of the Unarius Academy is helping people to discover their previous lives.

Although these early incarnations are of great importance to Unarians, Norman's eye is on that future day when Earth becomes a fully enlightened member of the Intergalactic Confederation. Unarians believe that the world is a repository for violent and untrustworthy souls that must be reborn numerous times before they will be fully welcomed by the confederation's thirty-two other planets, whose inhabitants have already attained a high moral plane. When the Unarians' work is completed, the Earth will emit a more pleasing high-frequency signal, summoning 33,000 Space Brothers in thirty-three interlocking city-ships, who will welcome the earthlings into the fold.

After receiving what she interpreted as an alert to their imminent arrival, Norman held several vigils at the California landing site during the 1970s. When the event did not materialize, she became the butt of media ridicule and broke off the space watches.

Norman still presides over the annual Conclave of Light, which draws hundreds of Unarians from all over the United States and Canada to San Diego. In the opening procession that celebrates the participants' past existences on other planets, everyone wears an appropriate costume and carries a banner emblazoned with the name of the one-time home planet.

As the twentieth century draws to an end, Unarians look forward to the fulfillment of Ruth Norman's momentous prediction. Although the thirty-three confederation starships failed to appear during the 1970s, she is now confident that they will land sometime in the year 2001. The mystic is determined that she will still be living her present corporeal life as Ruth Norman, the spiritual incarnation of the archangel Uriel, when the great day finally arrives. Norman wrote to one of her followers that she will then pack her bags and take off with the Space Brothers for a new home, and yet another life, somewhere across the universe. □

Trouble in Paradise

The several thousand adherents to the Church Universal and Triumphant living in Montana's Paradise Valley are well-prepared for a nuclear apocalypse. Shepherded by Guru Ma, their affectionate nickname for church leader Elizabeth Clare Prophet, they have built scores of well-stocked, state-of-the-art fallout shelters on CUT's 30,000 acres. The largest of these is gargantuan, with room for 750 souls. Some followers, perhaps desirous of more privacy, have constructed shelters on their own property.

The congregation is confident that Prophet will give them ample advance warning of catastrophe. She herself was impelled to move the group from Malibu, California, to Montana by a conversation in 1986 with eighteenth-century occultist the comte de Saint-Germain, who also reportedly counseled the I AM movement *(pages 73-74)*. Between 1987 and 1990, Prophet announced several intervals of imminent nuclear peril that came and went uneventfully—without altering the faith of true believers.

Calling herself the Mistress of the Universe, Prophet says that she has received messages from many other historical figures, among them Confucius, Merlin the magician, Pope John XXIII, Shakespeare, Jesus Christ, Buddha, and Christopher Columbus. A firm believer in reincarnation, Prophet asserts that she was once Marie Antoinette, the unhappy queen who was beheaded during the French Revolution. The late Mark Prophet, her second husband and the founder of the church, claimed to have been the reincar- ◊

nation of the knight Lancelot.

Although they may not be disturbed by CUT's unusual theology, many residents of Paradise Valley are angry about the fuel stored against the holocaust in leaky tanks, which has contaminated ground water and the nearby Yellowstone River. There is also alarm about the church's apparent militarism. Although it says that its members are as peaceable as any other gun-toting Montanans, the church is extremely well-armed, and it has not always acquired its ordnance legally. For example, Edward Francis, Prophet's current husband, was found guilty in 1989 of conspiring to buy armor-piercing ammunition and semiautomatic rifles under an assumed name. Speaking as a fierce foe of Communism, the Mistress of the Universe stoutly defends her huge arms caches: "If the people in China in Tiananmen Square had had guns, they wouldn't have been massacred by the Communists." Meanwhile, Prophet's flock is primed to hunker down in their bunkers whenever Guru Ma issues the alert—then emerge to inherit the earth. □

Adherent Eleanor Schieffelin shows one of the family bomb shelters built by the Church Universal and Triumphant to prepare for the nuclear disaster Elizabeth Prophet predicts.

GALLERY OF THE MAD

Everyone has moments that might pass for insanity—obsession, envy, suspicion, depression, cruelty, euphoria, and despair are all part of the human condition. Such moments are ephemeral for most people, molehills of excess upon a level horizon of sanity. But in the minds of others, disembodied voices, plots, and baseless fears are the very stuff of life—and lifelong companions.

Among the melancholy denizens of that dark realm there exists a kind of aristocracy: extraordinarily unbalanced souls who, by virtue of their aberrant perceptions and behavior, have burned their way forever into human memory. Some of them have caused suffering on a scale almost beyond human imagination, wielding absolute power like a scythe. Some have created high art or built outlandish monuments, subtly inspired by the maladies that eventually destroyed them. The grandly mad have given much to history but often too little of themselves. Their tormented passage leaves only a thin wake of legend, folk tale, or superstition—not enough for clinical analysis, perhaps, but a haunting reminder of the unreason that dwells in our collective past.

Little Boots

"If only the Roman people had a single neck," mused Gaius Caesar, better known as Caligula, when the audience at one of his spectacles applauded out of turn. Witticisms such as that came easily to Caligula, and few Romans doubted that if the collective neck were offered, their emperor would not hesitate to have it chopped through with an ax. Unpredictably capable of anything, he has been ranked among the most deranged rulers of Rome.

He earned the distinction in a crowded, competitive field. Caligula's four short years on the throne had been preceded by the grim, bloody reign of Tiberius and were followed some thirteen years later by murderous Nero and, still further down the road, such teenage apparitions as Elagabalus. Yet Caligula's whimsical sadism, megalomania, extravagance, outrageous flouting of Roman convention, and delusions of divinity put him in a class by himself. "I can do anything, and to anyone," he once told his grandmother, the empress Livia.

Caligula's chief biographer is the historian Suetonius, who lived decades later and who was strongly biased against the second emperor of the dynasty established by Augustus Caesar. At that remove, the scholar was often dealing less with history than with legend. Some revisionist historians now argue that Caligula was not the terrible brute of myth but the victim of a bad press and deny that many of the monstrous anecdotes relayed by Suetonius really happened. They doubt, for example, that Caligula married his sister Drusilla, as Suetonius maintained, or that, as people have believed for centuries, he

named his horse, Incitatus, a Roman consul. Such disclaimers, however, barely scratch the enduring portrait of Caligula: a man of monumental instability, ruthlessness, and unpredictability, nightmare enough for anyone. No one quibbles with Suetonius's laconic appraisal that Caligula was "healthy neither in body nor in mind."

When Caligula took the throne, his subjects expected a sharp break with the mad dictatorship of old Tiberius. Caligula, most believed, would prove a reasonable, benevolent ruler and restore to Rome some of the stability it had enjoyed during the long reign of Augustus Caesar. Although the new emperor suffered from occasional convulsions—perhaps a sign of epilepsy—he was a strong and handsome young man whose bloodline and behavior were auspicious. Born in AD 12, he was the son of Tiberius's nephew and adopted son, Germanicus, a popular soldier who had incorporated Germany into the empire. Young Gaius was nicknamed Caligula, which means "Little Boots," by his father's soldiers when they saw him dressed in a miniature version of their gear. When Germanicus suddenly died, probably the victim of poison, Tiberius adopted the boy as a son and coheir.

Unfortunately, the imperial uncle was not the sort of foster father to teach anyone good habits of body or mind. Sexually degenerate, he showed increasing signs of rapaciousness and paranoia as he grew older. Those he sus-

pected of threatening his person he had killed. As his lists of victims lengthened, however, and his heavy taxes grew more onerous, his subjects began to mutter against him. Ignoring the rising chorus of dissent, in AD 26 he moved to the isle of Capri, where Caligula joined him five years later. There, the boy witnessed Tiberius's dissipated behavior at close hand and became himself a master of dissimulation. "Under an artificial gentleness," the historian Tacitus noted, Caligula "concealed an atrocious soul." One of his pastimes was to disguise himself and go slumming through various rough taverns. He also liked to sing, dance, go to the theater—and witness executions.

His main goal in those years had

Roman Emperor Gaius Caesar, called Caligula, shows the haughty face of imperial caprice in this marble bust from the first century AD.

been to outlive Tiberius, which he finally achieved in AD 37, with the tyrant's death at seventy-eight. Tiberius had shown signs of reviving, Suetonius claimed, only to be smothered by his heir. In his will, Tiberius had named Caligula and another nephew, Tiberius Gemellus, as corulers of Rome. But the Roman Senate broke the testament and gave power to Caligula alone.

At first that had seemed an inspired decision. The twenty-five-year-old emperor started off as a model ruler. He cut Tiberius's extortionate taxes, restored an independent judiciary, abolished censorship, declared a general amnesty, and revised the aristocratic rolls to restore Rome's blue-blooded families, who had watched Tiberius sell off patents of nobility to fatten his treasury. Caligula was also open-handed with the common folk, handing out copious amounts of the gold he had inherited from his miserly uncle.

Six months into his reign, however, Caligula fell seriously ill with a fever that rendered him delirious. When he recovered, he was a changed man. The new Caligula, according to his hostile chroniclers, became intent on establishing an absolute monarchy along the lines of the classical Egyptian pharaohs. He began dressing up as a demigod—Hercules, for example—and then moved to a higher plane, appearing in the raiment of Mars or Apollo. He soon ordered that he be worshiped as a living god—a break with Roman practice, which had allowed the worship of Augustus only after his death. In a famous—and disputed—act of sacrilege, Caligula was said to have cut the head off a statue of Jupiter and replaced it with a likeness of his own. It was at this time, according to Suetonius, that Caligula decided to marry his sister, in line with the royal custom of the Egyptians.

His extravagance mounted. At one point, he built a bridge of ships across the entire Bay of Naples in order to stage a mock battle. He spent lavishly on such curiosities as a warship with ten banks of oars and kept the Roman people well supplied with bread and circuses, not to mention elaborate theatrical entertainments, which he adored. Retaining the loyalty of the Roman army was also ruinously expensive. When he had run through his uncle's hoarded millions, he discovered the same gold mine Tiberius had tapped: the aristocracy. In a reversal of policy, he raised taxes inordinately, then began seizing and selling off the estates of the wealthy, often on the pretext that they had committed treason. He would sometimes send a poisoned suicide cake to the unlucky noble whose property was about to become forfeit. Still short of funds, Caligula added sales taxes, a prostitution tax, and even opened a casino and bordello in the imperial palace itself.

His sadistic willingness to torment others pervaded all his dealings. When one patrician's son was sentenced to torture for some imagined crime, the emperor provided the deftly cruel touch of ordering the father to attend and sent a litter to fetch the man when he said he was too ill. Once, when a priest was about to sacrifice an ox in a religious rite, the emperor stepped forward and stabbed the man instead, joking as he slew: "Everyone in turn." Notorious for his transvestite passions—he occasionally liked to wear dresses with trains and women's shoes—Caligula was also a lecher who delighted in humiliating his conquests and their spouses. Women were compelled to accept his advances; later, Caligula would brazenly analyze the unfortunate wives' amatory skills for their husbands.

As commander in chief, Caligula was equally capricious. Alone among emperors to that time, he had no military conquest to his credit. To correct that deficiency, he sent his legions to the English Channel to wage war against Neptune and ordered them to return to Rome laden with seashells as proof of their triumph. But such handling of the imperial Roman army proved his undoing. In particular, he made a bitter enemy of Cassius Charea, a tribune of the Praetorian Guard, by repeatedly addressing the warrior as if he were a woman.

By then, the gilded youth who had once stirred such hopes among his subjects had become a prematurely middle-aged man of twenty-nine, balding, insomniac, subject to raging migraine headaches, and twitching with nervous tremors. Yet for all his degeneracy and jitters, Caligula never lost his mad brand of courage. Toward the end of his reign, he took long, unguarded walks through the imperial stables, as if daring his assassins.

Death overtook the emperor not at the stables but at the imperial theater, where a group of conspirators—led by the insulted tribune Cassius Charea—surrounded Caligula and stabbed him some thirty times. When the first of the blows fell, Caligula screamed, "I'm still alive!"—whether he was flaunting his divine immortality or goading his murderers onward, no one knows for sure. □

Czar Tissue

Russia has never lacked for bloodthirsty and even demented rulers. Yet over the centuries, one name has risen above all of the others: Ivan IV, better known as the Terrible. That title applied to him by history is, in fact, a mistranslation of the Russian term *grozny,* which means "the awe-inspiring." The mistake endures, however, because it so aptly describes the man and his legacy of mad suspicion, capricious rule, torture, and terror.

According to some historians, Ivan's cruelties were no worse than those practiced by many other despots, especially in Asia. But his arose less from imperial necessity than from a profoundly disturbed mind. He was subject to screaming fits and frothing, uncontrollable rages, and flurries of sadistic inspiration. These were punctuated by bouts of deep depression, insomnia, nightmares, and self-loathing. At one of those low moments, he called himself, not inaccurately, a "stinking dog living in drunkenness, adultery, murder, and brigandage." Some experts have speculated that Ivan the Terrible's mind was eaten away by syphilis.

Ivan's upbringing offers other morbid possibilities. A direct descendant of the Russian hero Ivan Nevsky, he was the penultimate ruler of the Danilovich dynasty, the line of czars that preceded the Romanovs, who reigned until the 1917 revolution. His father died when Ivan was three, and his strong-willed mother ruled in his name until her death—perhaps by poisoning—in 1538. Ivan's relatives, the

Glinskys, became the adult powers behind the uncrowned emperor's throne. By some accounts, young Ivan was badly abused and beaten and soon began to display strange and sadistic tendencies. One of his favorite boyhood pursuits was said to be dropping dogs out of a tower onto passersby. Another version has it that he set his hounds on prisoners and rode his horse full tilt into crowds. But he was also a shrewd intriguer. Gradually, as he grew to manhood, he began to take back power from his boyar relatives. In 1547, seventeen-year-old Ivan, after quelling a mob rebellion, was finally crowned czar.

The next six years were something of a golden age for Ivan. He was happily married and eventually fathered six children. To leach power away from the boyars, he promulgated a new and relatively liberal legal code, reformed the army, and instituted local self-government. He created an advisory national assembly, giving commoners an indirect say in affairs of state, and became the first Russian ruler to extend his sway beyond the Slavic people. Like Peter the Great, his aim was to

push Russia toward western Europe in the spirit of liberal absolutism. At one point, he even toyed with the notion of giving up the throne and living in England.

Russia was not to be so lucky. In 1553, Ivan fell severely ill. On his sickbed—what he believed was his deathbed—he demanded that the nobility he had so recently subdued swear allegiance to his infant son Dmitri. Many refused; Dmitri subsequently died. The loss of the boy marked a watershed in Ivan's personal decay: He became withdrawn and chronically suspicious. He received a second shock seven years later when his beloved wife, Anastasia, a calming presence in his life, died. Ivan became reclusive and subject to screaming fits. By some accounts, he began to have nightmares in which he was poisoned or impaled. Thereafter, his mental condition never improved, and his reign moved inexorably into the domain of madness.

No aberration seemed beyond him now. He stabbed his favorite son to death in a rage and had a hat nailed to the French ambassador's head when the diplomat failed to raise it promptly in the imperial presence. One of Ivan's notorious tests was to engage a candidate for his respect in conversation, then, without warning, drive an iron-tipped scepter through the man's foot. Those who flinched—or screamed—he judged to be unworthy of his esteem. People whose look Ivan did not like were summarily put to death.

In 1565, Ivan suddenly announced the most radical and sinister political reform of his reign. He divided his kingdom into two types of state: one to be ruled by normal feudal means, the other, known as the Oprichnina, under his total personal control. A cadre of some 2,000 black-uniformed oprichniki with absolute police powers helped him rule these special zones, where people disappeared arbitrarily and without notice and informers were everywhere. It was as part of his campaign to consolidate the Oprichnina that Ivan launched his 1565 siege of the semi-independent city of Novgorod, where some 30,000 people died in an orgy of torture and carefully choreographed mayhem. Thousands were impaled, sliced to pieces, or pushed into the icy Volkhov River to be clubbed and drowned. Tens of thousands more died of starvation. Yet, while marching to serve the same fate on the neighboring city of Pskov, Ivan suddenly stopped, turned around, and headed toward home. One story has it that the superstitious czar was warned by a hermit that he would be struck by lightning if any harm came to Pskov.

Like his totalitarian successors, Ivan finally turned on his own loyalists and sliced, boiled, and otherwise murdered hundreds of oprichniki before declaring an end to his grand political experiment in 1572. His reign was far from over, but it staggered with exhaustion. As part of his westward push, Ivan had been embroiled in an on-again, off-again war in the Baltic states since 1558; it dragged on until 1582. He ruled on, a fearsome husk, until 1584. Before he died, in a lucid moment of contrition, the Awe Inspirer created memorials at several monasteries for more than 3,000 of his victims and paid for prayers for their souls. □

Building Rage

As the splendid twilight of the Italian Renaissance blended into the baroque period, Francesco Borromini burst upon the world of architecture like a thunderclap. He is credited with developing almost single-handedly the baroque architectural style, a mixture of geometric repetition and radical eclecticism of design that set aesthetes gasping when they viewed his first masterwork, the Roman church of San Carlo alle Quattro Fontane, whose main structure was completed in 1639. But his triumph was tainted. Although Borromini was considered a great architect, one other was considered greater: the multitalented Gian Lorenzo Bernini. Living in Bernini's shadow was evidently more than Borromini could stand. His spirit withered, and his mind sank toward madness and rage. Modern scholars have suggested that the unstable baroque genius fell victim to schizophrenia, a mental disorder that is marked by aberrant behavior, isolation, and delusions. Whatever the technical term applied, the source of Francesco Borromini's mental disturbance is an obvious one: In part, at least, it had its roots in the cardinal sin of envy.

Born in the duchy of Lombardy in 1599, Borromini was originally named Castelli and began his career as a stonecutter's apprentice in Milan. After several years, he fled to Rome and became a draftsman in the office of his relative Carlo Maderno, then Italy's most prominent architect and the man who revised the fundamental plans for Christendom's greatest church, St. Peter's. Borromini met his lifelong rival when Bernini assumed a Maderno commission after Maderno died in ◊

Beset by jealousy, Renaissance architect Francesco Borromini produced such masterworks as this eccentric spire based on the Tower of Babel.

Flanked by the drafting tools of an architect, Francesco Borromini was portrayed by an unknown artist, possibly a contemporary.

1629. The two men worked together on one of the most spectacular aspects of St. Peter's: the great canopy, or baldachin, raised over the church's central tomb. Five years after the project was completed, Borromini launched into the edifice that made his professional reputation, the church of San Carlo.

But by that time, Borromini had acquired another kind of reputation as well. A dour, irascible, and aloof man who remained forever unmarried, he was already known for his stubbornness, long periods of melancholy, and ferocious fits of rage. Those cankers on his personality festered as his stature grew. His sponsors included some of Italy's wealthiest families, as well as Pope Innocent X, but they found him increasingly argumentative, defiant, and stormy. His rages became notorious: He once had a worker who damaged building materials beaten so severely that the man died. In contrast, Bernini was the consummate courtier-architect: He mixed smoothly and well with the highborn, and his talents were but-tressed by his additional genius as a sculptor and painter. Bernini easily won the popularity contest and attracted commissions that Borromini's behavior drove away.

The thwarted architect's resentment became cancerous. He accused Bernini of cheating him of money for work the pair of men had done on St. Peter's, then broadened the charges to include incompetence in the construction of elements of the cathedral that were later removed. Bernini, ever the diplomat, held his tongue for years but finally accused Borromini of having abandoned the humanistic proportions of Renaissance architecture. In fact, the basis of Borromini's great contribution was exactly that he had replaced those notions with relationships borrowed from geometry. But Bernini had deftly negated his radical competitor's achievement.

The people who commissioned great works of architecture began to follow Bernini's lead. As Borromini's work dried up, the gloomy architect slipped into a profound depression—and worse. As one biographer reported, "No one recognized him as Borromini, so distorted was his body and so terrifying his face. He twisted his mouth in a thousand horrible grimaces, and from time to time rolled his eyes in a terrifying manner and sometimes shook and roared like a lion."

Finally, in 1667, he reached the end of his tether. On a fateful August night, he suddenly decided to write out his will, until a servant-nurse ordered him to put out his candle and sleep. At 5:00 a.m., he awoke and demanded light; the servant refused to give it. "I suddenly became impatient," Borromini related, "and began to wonder how I could do myself some bodily harm." He remembered a sword hanging in his bedroom. "In despair I took the sword and, pulling it out of the scabbard, leant the hilt on the bed and put the point to my side and then fell on it with such force that it ran into my body, from one side to the other." Discovered by a servant, Borromini was taken to bed, where, in dreadful agony, he dictated the melancholy narrative of his own suicide. A few hours later, he was dead. His will, like his death, was an acceptance of failure. In accordance with his wishes, Borromini was buried anonymously in the same grave as his former master, Maderno—a final tortured comment, perhaps, on the lack of recognition that had shattered his sanity. □

Convinced that "we human beings, through the history of the world, have protected our continents from cataclysmic earthquakes by murder," Herbert Mullin did what he could to spare California another seismic disaster: In a five-month killing spree during 1972 and 1973, Mullin killed some thirteen people before being caught, tried, and sentenced to life imprisonment—for murder, however, not madness.

The Japanese shogun Tokugawa Tsunayoshi appears in a woodcut by an unknown contemporary artist.

Humane Society

Few Japanese rulers have been as unpopular as Tokugawa Tsunayoshi, whose mania about animals drove his subjects wild for twenty-four years. Tsunayoshi was the fifth of the Tokugawa shoguns, or warlords, who ruled Japan from behind the Chrysanthemum Throne from 1600 to 1868. He took power in 1680 and for the first five years of his reign was deemed a competent ruler, largely due to the support of one of Japan's great courtier-statesmen, Hotta Masatoshi. After Hotta died, however, Tsunayoshi's government—and mind—began to fall apart. The openly bisexual warlord had produced only one son, who had died as a youngster; now, troubled by the absence of heirs, the warlord consulted a priest and was told that he was being punished because an ancestor had killed a dog. For Tsunayoshi, this was the stuff of obsession.

Starting in 1685, he enacted the *Edicts on Compassion for Living Things,* a code that eventually totaled thirty-six laws and set out a variety of horrid punishments for anyone who mistreated a dog and all manner of other animals. Among other things, Tsunayoshi made it a crime punishable by decapitation or enforced suicide to hit a dog that had bitten anyone. Even failing to stop for a dog crossing a street became a punishable offense. To ensure that authorities knew exactly what canine population was at risk, dog owners were required to register them and deposit a hair sample as proof of ownership. They were also required to report how many times a day the animal urinated. Tsunayoshi set up a system of shelters for stray pooches that eventually housed some 82,000 animals.

Persons convicted of mistreating other creatures were likewise punished. One man whose cat fell down a well was exiled to a barren volcanic island where he presumably starved to death. Farmers were forbidden to raise poultry for food—wildly popular ordinances, no doubt, in a country where the fare has always been frugal. Wolves and birds of prey that threatened flocks were decreed immune from attack. The obsessed ruler finally made it illegal even to clap hands to scare pigeons away.

In his mad determination to make things up to the world of animals, however, the shogun may have overlooked an ancestral slight to another, less visible, species. He was killed in 1709 by a host of tiny creatures: variola viruses, the bearers of smallpox. □

Rack of Lamb

At least in the popular imagination, madness and artistry are often linked. But rarely has such a linkage been more poignant, or more productive, than in the case of Charles and Mary Lamb. One of English literature's most devoted brother and sister teams, their essays, poems, and children's stories have charmed millions since the early nineteenth century. Charles Lamb was one of Britain's most accomplished essayists and literary critics, whose whimsical, humorous personal writings brought a new grace and delicacy to the language of self-expression. Mary Lamb was a talented and thoughtful feminist writer and the driving force behind such classical Lamb collaborations as *Tales from Shakespeare, The Adventures of Ulysses,* and *Poetry for Children.* Yet all of those delightful works were produced amid personal suffering on a Victorian Gothic scale, as the siblings were variously beset by violent manic-depression, melancholia, nervous breakdown, and alcoholism.

Insanity and tragedy were part of the Lambs' lives virtually from the moment they were born. Their father was the personal clerk of Samuel Salt, a famous parliamentarian and a director of the wealthy East India Company. The senior Lambs had eight children, five of whom died at birth. Mary, the eldest survivor, was born in 1764, and helped to educate her youngest brother, Charles, born in 1775. He was small and delicate, afflicted with a lifelong stammer and asthma. Yet Mary soon proved to have the worse disease: She had inherited from her mother's side of the family a predisposition to manic- ◊

This dog-shaped copper foot warmer was filled with hot water and used by shogun Tokugawa Tsunayoshi.

depression. During her lucid periods she was warm, humorous, and intelligent. During her attacks she was inarticulate and staring, prone to screaming fits and outbursts of violence.

Insanity gnawed deeply into both sides of the Lamb family. The father also was progressively afflicted with senile dementia that rendered him tyrannically dependent after age fifty; when Charles was twenty-one, his mother became a bedridden paralytic, possibly the result of hysteria. Charles, who left school at fifteen to clerk at India House, became their guardian and main source of support. But he also possessed his family's low resiliency. In late 1795, he had a nervous breakdown and was institutionalized for six weeks. He later wrote to his closest friend, the poet Samuel Taylor Coleridge, that the incident inspired in him a "gloomy kind of envy, for while it lasted, I had many, many hours of pure happiness. Dream not, Coleridge, of having tasted all the grandeur and wildness of fancy till you have gone mad."

There was worse to come. The following year, Charles returned home to discover his sister in a violent fit, with a bloody knife in her hand. She had wounded her aunt, cut her father—and stabbed her mother to death. She was committed to an asylum—she would return to one twenty times during her life—but when she had recovered sufficiently, her brother brought her home, with a promise to the government that he would "take her under his care for life."

Literature was Charles's solace. His first published verses appeared in the year of his mother's death; two years later he commemorated her in his most famous poem, "The Old Familiar Faces," which began: "I had a mother, but she died, and left me." Mary, meantime, regained lucidity, often for months at a time. She also began to write witty and ironic essays on the female condition and provided the main impetus for the duo's first commercial success, the Shakespeare adaptations. Of the twenty slimmed-down dramas, fourteen were modified by her, though her name did not appear on the title page until the seventh edition. She also wrote seven of the ten children's stories in their next great commercial success, *Mrs. Leicester's School.* The sister and brother shared a single writing table, their joint labors marked, Mary recalled, by her "taking snuff and he groaning all the while, and saying he can make nothing of it."

Charles's most accomplished works were his own essays, published in the 1820s and 1830s, under the pseudonym Elia in order to avoid embarrassing his elder brother, Jo. The engagingly personal, elaborate pieces discussed everything from Charles Lamb's early childhood to his intensifying love affair with alcohol. The vituperative historian Thomas Carlyle, who hated Charles, once called him a "shuffling, stuttering, drunken, insane person."

And, in fact, life for the siblings was quietly growing worse, though the couple somehow managed to adopt and raise an orphan girl for twelve years, until her marriage. Mary's manic-depression would lift and then close in, sending her back to the madhouse. Her literary output largely dried up. Charles retired from his clerkship in 1825, rendering their financial condition more fragile. Finally, in 1835, he died suddenly of an infection after injuring his foot on a stone. By that time, Mary had become so withdrawn into madness that she was not aware of the loss. Without knowing that her other half was gone, she lived numbly on for another thirteen years. □

Death Wish

By the end of the eighteenth century, legal codes had acknowledged that insane people who committed criminal acts were not guilty by reason of their illness. But what to do about the dangerously unbalanced, once their lack of culpability had been established? The man who finally moved British law to address that issue was James Hadfield, a soldier driven mad by his war wounds, who believed that he could save the world from its sins only as an assassin.

James Hadfield became one of England's most famous would-be regicides on May 15, 1800, when he snapped off two shots at King George III as the Hanoverian monarch entered the royal box at London's Drury Lane Theatre. Both of the bullets missed the king, and Hadfield was immediately seized. He was charged with high treason, a crime that demanded the death penalty. Yet it was clear virtually from the start that Hadfield suffered from madness—brought on, ironically enough, by his service to king and country.

Hadfield had been a professional soldier and a member of the duke of York's personal guard, until badly wounded on a campaign in Flanders. During a battle, his head was brutally hacked open with a sword; when he recovered, he began to experience recurring fits, often violent, that led to his discharge from the army. Hadfield's overriding delusion was that he was a new savior and that he had to die to cleanse the world of its sins. Yet his madness took a further peculiar twist: His mystical status somehow prevented him from committing suicide; therefore, he had to commit a crime—like attempted regicide—that guaranteed his execution.

The details of Hadfield's malady were carefully brought out at the treason trial by his attorney, Thomas Erskine, one of the most brilliant legal minds of the day. Among other things, Erskine showed that Hadfield had first tried to kill his infant son for the same reason and that even in his insanity the wounded soldier was loudly insistent on his loyalty to the Crown. Finally, both prosecutor and judge joined Erskine in the insanity verdict and in the view that Hadfield could not be safely returned to society.

As the law then stood, criminally insane defendants could only be remanded back to their last place of confinement, which meant ordinary prison. But as a result of the publicity the demented dragoon's case had generated, new legislation passed Parliament within the year, allowing criminally insane defendants to be detained in asylums. The first person to benefit from the new, humane law was Hadfield himself, who was sent to the famed mental hospital at Bethlem—familiarly, Bedlam.

Hadfield evidently did not like it there; two years later, he escaped, was captured, and returned to Newgate Prison. Eventually, he was sent back to Bethlem, this time remaining there for nearly four decades until his death in 1841. During most of that time, he was deemed a model inmate. A French woman, Flora Tristan, who struck up a visiting relationship with Hadfield, observed that he had "a loving heart, an absolute need for affection." He kept two dogs, three cats, a number of birds, and a squirrel as pets, and when they died, stuffed them and wrote verse epitaphs to their memory. His sentimentality, though, had its practical side. Hadfield also sold copies of the touching funereal verses to tourists and, according to another contemporary, would sometimes breed and sell his feathered friends as well. □

Put away as a mad would-be regicide, James Hadfield produced touching poems, including the 1826 "Epitaph for my poor Jack, Squirrel," which he illustrated with this watercolor.

Mad about the Bard

Who really wrote William Shakespeare's plays? Nearly 400 years after the Bard was buried in the church at Stratford-on-Avon, furious literary wars are still raging over the authorship of his work, with nearly sixty different candidates vying for the honor. The heat and intensity of the debate is a tribute to Delia Salter Bacon, a determined Connecticut schoolteacher and historian who, nearly 150 years ago, pioneered this controversial quest. But there was little comfort in it for Delia Bacon, whose efforts brought her only a dubious kind of fame and fatal madness.

Bacon was an extreme rarity in mid-nineteenth-century America: an independent female intellectual. The daughter of a dreamy and feckless Congregational minister, she was born in 1811 and raised by a wealthy Hartford matron after the death of her father, who bankrupted himself trying to found a utopian religious colony in Ohio. She was intelligent and talented as well as strong-willed: An aspiring historian, novelist, and short-story writer, Bacon once won a prize in literary competition against the young Edgar Allan Poe. As one of her brothers put it later, "From her childhood, she has had a passion for literature, and perhaps I should say a longing for celebrity." She moved out on her own at age fifteen and attempted, unsuccessfully, to set up her own girls' school. Then Bacon took a usual step in those days for unmarried females and became a teacher.

To augment her income, Bacon also began giving public history lectures for an admission fee, a popular form of middle-class entertainment. Audiences found her combination of presence, erudition, eloquence, and wit irresistible. But she shocked them when, in conversations following her talks, she referred to the great William Shakespeare contemptuously as "Will the Jester," a "vulgar, illiterate deer poacher," and opined that the plays were too brilliant, and too pregnant with philosophical meaning, for any one person to have written them. The attractive thirty-four-year-old spinster also shocked her world when, in 1845, she had an affair with a divinity student ten years her junior—a terrible breach of propriety in her circles. Her life and her ability to make a living were shattered by the ensuing publicity. Bacon went into seclusion in Ohio, tough-mindedly nursing her emotional wounds and tuning her Shakespearean speculations.

The basis for Bacon's—and most other—Shakespeare conjecture is the near-complete lack of information about the man himself and the even greater lack of evidence tying Shakespeare the man to the plays offered under his name. Only six copies of Shakespeare's autograph, for example, are known to exist; most of the evidence about him indicates that he was a shrewd, pragmatic businessman—hardly the type, in Bacon's view, to have produced the sublime human and philosophical insights of the Shakespeare plays. The man from Stratford, she reasoned, must have been a stand-in for someone else. The real authors, Bacon became convinced, were actually a cabal of highborn Englishmen, including Sir Francis Bacon (no relation), Sir Philip Sydney, Edward de Vere, Sir Walter Raleigh, and the poet Edmund Spenser, many of whom are still in contention individually for the title.

As she turned over her own theories, Bacon began to flavor them with imagined conspiracy. Gradually she came to the view that Raleigh, Bacon, and the others had political, not literary, motives for writing the plays. The secret authors were nothing less than a cell of liberal-minded subversives, she decided, intent on spreading a democratic doctrine of constitutional government under the nose of their absolute monarch, Elizabeth I. They carried out their effort, Bacon theorized, until Elizabeth finally uncovered their enterprise and gently persuaded the group to disband.

The obsessed sleuth also became convinced that the evidence to back her theory could be found in Shakespeare's tomb. She put that possi-

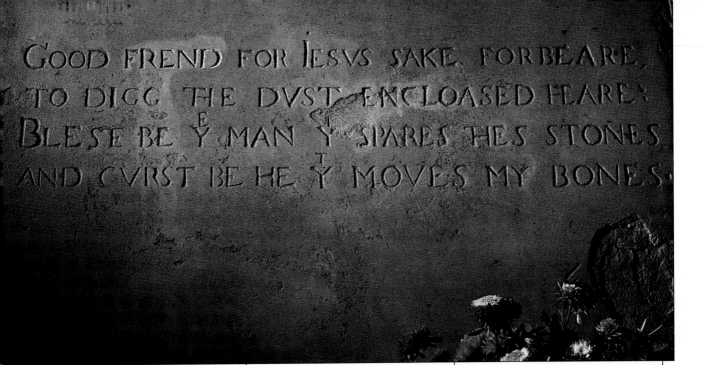

GOOD FREND FOR IESVS SAKE FORBEARE,
TO DIGG THE DVST ENCLOASED HEARE:
BLESE BE Y MAN Y SPARES THES STONES
AND CVRST BE HE Y MOVES MY BONES.

bility, among others, to Ralph Waldo Emerson when she first met the thinker in Cambridge, Massachusetts. Emerson was intrigued—later he declared that she and poet Walt Whitman were "the sole producers America has yielded in ten years." He introduced her to a banker, Charles Butler, who promised to pay for her trip to England and finance half a year's research. Emerson also provided introductions to the irascible British historian Thomas Carlyle and talked *Putnam's Magazine* into serializing chapters of Bacon's future book on the Shakespeare mystery. In 1853, Delia Bacon, now forty-two, set sail for England.

Once there, however, her quest became confused. She quarreled about her project with Carlyle, who expressed his view that "truly there can be no madder enterprise." And she refused to examine any of the voluminous documentation on Shakespeare in the British Museum. An undisciplined researcher, she relied mainly on her own hunches—she concluded, for example, that Sir Francis Bacon and Shakespeare must have been the same person because they showed great congruity of belief. She tried, without

success, to have Bacon's coffin opened. Then she locked herself away and wrote furiously. A year passed; her support from Charles Butler evaporated. Penniless, but increasingly gripped by her theory, Bacon moved to London, where she luckily found rooms above a grocery store where the landlord lent her money and forgave her the rent. In 1856, a chapter of her manuscript was published in *Putnam's Magazine,* but the agreement to publish other chapters dissolved. Again, she invented agents of conspiracy, hinting at a plot by pro-Shakespeare forces to prevent her theories from being aired.

As her desperation mounted, Bacon found a new patron: Nathaniel Hawthorne. The author of *The Scarlet Letter* had been named American consul in Liverpool, a well-paying job that allowed him creative freedom. Bacon wrote him a despairing plea for help. The good-hearted novelist sympathized with her plight and agreed to help her publish her manuscript. Bacon, meanwhile, finally announced that she would visit the Bard's grave, where she was certain evidence supporting her theory lay beneath the flagstone covering. She traveled to Stratford

and immediately fell ill for six weeks. Hawthorne, meanwhile, forced her book upon his publisher and agreed to spend $1,000 of his own money to cover the printing costs. Bacon was anything but grateful: She fought constantly with the book's editors and refused to rewrite a line.

Her climactic moment came in late 1856, when she finally visited Shakespeare's grave. Once again, her unusual ability to persuade others to do her will stood her in good stead: The vicar not only allowed her to stay at the grave site after hours but granted permission for the Bard's bitterest foe to lift the flagstone off the tomb, so long as she did not disturb the coffin that lay underneath it. Bacon agreed and did—nothing. Inexplicably unable to take the definitive step, she merely stole away.

In 1857, *The Philosophy of the Plays of Shakspere Unfolded,* by Delia Bacon, with a kind but skeptical preface by Nathaniel Hawthorne, finally appeared. The 700-page book was a rambling disaster, built around a theory that had taken a sharply conspiratorial turn. Her thesis was that the highborn alternative authors had entered into a se- ◊

cret compact to propagandize the English masses with radical democratic views disguised as plays: "great philosophic poems," as she described them. It was Sir Francis Bacon, she declared, who first had the idea of using drama as a masquerade for a "great scientific enterprise," and the aristocratic company settled on Shakespeare as their figurehead after he was introduced to the group by playwright Ben Jonson. Turgid and unreadable, Bacon's book drew outraged fire from Shakespeare adherents and incomprehension from everyone else. The tome "fell with a dead thump at the feet of the public, and has never been picked up," wrote Hawthorne. "If any American ever wrote a word in her behalf, Miss Bacon never knew it, nor did I."

But by then, the author must have been numb to criticism. Living in the home of a charitable shoemaker in Stratford, she had begun to suffer from hallucinations. Two months after her book was published, Hawthorne received a letter from Stratford's mayor, announcing that "there is much reason to fear that she will become decidedly insane." The loyal Hawthorne tried to have her repatriated to the United States, but Bacon's condition deteriorated; she remained in England, in a private asylum eight miles outside Shakespeare's hometown. Finally, in 1858, a nephew brought her home—too late. Her family put the ailing woman into a Hartford sanitarium, where she sank deeper into insanity. She died the following year, after briefly recognizing some of her relatives. Not once, in her period of institutionalization, did she mention the man whose ambiguities had defeated her: William Shakespeare. □

Hospital Rounds

Karl Friedrich Hieronymus, Baron von Munchausen, the fictional counterpart of an eighteenth-century German cavalry officer and minor grandee, was famous for his globe-spanning travels—and for the fanciful tales he told about them. In the 1950s, the noble's name was revived by medical researchers trying to name a strange mania they had discovered. Munchausen Syndrome seemed a good fit.

Like the baron, many victims of the strange disorder travel widely—not from country to country but from hospital to hospital. In another nod to Hieronymus, the modern Munchausens lie outrageously, and convincingly, about their supposed afflictions. And they take great pains—often literal ones—to fake symptoms that lead them toward treatments that may be dangerous, disfiguring, or even life-threatening. Munchausen Syndrome is hypochondria gone mad.

In one documented case, for example, a forty-year-old man entered the hospital claiming severe pain, occasional numbness, and weakness in his right leg. Ten days earlier, he said, he had received surgery on the artery in that leg to remove a blood clot, and he had suffered many similar operations on his left arm, ending with a below-the-elbow amputation of the limb. All the surgery, he claimed, had been performed abroad. The patient also reported a long history of angina and a family history of heart disease. Doctors examined the man and found that his right leg was certainly damaged by arterial clotting and subjected the patient to a series of emergency bypass operations and medication in order to prevent more

clots from forming in the artery. Despite their efforts, however, he developed gangrene, and the leg had to be amputated.

But during the surgical preparation, doctors had discovered something else about their patient: He showed no evidence of heart or vascular disease. Upon further scrutiny, the man's stories of foreign surgery turned out to be lies. The real cause of his disastrous amputations, it seemed, was the fact that he kept appearing at different hospitals and making repeated claims, replete with symptoms of severe angina, in order to have his heart probed. His knowledge of medicine was good enough that at least four times doctors inserted catheters into his heart for inspections—the probing, in fact, was all he really wanted. His clotting problems were side effects of the repeated invasions of his heart; floating blood clots set adrift by the catheters lodged in arteries, blocking circulation so badly that only drastic surgery could save the patient. In all, the man had been admitted twenty-three times to fifteen hospitals in less than three years—all in the New York area.

Victims of Munchausen Syndrome also go by less flattering names: hospital hobos and medicine addicts. What they have in common is a compulsive desire to undergo medical treatment for fictitious ailments that somehow have attracted them. In order to get the treatments that they desire, they must fake physical symptoms, as in the double amputee's imitation of the sharp chest pains of angina. Other Munchausen tricks can range from tampering with thermometer

quently their own child, to satisfy their twisted Munchausen longing.

The syndrome poses a special challenge to the medical profession because it makes a diagnostic physician into a complicitous partner in a rare but dangerous mental disease. The mental disturbance also can go undetected for long periods of time, concealed by both the victim's skill at faking illness and the scant likelihood that anyone would voluntarily undergo painful and sometimes dangerous medical treatment for no reason.

Munchausen strikes men and women equally, usually in early adult life. At some time before the onset of the malady, its victims have usually been hospitalized for a genuine health problem. Little is known about how the ailment then proceeds. Abandonment, parental abuse, and rejection crop up frequently in the histories of Munchausen victims. But they do not explain the disorder. Nor is it easy to treat. Psychiatric methods do not work very well. For one thing, when victims are confronted with their real, rather than imaginary, illness, they tend to become angry, evasive, and manipulative—and walk away from treatment. For them, the cure is truly worse than the disease. □

readings and urine specimens to faked epilepsy, poison injections, and self-mutilation. In many cases, mutilation is all that the syndrome's victims are after.

One tip-off to the syndrome is the calm and unconcerned manner in which they discuss the hazardous medical procedures ahead of them. Many extreme sufferers of Munchausen Syndrome are covered with scars from old operations and may develop genuine illnesses, such as abscesses, gangrene, or organ failure, from repeated treatments. Like obsessed lovers, Munchausen victims crave someone's—a physician's—undivided attention and will often do anything to get it. Sometimes, victims use a proxy, fre-

Stressed to Kill

The term *running amok* has become a commonplace in English, colloquially taken to mean "out of control." Behind that euphemistic usage lies something much more extreme: An explosive form of homicidal mania that was formerly endemic in Malaysia and that is still reported in parts of the country—but which also shows up in other cultures of the Pacific Rim region.

Amok was originally a Malaysian word that meant "to engage furiously in battle," except that in the insane form, the battle was usually against unarmed and terrified family members or neighbors who were caught in a swath of murder. Another term for the malady is *mata gelap*, literally, "darkened eye." Persons afflicted with amok suddenly become withdrawn and isolated, then, after a period of hours or days, explode in violence, using whatever weapons are at hand against anyone within reach. The murderous fury lasts until the victim is either killed or overpowered. Once rendered harmless, the formerly homicidal maniac usually falls into a sleep or stupor for hours, even days. Many awaken with no memory of their killing spree. Some become suicidal. Strangely, the violent attacks almost never recur.

Since the 1930s, the disorder has been a rarity in the urbanized portions of Malaysia and Indonesia; the best-documented cases occurred earlier, when colonial rule was rubbing up against a less diluted native culture. One study, written in 1891, reported the mania of a peasant who suddenly entered the house of his brother-in-law with a spear ◊

and another bladed weapon in his hands. The man asked his in-law's pardon, then stabbed his own wife, who was present. Now the killer turned on the brother-in-law, killing him, before pursuing the man's wife and four children. The woman and two children were butchered, as were two villagers who unfortunately happened along. The afflicted person, or *pengamok,* disappeared into the jungle but returned the following night to attack another family. He was fatally wounded and, witnesses reported, died saying "he did not know what he was doing, only his head went round and the devil told him to do it."

These days, when amok occurs in Malaysia, it is usually in remote rural communities, far from the influence of modernity. But over time, enough evidence has been gathered to compile an approximate portrait of the victims. They are usually men—there is only one recorded instance of a female amok—between the ages of twenty and forty-five. The persons most likely to fall victim to the pengamok are, not surprisingly, those who live closest to them. Another high-risk group are inmates of old-fashioned, penal-type mental hospitals, where amok cases occur far more often than in modern therapeutic ones.

The cause of the disease, once considered a form of spirit possession, is not precisely known. Modern investigators have tended to point to peculiarities of Malaysian culture, which is extremely indulgent to young chil-

dren but suddenly becomes stern and admonitory to adolescents, stressing their social duty. Psychiatrists point to this as a source of inner conflict, which causes grave difficulty in expressing hostility and causes blame to be directed outward, at the community, rather than at oneself. Social psychologists, on the other hand, point to such possible causes as a loss of social standing or the effects of a major life change over the previous two or more years.

Even as amok has declined in Malaysia, it, or something like it, has appeared in the nearby Philippines, Thailand, and Laos. There, the weapons are less traditional: They may be guns, automatic weapons, or even grenades; but the syndrome of social withdrawal, explosive violence, and subsequent stupor seems remarkably similar. The shifting patterns suggest that there may be something socially contagious about certain aberrations of behavior. For example, amok may even have spread to parts of the United States, where, without warning or explanation, an inner detonation of secret violence sometimes compels an individual to murder crowds of strangers. □

The *kris*, a familiar Malaysian implement, is typically the weapon of choice by homicidal *pengamoks.*

Biting Cold

The long, harsh, desolate winters of the subarctic region would be a test of anyone's sanity. But it has been an especially extreme test for a small number of Indian tribes that eke their lonely livings from that unyielding land. Sometimes the struggle has become too much, and tribal members have been swept away in a rare form of homicidal mania, coupled with cannibalism, known as windigo.

By no coincidence, windigo is also the mythological personification of starvation among the Cree, Ojibwa, and Salteaux Indians: a giant, living skeleton of ice who murders and devours all in his path. Human victims of the eponymous madness are considered to be possessed of the evil spirit, unable to resist its murderous dictates and unable to stop killing. The cure usually administered is death at the hands of the rest of the community.

The victims, mostly male, enter into a depression in wintertime, brought on by bad hunting. They become melancholic and withdrawn, lose their appetite, and are restless and unable to sleep. Then they erupt in violence, usually against members of their immediate family. Murder is followed by cannibalism; then the windigo sufferer stalks other victims. Sometimes the murderous seizures are reinforced by delusions that the victims had turned into game animals.

Windigo is unique in another regard: Other native peoples, living under conditions just as harsh, or worse, do not seem to suffer from it. It is unknown, for example, among the Eskimo tribes who live even farther to the north and under more desolate conditions. Windigo

Windigo, the Ojib-
wa's specter of
starvation, was
drawn by Norval
Morrisseau, a self-
taught tribal artist.

seems to depend on cultural conditions unique to the tribes that believe in the windigo monster.

According to anthropologists who have studied the Ojibwa, the culture is indeed a unique one. It is, as one put it, "saturated with anxiety." Much of that anxiety has to do with how the Ojibwa live. The land that they occupy is immense, but it is sparsely populated with game, especially in winter. Thus, the Ojibwa life has always been an extremely solitary one. During wintertime especially, Ojibwa families have almost nothing to do with one another, and family lives reflect that isolated aloofness. Affectionate demonstrations are taboo, even between parents and children.

From an early age, youngsters are trained to hardship; experimental starvation is encouraged, and they rely upon supernatural companionship—a guardian spirit—rather than on their fellow human beings. Each hunter's prowess is deemed a reflection of his spiritual potency: The best hunters make the most powerful medicine men. This cultural training, however, produces individuals who are profoundly egocentric, suspicious of fellow tribesmen, and dependent on the achievements of hunting not only for their livelihood but for their community standing and even their sense of identity. Members of the tribe are extremely sensitive to insults or personal slights and wary of all others. As one expert on the culture put it: "The price of success to the Ojibway is psychiatric insecurity, which increases with increasing flights of ambition."

When the Ojibwa join in larger communities, almost always in summertime, the tides of this suspicion swell, usually focused on the

most successful hunters in the group, whose attainments, paradoxically, diminish the sense of self of other members of the tribe. If they become too successful, they might be killed by their fellows. One anthropologist records the case of a medicine man who had inspired such fear in the tribe that he was surreptitiously poisoned and kicked by his comrades as he lay dying. One was his own daughter, who had given permission for the murder.

In such an atmosphere of hostile, hypercompetitive egos, laying curses is a common pastime. The commonest curse is "You will starve." Thus, when winter returns, and an isolated Ojibwa faces actual hunger, the most plausible explanation is that the curse worked. At the same time, the hunger brought on by failure at hunting, the most basic Ojibwa activity, is an almost intolerable admission of defeat. This, many experts believe, leads to the depres-

sion, psychosis, and violence of the windigo malady.

Although the victims of windigo are overwhelmingly male, women too can fall victim on occasion. But in those cases, the women are filling traditionally male roles: widows who have taken up a hunter's life, for example. Nor is melancholy a necessary precursor to the onset of madness. In one case, a mother ordered her son to kill his father one winter, and the boy complied. Then the mania took over. Before spring, the boy had eaten all his siblings except one girl, who was his accomplice in killing their mother—and her brother's final victim. That summer, when the boy returned alone to the Ojibwa community encampment, he was finally found out and killed in turn.

The Ojibwa themselves draw diagnostic distinctions about the degree and severity of windigo. In most cases, usually involving powerful community members, the madness is deemed severe enough to warrant immediate death. In some instances, however, the tribe tries to restrain the sufferer into the summer, when the windigo seems to weaken. In at least one case, where an afflicted man hallucinated that he saw a beaver in his pregnant wife's uterus—a cannibalistic delusion—he was not slain but nursed back to health.

Today, windigo is likely an extinct form of madness. As recently as 1961, Canadian researchers were able to assemble a total history of only seventy cases; only ten of these occurred in the twentieth century. Perhaps the frequently destructive touch of western culture has eased the Ojibwa's isolation—and reduced their anxieties below the saturation point. □

Bestial Acts

For fans of horror movies and the occult, there is something eternally alluring about the cliché of creatures doomed to roam the night as werewolves, spreading death and fear among their fellow humans. Yet something akin to this does exist. Called lycanthropy, it is a relatively rare mental disorder, often curable, whose victims believe they are animals—though not always members of the species *lupus*.

The notion of people turning into beasts is almost as old as human history. The term *lycanthropy* itself derives from the Greek myth of Lycaon, who was turned into a wolf by Zeus as punishment for trying to trick the god into the crime of cannibalism. In the Middle Ages, fear of werewolves became a form of mass hysteria that lasted into the 1500s; one French judge named Henri Boguet alone burned hundreds of men and women for the offense during his career.

But there were also early attempts to create a scientific understanding of the phenomenon. A sixteenth-century physician, Jena Fernel, argued the case for werewolves as being created by forces of evil; his contemporary Pierre Leloyer argued that demonic powers could not turn humans into animals, but could cause animal-like *behavior*—in effect identifying the disorder as mental rather than supernatural. In seventeenth-century Britain, when cases occurred of people who thought they were wolves, the victims were treated as sufferers from delusion brought on by melancholy. In 1700, an interesting variation occurred when a group of nuns in a French convent were said to mew and behave as if they had suddenly been changed into cats. As science progressed, the rare instances of humans who behaved like animals were increasingly treated as cases of outright mental disorder. Earlier in this century, for example, Swiss psychoanalyst Carl Jung diagnosed as merely insane a woman who "would exhibit a sort of lycanthropy in which she crawled on all fours and imitated the grunting of pigs, the barking of dogs, and the growling of bears." But such cases were rare, and experts began to consider the aberration extinct.

They were somewhat premature. In 1988, a group of Massachusetts psychiatric researchers found a dozen mental patients who could reliably be described as showing lycanthropic behavior. Each exhibited different symptoms, for varying lengths of time. Among the twelve were two delusional wolves, two dogs, a bird, two cats, a rabbit, a gerbil, two multipurpose beasts that variously howled, crawled, hooted, and clawed—and one remarkable tiger.

This giant cat was a twenty-six-year-old man who had believed for roughly half his life that he was a cat trapped inside a human body. The knowledge, he said, had been passed on to him by his family cat, who taught him cat language, trained him to mimic human behavior, and served as his surrogate parent. The patient claimed that when left alone as a child he had hunted regularly with cats, eaten small animals and raw meat, and had sex with cats. He used to visit tigers at zoos, he said, where he spoke to them in their language and petted them through the bars. At age seventeen, he had decided that, because of his large size, he must be a tiger himself, albeit one with a very untiger-like body. For seven years, he pined for a female zoo tiger named Dolly and attempted suicide when she was sold to a zoo in Asia. The tiger-man had also begun to dress the part, in striped orange-and-black clothes and bushy hair, sideburns, and beard. He grew his nails long and loudly regretted the absence of a tail. Eventually, he came to believe his true parents had been tigers or, at the very least, there had been a tiger ancestor.

When the man was first hospitalized, he had hallucinated that he was accompanied by another tiger. This gradually changed into a belief that his old feline flame, Dolly, had escaped from the zoo, was living on the hospital grounds, and would have sex with him in the shower in the early morning. And he worried that there might be something wrong with his mind—that he was a "crazy tiger."

As a child, the tiger-man had lived in a broken, angry home. He had early childhood memories of being tied in a harness to a tree and imagining himself a dog. He hated his parents, particularly his mother, and speculated wishfully that he might have been adopted. None of those details did much to explain his delusion, which may have had a genetic basis: Both his grandfather and his first cousin had committed suicide, and two aunts had died in psychiatric institutions.

Remarkably, the tiger-man's delusion did not prevent him from living something close to a normal life. He attended high school and college, served as president of his class for one year, and edited his high-school newspaper and yearbook. Between the ages of fifteen and twenty-one, he had a number of sexual relations with women, some lasting for years. They had been fine, he reported, although he found them less attractive than felines.

During eight years of treatment, the were-tiger received a variety of chemical treatments that did nothing to lessen his fundamental belief in his beastliness, though they did cause his imaginary tiger companion to disappear. Eventually, he was released on medication back into the human world. According to the medical researchers, as of 1990 the man was working as a research scientist, functioning well, and sharing an apartment with two friends—plus, of course, a cat. □

Madhouse Flower

In his day, Richard Dadd was ranked among the most promising young artists on the British scene. Bright prospects beckoned. By the time of his death, however, he had become something more singular: artist-in-residence at the British insane asylums of Bethlem and Broadmoor and a famous patricide.

The doomed artist's difficult journey began in Chatham, where Dadd was born in 1817, one of seven children, four of whom died insane. By age thirteen, Richard had already begun to show distinct drawing talent. Seven years later, after his father, a small businessman, moved the family to London, the son's skills impressed the masters of the Royal Academy enough that they admitted him as a student. He was immediately popular with his peers, "a man of genius that would assuredly have placed him high in the first rank of painters," as a fellow student wrote, "one of the noblest natures and brightest minds that ever existed." In person, too, he was considered something of a paragon. Tall, handsome, and energetic, he was described by a family friend as "invariably gentle, kind, considerate and affectionate"; another said he was "one of the kindest and the best, as well as the most gifted, of the children of genius it has ever been our lot to know."

Dadd had already begun exhibiting publicly as a student, with a marked preference for fanciful scenes from Shakespeare as subjects. By the time he left the academy, he was winning commissions as a decorator, an etcher, and an illustrator. Then, in 1842, he was offered a fateful assignment: to travel as an artist with Sir Thomas Phillips, a well-to-do lawyer who wanted to make a grand tour of the Middle East before settling back into harness as a London barrister. Dadd seized the opportunity—and began to discover a madman within.

His early symptoms came upon him more than halfway through the journey, in Egypt, and he attributed them to sunstroke and what he called his "nervous depression." Increasingly, he began to feel that he was being pursued by spirits who appeared to him in the guise of fellow travelers and finally as his patron, Sir Thomas. In Rome, the young artist felt a sudden urge to attack the pope. On the final leg of the trip, his symptoms became so disturbing that he left the main party and returned to England alone.

The man who arrived back in London was vastly changed. Dadd had become suspicious, unpredictable, violent. Once he locked himself in his room and waved a knife under the door at all would-be visitors. He cut a "birthmark" on his forehead and claimed it came from the devil and much later declared that he considered himself a descendant of the Egyptian god Osiris. Friends who later entered his rooms discovered the floor littered with eggshells and ale bottles, his main source of food. They also discovered pictures of themselves with their throats cut.

Doctors advised his father that Richard was dangerous and no longer responsible for his actions. The elder Dadd, devoted to his son, made a fatal decision to care for Richard himself. Two days after the warning, the son called on his father and asked him to visit an old ◊

One of artist Richard Dadd's fantasies was *The Fairy Feller's Master Stroke,* in which a feller, or woodsman, works in a fairy landscape.

haunt near Chatham. The older man agreed, and as they walked in a park, Richard pulled a knife and stabbed his father to death. He believed his father was a devil and that his own task on earth was to "exterminate the men most possessed with the demon." The painter then fled to France—where he was arrested after trying to murder a fellow passenger in a coach.

Within a year, Dadd was committed to Bethlem, where his creative juices, which had evaporated during his mental decline, once again began to flow. He produced watercolors, then oils, that repeated his favorite fairy themes. He still suffered sudden fits of violence and the al-

ternate gorging and vomiting symptoms seen in bulimia. But little in his work hinted at the murderous disturbances still raging within, except perhaps some subtle alterations of the human form: His imaginary figures often had no necks, misshapen legs, and tiny feet.

After twenty years at Bethlem, Dadd was transferred to another hospital, Broadmoor, where he played the violin, read classical history, and experimented with such techniques as decorating glass panels. Every now and then, he would have a violent outburst and attack an inmate. He would invariably apologize afterward. His belief in being controlled by the spirit world never disappeared, but by the end of his life—he died of consumption in 1886—Dadd was remembered by a visitor merely as "a pleasant-visaged old man, with a long and flowing snow-white beard, with mild blue eyes that beam benignly through spectacles."

Little by little after his death, the paintings done during his forty-year confinement began to trickle into public view. In 1974, a major retrospective of his work was mounted and toured parts of England, in tribute to the creative spirit that had flourished in a madhouse. □

Black Forest Fantasies

Compared with the manias of some despots, the obsessions of "Mad King" Ludwig II of Bavaria were as tame as his other, gentler sobriquet: the Fairy-Tale King. He was consumed by opera and building castles, on a ruinous scale. Inspired by medieval romances, Wagnerian operas, and the opulent absolutism of French kings, Ludwig's castles were also his alternative reality—a world into which he increasingly disappeared.

A member of the Wittelsbach dynasty that ruled Bavaria from 1180 onward, Ludwig gave early intimations of where his true passions lay. As a youngster, he preferred acting and dressing up as a nun—and he loved building with toy bricks. But the family was tainted by insanity. Ludwig's aunt, Princess Alexandra, firmly believed that she had swallowed a grand piano made of glass. Ludwig's brother Otto would be declared insane in 1875. In 1859, at age fourteen, Ludwig himself started to have mild hallucinations and to hear imaginary voices.

A year later, Ludwig was smitten by his first grand obsession. He attended a performance of *Lohengrin,* the tale of a German knight guided by a swan to rescue a maiden in distress. The young prince came away thunderstruck by the extravagant romantic genius of the opera's composer, Richard Wagner. For the rest of his life, Ludwig had swan motifs from the work engraved on his bedsteads and coaches, embroidered on his bedclothes, and painted everywhere. But such foibles seemed trivial when the tall, handsome young king finally took the

Neuschwanstein—"New Swan-Crag"— was one of three fabulous castles built by Bavaria's King Ludwig II, who strikes a pose in an 1887 painting *(inset)* by Gabriel von Schachinger, seen against Ludwig's ubiquitous swan and lily motif.

throne at nineteen, in 1864. "This man has something great and poetic about him," his cousin-in-law, the infanta of Spain, once wrote, and "has powers of imagination such as one rarely finds in anyone." As Bavarians would discover, Ludwig was almost all imagination, a dreamy introvert who preferred myth, poetry, and architecture to the dreary everyday business of running the state.

One of his first kingly acts was to dispatch his cabinet secretary to find the egotistical and extravagant Wagner, who was on the run from creditors. Ludwig brought him to Munich, where, Wagner related, "he offers me everything I need to live, to create, to perform my works. I am only expected to be his friend." Under the young king's patronage, Wagner completed the scores of *Die Meistersinger von Nürnberg, Siegfried, Götterdämmerung,* and *Parsifal* in something approaching princely comfort. But Bavarians began to murmur, especially after Ludwig underwrote a large part of the cost of Wagner's festival performance house in Bayreuth, located about 100 miles north of Munich— an unpopular project that fizzled out after a couple of years. Gravely concerned about the composer's hold over the dreamy monarch, the people finally acted. Wagner was expelled

from the capital and fled to rural Bavaria, but he continued a feverish correspondence with Ludwig, who still sent the composer money.

By then, other royal quirks had begun to surface. Even when attending one of his beloved operas, he suffered from the excessive attentions of his subjects. "I can get no sense of illusion so long as the public ogles me," he complained. As a solution, he commanded performances in which entire theatrical and singing troupes performed to a darkened, empty house, while Ludwig watched from behind the drawn curtains of his royal box. He ordered more than 200 of these lonely encounters with the arts.

A similar uneasiness afflicted his appearances of state. He would often cancel dinner parties at the last minute. When he did bother to attend, he would build a wall of flowers and table decorations in front of his place and order musicians to play louder than usual to preclude conversation. A Roman Catholic, he had his own chapels built so that he could hear Mass alone. Because court protocol bored him, Ludwig had the entire roof of the royal palace in Munich converted into a Winter Garden, where only his closest friends were invited. The awestruck Spanish infanta described a visit there: "Before me was an enormous garden, illuminated in Venetian style, with palms, a lake, bridges, huts and castellated buildings." An artificial moon reflected on the waters, and a hidden orchestra played Spanish music in her honor. At one point, a rainbow appeared.

The Winter Garden was an escape but a limited one. Ludwig increasingly longed for ◊

a world that was entirely fantasy. His first attempt to create that dream world was the castle at Neuschwanstein, purportedly a medieval restoration but in fact a wild jumble of baroque architecture decorated in a variety of exotic fantasy styles, from Turkish to Byzantine to Moroccan. While the castle was still under construction, Ludwig ordered the building of Linderhof, a conscious imitation of Louis XIV's palace at Versailles, on the site of a hunting lodge. But Linderhof was a mere pastiche. Ludwig's last project, Herrenchiemsee, was intended to be a faithful reproduction in stone of the real thing, complete with a virtual duplicate of the great Hall of Mirrors and the French king's private apartments.

Too busy creating fantasy worlds to rule his real one, Ludwig gradually withdrew from sight and became nocturnal. The king would wake at 7:00 p.m., have lunch at midnight and supper in the early morning hours, then retire before his cabinet and his subjects awoke. When he left his dream environments for the outside world, he kept to the solitude of the Bavarian woods. His subjects sometimes spotted him at night, traveling in a gilded coach or sleigh pulled by white horses and surrounded by elaborately clad lackeys in wigs—more a baroque ghost than a king. At times he would stop and invite himself into the homes of peasant families, who had begun to call him the Dream King. Ludwig also *pretended* to travel. One account has it that he would calculate the distance from Munich to wherever he wanted to go, then spend the night driving around the arena of the court riding school until he had covered the required distance. Halfway along the "route" he would stop his carriage, leap out, have a picnic, then move on.

Along with imaginary destinations, Ludwig spent more and more time with invented people. He was often discovered roaring with laughter and talking to himself, as if in an intellectual salon. He invited his favorite gray mare to dinner in the palace, where she fed off the state porcelain. Many of his other dinner guests were entirely invisible. When these entertainments flagged, Ludwig would often dress up as another king—Louis XIV was a favorite—and then dash through his palace in costume.

As his mind deteriorated, Ludwig became increasingly tyrannical. The slightest imagined offense would cause him to strike or kick his servants. It was forbidden to cough, sneeze, or speak Bavarian dialect in the royal presence: Those who disobeyed were ordered to be flogged, jailed, or executed, although the sentences were never carried out. The imaginary noises he had heard in his youth recurred, only louder. He began suffering from severe headaches. The dashing youth of his coronation was replaced by a morose, heavyset man with a wispy mustache. Even his self-imposed isolation began to weigh on him. One visitor recalls the king telling him sadly that "sometimes, I have an irresistible urge to hear a human voice. Then I call one of the domestic servants or outriders and ask him to tell me about his home and his family. Otherwise I would completely forget the art of speech."

Bavaria suffered its mad king bravely, partly because the state was a limited monarchy, and the civilian cabinet, rather than the king, handled most matters of importance. For most of his rule, he had managed to avoid conflict with the Bavarian bourgeoisie by paying for his fantasies out of the Wittelsbach privy purse. But the outrageously expensive castles were more than private wealth could bear. Ludwig secretly began taking a subsidy from Prussian chancellor Otto von Bismarck, a move that imperiled Bavarian sovereignty. He searched the world for bankers who would continue to lend him money. Courtiers were sent on a lunatic mission to Persia to find an imagined multimillionaire who would help the king stay afloat. Other emissaries went to Sweden, Turkey, Brazil—one group was even dispatched to Frankfurt, pretending to comply with royal instructions to rob the Rothschild bank.

At last, in 1886, as creditors prepared to take action, the Bavarian cabinet turned upon its king. Ludwig was arrested at Neuschwanstein and brought to the palace of Berg on Lake Starnberg. A psychiatrist, Dr. Bernard von Gudden, certified that the king was insane, and a regency was declared.

The characterization of his fantasies as madness was evidently too much for Ludwig. As he told his jailers: "I can bear that they take the government from me, but not that they declare me insane." On a June afternoon in 1886, the forty-one-year-old monarch and his psychiatrist went for a walk along the lakeshore. Later that night, they were both found drowned. The exact circumstances of their deaths were never discovered, but the likeliest explanation was that Ludwig had murdered his companion and then killed himself. But the king had foreshadowed his death years earlier. "I must build," young Ludwig had declared, "or die." □

Vice Guys Finish Last

The literary creations of Guy de Maupassant, France's nineteenth-century master of the short story, brought him fame, adulation, and wealth that allowed him to build a reputation for legendary extravagance and sexual profligacy. But some of his most powerful works grew out of the demented obverse of his volatile life, the gnawing progress of the venereal disease that would drive the author mad and finally kill him.

Born in 1850 near the Norman city of Rouen, Maupassant was brilliant, self-confident, a master of irony and the macabre—and thoroughly depraved. "A foul-mouthed, offensive individual," he was described in one account. Sex and literature were his obsessions. He got help with the latter from French novelist Gustave Flaubert, who taught the young would-be writer the value of minute observation as a way to create accuracy and vividness in his art.

He picked up depravity on his own. Maupassant was the product of a broken home; raised by an adored but neurotic mother, he despised married men and created a compulsive cult of promiscuous virility for himself. By age twenty-four, he had begun to show the skin lesions of syphilis. He had the blemishes treated and evidently believed that he was cured, for he continued to boast of hundreds of seductions.

But his presumption of a cure was in fact a long-term death warrant. As his illness revived, the indomitable writer was slowly and insidiously conquered from within—a process reflected in the growing psychological anguish of his fictional protagonists. In 1884, for example, Maupassant published *Lui*, in which the narrator describes his fears "of walls, of furniture, of familiar objects which seem to me to assume a kind of animal life. Above all I fear the horrible confusion of my thought, of my reason escaping, entangled and scattered by an invisible and mysterious anguish." Off of the printed page, Maupassant drowned those anxieties not only in sex but in drugs, especially ether.

Three years later, the writer published *La Horla*, a mesmerizing, paranoid tale, written in the style of a diary, of a man who is gradually possessed by an invisible and all-powerful spirit. "I am lost!" cries the character. "Somebody possesses my soul and dominates it. Somebody orders all my acts, all my movements, all my thoughts. I am no longer anything in myself, nothing except an enslaved and terrified spectator of all the things I do."

Within two years, Maupassant himself had begun the slide into a similar hell. He experienced feelings of extreme cold, sensitivity to noise, insomnia, and pains in his limbs. He complained of headache that "tortures as no torments have ever been able to torture, which grinds the head into atoms." He began to see spiders. He had long moments of depression and confusion, which were coupled with general mental agony—and blamed all of it on a "softening of the brain brought on by my bathing my nostrils with salt-water. The salt has fermented in my brain and every night my brains are dripping through my nose and mouth in a sticky paste. It means I am going mad."

Even more of an agony was the inability of his mind to string consecutive thoughts together. "There are whole days on which I feel I am done for, finished, blind, my brain used up and yet still alive," he wrote in a lucid moment. Soon, like the protagonist in *La Horla*, he contemplated suicide. Ensconced in one of his villas, he decided to shoot himself, as a friend related it, "to kill the flies devouring the salt in his brain." But his loyal valet had stolen his bullets. Frustrated, the writer jabbed a paper knife into his throat. The attempt failed, and he was restrained. In January 1892, he was consigned to a clinic in Paris.

Maupassant lasted an entire year there before he entered the final phase of his syphilitic dementia. Then, as the writer Rene de Goncourt noted unsympathetically, he began to turn "into an animal." He declared that he was the younger son of the Virgin Mary and planted twigs around the clinic, insisting that they would grow into little Maupassants. At times, he would howl like a dog and lick the walls of his cell or retain his urine because it was "all diamonds." Sometimes, imagining that his thoughts had physically escaped his head, he would go searching for them—and rediscover them as butterflies.

Finally, even his delusions collapsed into hours of screaming, interspersed with convulsions. He died, aged forty-three, in July 1893, uttering the words "darkness . . . darkness." □

Musical Murmurings

Robert Schumann, one of the nineteenth century's most influential German romantic composers, was a pioneer in an intensely subjective form of classical music that attempted to give voice to the inner moods and feelings of its creator. A friend of Brahms and Chopin, Schumann often claimed that he got help from "inner voices" that provided him with themes and melodies—but at a terrible price. The voices became a never-ending clangor in his brain that drove the musical genius to attempted suicide, madness, and an early grave.

Schumann was born in 1810 in the state of Saxony, the son of a prosperous bookseller and publisher. He showed musical talent at an early age and published his first composition at twelve, an accompaniment for the 150th Psalm. He also displayed considerable literary ability, turning out plays and a variety of poems, including translations of classical verse. When his father died, the aspiring sixteen-year-old musician promised his mother that he would follow a more practical career than music and enrolled in law at the University of Leipzig—where he continued to write romantic plays and compose songs. He also studied piano under the noted teacher Friedrich Wieck. For the first time, the composer-to-be met Clara Wieck, his teacher's nine-year-old daughter, who was also showing signs of extraordinary talent.

He moved on to legal studies at Heidelberg—and composed waltzes. Finally, his mother acknowledged defeat and sent him back to study again with Wieck, with the aim of making the boy a composer-pianist. Schumann himself foreclosed that prospect through a bizarre exercise in self-discipline. In an attempt to strengthen his right hand, he tied the third and fourth fingers together while playing and left them like that for months. Gradually, the third finger became paralyzed, and a star turn at the keyboard became impossible. Composition was the remaining avenue for his talent: In the same year, Schumann published his first professional work, *Opus I*, a series of musical variations.

The next few years were fruitful ones for the young composer, as a number of his piano pieces were published, some of them inspired by his affair with one of Professor Wieck's students, Ernestine von Fricken. He also suffered from a nervous breakdown, in which he claimed to have wild musical flights of fancy; he brought them under control by writing them down.

Neither love affairs nor mental turmoil could keep Schumann from noticing the young, beautiful, and increasingly independent Clara, who was frequently at her father's side. In 1836, when she was sixteen, the couple fell in love. Her father was not enthralled. Dutiful Clara obeyed when he ordered her to cease seeing the composer, and for sixteen months, Schumann wrote his disconsolate *Fantasy in C Major*, drank heavily, and chased other women. By 1837, however, the couple was trysting again, and Schumann formally asked Professor Wieck for permission to marry his daughter. The parent again said no. Eventually, Clara herself broke the impasse by taking her intransigent father to court; the couple was finally wed in 1840.

The next few years were the most productive of Schumann's life as he composed many of the solo songs, or *lieder*, on which his modern reputation rests. Again, the inspiration often came from his inner voices. At Clara's urging he also transmuted some of those inner themes into major orchestrated works. He tried his hand at chamber music and even attempted an oratorio.

By this time, the twin sides of Schumann's inner voices had begun to show themselves more clearly. Naturally shy and uncommunicative, his control over the font of inspiration was weak, and as he tried to teach and conduct in public, the inner voices sometimes got in his way. On one occasion, as Schumann conducted an orchestra practice, when the music stopped he kept right on—directing music that only he could hear. His conducting skills were thus not much in demand.

There was not much money in composing, and the Schumann family would eventually include eight children. Clara began to take up the slack, returning to the concert-piano circuit she had abandoned.

She became a raging success—which only depressed

In this contemporary lithograph by J. Hofelich, Robert Schumann sits with his pianist wife, Clara, for whom he wrote many scores, among them *Phantasiestucke, Opus 12, No. 2*, the music overprinted here.

her husband. In 1844, after the family returned from Clara's triumphant concert tour of Russia, Schumann suffered a nervous collapse. He found that he could no longer focus on musical ideas. His inner voices began to turn into auditory hallucinations: For hours, Schumann would hear nothing but tonal sounds, interspersed with snatches of strange, sometimes disturbing music. The Schumanns decided to leave Leipzig.

For nearly six years, the family lived in Dresden, where Clara pursued her concert career and her husband gradually recovered his equilibrium, though never entirely. Starting in 1845, he composed *Symphony Number Two in C Major*, but for ten months, continuing auditory hallucinations—he called them "distortions"—made completion of the score impossible. The composer desperately sought another musical post and finally found one as municipal director of music in the city of Dusseldorf, in 1850.

Once again, it seemed that his creative powers were on the mend. He composed a cello concerto and a new symphony—then failed again as a conductor. By 1852, he was complaining of "strange afflictions of hearing"—a repetition, apparently, of nonstop tonal sounds. The sounds would come back whenever Schumann felt himself under extreme emotional stress. As one friend later put it, "He is constantly so filled up with music that I really can't blame the man for preferring not to be disturbed by the sounds of the outer world." As his mental afflictions worsened, Schumann sought solace in séances, which provided some temporary relief. But soon he was complaining of a "strange weakness of the speech organ" that produced a transient bout of inarticulacy.

The tide of music within Schumann now began to drown him. The sounds in his brain became voices. He talked of angels dictating a musical theme to him, which turned out, on inspection, to be one of his own violin concertos. On some nights, according to Clara, he hallucinated "music that is so glorious, and with instruments sounding more wonderful than one ever hears on earth." The composer himself enthused to a friend that his affliction was "the inner hearing of wondrously beautiful pieces of music, fully formed and complete! The sound is like distant brasses, underscored by the most magnificent harmonies. This must be how it is in another life, after we've cast off our mortal coil."

Casting off that coil became a deepening fixation for Schumann. One night, Clara recalled, he spoke of signs that he would soon die. Angels, he told her, "called out to welcome us, and before the end of the year we would both be united with them." The next day, however, Schumann was quaking with terror. The angels had become demons, who "told him he was a sinner, and that they wanted to throw him to hell." He screamed in fear, as hallucinated tigers and hyenas rushed to seize him. At various times, he babbled constantly about being a criminal. And he began to fear that he would somehow harm Clara and urged her to leave him.

One night in February 1854, the composer spent an exultant evening playing the piano and eating hugely. Then he suddenly announced that he must go to an insane asylum because, Clara wrote, "he could no longer control his mind and did not know what he would do at night." Doctors were called, and he was calmed, but the next morning, Schumann walked out the door of his home in his robe and slippers, crying, and strode to the nearby Rhine River. Rushing down the incline, he threw himself into the water. Fishermen rescued him, but the composer's demand to be institutionalized could no longer be ignored. He was sent to Endenich, an asylum in Bonn.

Schumann never recovered his lucidity. His auditory hallucinations faded, replaced by other obsessive concerns, including a fear that he was being poisoned. But with his inner voices silenced, Schumann's musical creativity dried up. He wrote virtually nothing at Endenich. Instead, he invented a whole new world, talking aloud to imaginary critics who attacked his work. Finally, even this became too much for his mind to sustain. His ability to speak coherently began to disappear, and he refused to eat. In the spring of 1856, one of Schumann's closest friends, the composer Johannes Brahms, visited him and reported, "He spoke continuously, but I understood nothing. Often he just blabbered, sort of bababa-dadada. He will remain, at best, in this significantly apathetic state."

Three months later, for the first time since his attempted suicide, Schumann allowed Clara to come and visit him. "He smiled at me and embraced me with great effort," she wrote later, "because he could no longer control his limbs." The next day, he took a little food from her— a fatal mistake after months of self-starvation. On the third day, Robert Schumann joined the demonic angels who had poured their glorious music into his mind. □

Der Führer

The evidence for the insanity of German dictator Adolf Hitler is a virtual massif of mad behavior. Through his efforts, an entire continent, including his adoptive German homeland, was reduced to rubble, with tens of millions of people dead, many of them for their religion, race, or nationality. At the end of that destructive binge, the great leader was trembling, raving, increasingly robotlike as he huddled in his doomed Berlin bunker, left arm twitching, left leg semiparalyzed, hopelessly addicted to injected cocktails of drugs administered by his quack physician. Here he announced that he was finally ready for the "responsibility of marriage," blamed everything on others, and, as a final act, killed himself and his bride of two days, the compliant Eva Braun, in front of a portrait of his beloved, long-dead mother. It is madness monumentally personified.

And yet, a debate over Hitler's actual mental state has sputtered on for decades, fueled, in part, by the complicating circumstance that the Nazi dictator never underwent a psychiatric examination. In 1943, a psychiatric report prepared for American intelligence agencies labeled him a hysteric and a psy-

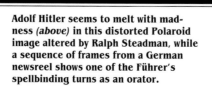

chopath—but without the benefit of a personal interview. In the aftermath of the Second World War, a prison psychiatrist at Nuremberg who interviewed a score of top Nazis about their leader declared that he was a "psychoneurotic of the obsessive and hysterical type," adding that he exhibited "paranoid or persecution patterns." Other theories abound, including the notion that he was afflicted with syphilis, which can produce megalomania, delusions of grandeur, and paranoia as the disease runs its fatal course.

All of those observations, however, can be no more than supposition. As a political leader, Hitler was undeniably an evil genius, one of the world's most compelling orators, who specialized in the mass psychology of hate. As a Swiss diplomat remarked, never had he met "any human capable of generating such a condensation of envy, vituperation, and malice." But his technical degree of madness remains elusive. As an individual, Hitler was a compulsive loner, sus-

picious and aloof, who was also such a nonentity in his formative years that little can be said for certain about his mental and emotional development. Hundreds of researchers, however, have combed over the scant evidence and uncovered glints of a personality warped in a number of surprising—and surprisingly banal—ways.

Most striking is the infantilism of Hitler's personality: He never grew up, emotionally, intellectually, or sexually. His favorite actress was Shirley Temple. His favorite films—and he doted on movies—were *Snow White and the Seven Dwarves* and *King Kong,* which he never tired of watching. When thwarted, especially over little things, he would beat tables and walls with his fists

Adolf Hitler seems to melt with madness *(above)* in this distorted Polaroid image altered by Ralph Steadman, while a sequence of frames from a German newsreel shows one of the Führer's spellbinding turns as an orator.

and scream. Despite his claims to be one of Germany's great thinkers, his favorite books were the Wild West thrillers of a German author who had never visited the United States, Karl May. Hitler once advised his generals to read May's books as a guide to fighting the Soviets on the eastern front.

Even when leading the Nazi war machine, the supreme German leader liked to retreat to his private quarters and play with toy buildings and cannons. He gorged himself on candy and chocolate—as the Soviet army closed in, he lived almost entirely on chocolate cake. The conqueror of Europe was fiercely afraid to be left alone at night: After he won political power, he kept guests up until morning, telling and retelling dull and pointless stories. Every morning and night, he played a game with his valet, seeing how fast he could dress and undress. Incandescent before a political audience, he was intensely uncomfortable at social events and only relaxed completely in the presence of children. Under stress, he would suck his little finger.

Throughout his life, Hitler lived in a variety of dream and fantasy worlds, to which he clung with remarkable tenacity. As he once told one of his doctors: "I suffer from tormenting self-deception." Some of his childhood acquaintances recalled Hitler getting up at night and going out to a nearby hill, where he made speeches to an invisible audience. At age sixteen, as a drifting artist in Vienna, a friend recalled, he

became convinced that he was about to win the Austrian lottery—so convinced that he found an elaborate new apartment, picked out new furniture, and planned lavish social events. When he failed to hit the jackpot after all, Hitler flew into a screaming rage at the perfidious cabal that had thwarted him. His greatest fantasy was that he was destined to be Germany's greatest leader: He claimed, in fact, to have had the idea for the Third Reich as early as 1906, inspired by a performance of the opera *Rienzi,* composed by his beloved fellow anti-Semite Richard Wagner.

With Hitler, fantasy was blended with extraordinary rigidity—a quality he extolled about himself as a basis of his political daring, calling it "unshakable obstinacy." But it was more than that. A friend recalled that from an early age, "there was in his nature something firm, inflexible, immoveable, obstinately rigid." Everything about his ordinary behavior smacked of monotonous regimentation. In his rise from obscurity, he wore the same suits, raincoat, shoes, and necktie for years. He listened incessantly to the same records and would fly into a rage if anyone violated the strictly assigned seating at his state dinners. Every day, when Hitler walked his dog at his mountain retreat, Berchtesgaden, he would pass through the same field and at the same spot would throw a stick of wood in exactly the same direction each time. Day after day, in his besieged bunker, Hitler told the identical story of his dog's toilet habits and shrilly defended his own policies and actions as having been inevitable. "Don't you see!" he cried out in the bunker as the end drew near, "I cannot change."

Hitler's minister of supply, Albert Speer, was convinced that his master had lost all ability to change and grow after about 1910. That, Speer believed, was when Hitler's intellectual development ended. Psychological investigators trace much of Hitler's infantilism back to the circumstances of his early upbringing. His father, Alois Hitler, was a stern and occasionally violent authority figure, twice married—the second time to his young niece Klara, the passive, obedient, obsessively clean woman who became Adolf's mother. Alois was an occasionally violent drunkard who beat his wife and son and used the same signal—a loud whistle—to call both Adolf and his favorite dog. Klara, on the other hand, doted on the boy, pandered to his adolescent artistic pretensions, and supported him long after Alois's death. Despite Hitler's later claims to have lived a life of grinding poverty, he never earned a wage until he was twenty-two years old. Although he idealized his mother, he imitated his father when he fell in love with his own sixteen-year-old niece, Angela "Geli" Raubel—who committed suicide after telling her friends she was unhappy because of what her uncle wanted her to do. Hitler, then in his early forties, was inconsolable.

The Geli episode was only one of a series of incidents that have pointed experts toward the possibility that Hitler, who made much of his ◊

emotional distance from women and hated all physical contact with them in public, was sexually perverted. Researcher Robert Waite has noted that of the seven women that Hitler had known intimately, six attempted or succeeded at suicide, impelled, perhaps, by the revulsion and self-hate sparked by his sexual demands. German screen star Renaté Mueller, who spent time with the Führer in his early triumphant days, claimed that he groveled on the floor of her apartment and asked her to kick him. He was also fascinated by the circumstances of women's deaths. During his early days as chancellor, at a time when he had reintroduced beheading as capital punishment for a variety of crimes, Hitler pardoned five wife murderers in a row, before his further acts of clemency were declared a state secret.

The name that psychological experts have most recently given to Hitler's perceived mental imbalance is curiously innocuous: borderline personality, a diagnosis that describes someone who is mentally ill but able to function normally in many areas of life. Such individuals are often infantile, selfish, and narcissistic, overcome with fantasies of omnipotence that are shaken by spasms of self-doubt. They are prone to sexual perversions involving bodily wastes. Often, the borderline personality seems to split into two distinct selves: one that is kind, sentimental, creative; the other, cruel, cold, destructive. All of that seems to apply to Hitler, but as a description of the century's preeminent monster, it still seems strangely inadequate. The fact is, psychiatry has not yet coined a term that fully evokes a man mad enough to push the world toward suicide. □

Leap into Darkness

Like Shakespeare and Picasso, Vaslav Nijinsky has a name forever wedded to his art. Arguably the greatest male ballet dancer of the twentieth century, Nijinsky left audiences agape at his prodigious leaps—he seemed to hang weightless for a moment in midair—and his inspired miming. He was also a revolutionary creator and choreographer who dragged ballet from its staid classical repertoire into the subversive realm of the avant-garde and shocked cultured Europe with the bold eroticism of a new kind of dance. All this came well before he turned thirty—then darkness.

Nijinsky was near the peak of his fame when he fell into madness, but his mental illness was no lightning bolt. Behind the glamour and achievement of his wondrous career, he had always been a withdrawn, inarticulate man whom one colleague referred to as an "idiot of genius." For most of his early life, Nijinsky had trouble with self-expression that led many to wonder about his mental competence. The composer Igor Stravinsky, whose wildly atonal music formed the basis of *Le Sacre du Printemps* (The Rite of Spring), observed that Nijinsky "spoke little and when he did speak, gave the impression of being a very backward youth, whose intelligence was very underdeveloped for his age." It was only while he was dancing that Nijinsky could be said to be in true command of his faculties and his fate.

He was born in 1889 to a pair of Polish-born dancers who made a precarious living in Russia as touring performers. Nijinsky's father soon abandoned his family; his mother struggled to bring up her three children in St. Petersburg under dire financial conditions. Then tragedy struck again: Nijinsky's older brother suffered crippling brain damage in a fall. It was a measure of his mother's fierce ambition and will that she fought for, and won, a place for her younger son in the country's premier dance academy, the Imperial Ballet School.

From the beginning, Nijinsky was known for his spectacular athletic abilities on stage and for his passive, quiescent character. The combination earned him the jealousy and malign attentions of classmates: Once, as he prepared to make a practice leap, a group of them soaped Nijinsky's approach. The head injuries he sustained kept him hospitalized for days. Nonetheless, when he graduated in 1908 and began his public career, the quiet young Pole was soon feted as a darling of Russia's balletomane aristocratic society—and met the man who was to shape his destiny, Sergey Diaghilev.

A flamboyant impresario possessed of florid ambition and an overweening sense of command, Sergey Diaghilev had already conceived of a traveling Russian dance company that would take western Europe by storm: Les Ballets Russes. He quickly saw that Nijinsky could become a centerpiece of his troupe; the two men became lovers within months. In 1909, the young dancer debuted in Paris as a slave in *Le Pavillon d'Armide* (Armide's Pavillion): His spectacular athleticism, mesmerizing presence, and palpable eroticism made him an immediate sensation. As the composer Richard Strauss was later to exclaim: "Among dancers, Nijinsky

is what Frederick the Great was among kings!"

Unlike the great king of Prussia, however, Nijinsky had trouble holding on to what he had conquered. Offstage, the dancer was a clumsy, uncommunicative wallflower who was prone to illness. Worse, from Diaghilev's point of view, the dancer was often tardy and disorganized in his work. Nonetheless, he and Diaghilev collaborated in a second Paris season that was more widely hailed than the first. Eventually, the duo brought their show home to Russia, where the more conservative audiences found it a scandal: Nijinsky's "slave" costume—an abbreviated loincloth—caused aristocrats to walk out of the performance. He was dismissed from the roster of the Imperial Ballet, which was fine in Diaghilev's opinion since it made his star the exclusive property of Les Ballets Russes.

But if he found rejection in Russia, Nijinsky found adulation abroad. The only place where Nijin-

sky escaped from his cage of failed self-expression was in dance, the medium in which he could express his profound but ambiguous eroticism. As he began to choreograph his own work, those feelings took a more explicit form. His portrayal of a satyr in *L'Après-midi d'un Faune* (The Afternoon of a Faun) caused an immense scandal. It also marked the beginning of new strains in his relationship with Diaghilev, since Nijinsky the choreographer was even more inarticulate than Nijinsky the private man. Lacking formal instruction, he could only teach dancers the steps to his work through example, a process of interminable repetition interrupted by spectacular outbursts of temper. Then a new complication entered the scene: Romola Pulszky.

The daughter of a prominent Hungarian family, Pulszky had once entertained dancing ambitions of her own, but they had dissipated by 1912, when she first saw Nijinsky perform. She became obsessed and

determined to claim him for her own. Despite his long relationship with Diaghilev, Nijinsky was uneasily bisexual. In 1913, when Nijinsky and Les Ballets Russes left by ocean liner on a South American tour, Diaghilev stayed behind—but Pulszky was on board. By the time the ship docked, she was pregnant. When Nijinsky and Pulszky married in Buenos Aires, the jealous impresario fired his top star.

Undaunted, Nijinsky went back to Budapest and tried to launch a career as an independent artist. He failed, and his mental health failed with him. He became chronically depressed and insomniac and complained of discomfort in his chest—a type of psychological invalidism that made him incapable of work. The birth of a daughter did not lift his spirits. Then came another jolt: The guns of August 1914 found Nijinsky, a Russian citizen, inside the hostile Austro-Hungarian empire. He became a virtual prisoner of war.

Over the next two years, the dancer spent much of his time creating an idiosyncratic, and ultimately useless, system of dance notation that was supposed to overcome his inability to communicate. Meanwhile, a campaign led by his friends and sympathizers—Diaghilev chief among them—sought to have him released from de facto detention. The campaign succeeded: He was allowed to leave for Vienna and thence on an unsuccessful tour of the United States. One of its few highlights, from Nijinsky's point of view, was a visit to the studios of Charlie Chaplin, whose silent comic genius Nijinsky adored. For his part, Chaplin found the dancer so depressed that while his famous guest was watching him on set, the comedian ordered the film taken out of ◊

the movie cameras, for fear that Nijinsky's dolefulness would "ruin my attempt to be funny."

By 1917, Nijinsky was back with Diaghilev—under a strict contract that made him liable for any performances that he failed to meet. The contract was soon flouted. Nijinsky had fallen under the influence of two disciples of the mystic Russian novelist Leo Tolstoy, who urged Nijinsky to forsake his family and his art for a life of asexual contemplation. He broke the contract and was again fired. Romola took him to Switzerland.

Nijinsky retreated to the ski-resort village of St. Moritz, where his mental deterioration accelerated. He ceased dancing in public and began walking the streets of the town with a cross around his neck, urging residents, Tolstoy fashion, to repent their sins. "I am what Christ felt," he declared. "I am Buddha and every kind of God." According to his wife, he felt responsible and guilt-ridden for the slaughter of World War I. At times he would demand that Romola dance with him, without ever telling her what steps to follow. He became increasingly suspicious and among other things imagined that his wife was

having an affair with a local psychiatrist. He suddenly took up the dangerous, icy sport of bobsledding and had several accidents. Finally, he was put under sedation, and a male nurse was hired to keep him under observation and restraint.

Then, in January 1919, Nijinsky announced he would dance again for a group of friends and local townspeople at a St. Moritz theater. There would be no program and no rehearsals; the dancer declared that he would improvise on stage. Those who attended pronounced the evening unforgettable. Nijinsky began by facing the audience seated in a chair for a half-hour. Finally, he stood with open arms in the pose of a crucified Christ and declared, "Now I will dance you the war, with its suffering, with its destruction, with its death. The war which you did not prevent, and so you are responsible for it." What followed was a wildly improvised performance of spectacular leaps and wild poses. Nijinsky later wrote: "I felt God throughout the evening. He loved me. I love Him. We were married."

That final evening was followed by profound depression. The former source of so much awe and aesthetic veneration became an object of pity, who obsessively chronicled his own disintegration in a series of diaries. "My ideas don't have any direction," Nijinsky wrote as his mental collapse gathered momentum. "They change all the time, my existence is ruined." He wrote furiously that he was a "clown," a "lunatic," and a "monster." He was sent to a sanitarium and diagnosed as a catatonic but soon released. Back at home, he suffered destructive spasms in which he would scribble on walls and throw furniture around. Increasingly, he declared

that "demons" were attacking him. Rehospitalized, he grew more violent and would attack attendants. He fell completely under the control of the possessive Romola, who could not bear, it seemed, to consign him to permanent institutional care. At one point, she even took him to the shrine at Lourdes to see if she could achieve a miracle cure.

Over the ensuing decades, Nijinsky's life became a pathetic series of pilgrimages from place to place, as he tried a succession of such dangerous therapies as insulin shock treatment in a vain effort to retrieve his sanity. When World War II began, Romola brought him back to the family home in Budapest, where he would remain passive most of the time, then occasionally rouse himself to assault his male nurse or unlucky passersby. His always faltering speech became unintelligible. At one point, he was placed in a Nazi-run hospital, where, as the war wound down, he barely escaped death when his captors decided to exterminate him as a "defective."

Sadly, one of his last few moments of animation came when Hungary was overrun by the Soviet army. In the presence of his Russian-speaking liberators, Nijinsky came to a dim kind of nostalgic life. One night, he suddenly jumped up among a crowd of them and began to whirl and dance; for a time, he could speak Russian without impediment. But this clearheaded interlude soon ended. The couple moved on to Vienna and eventually to London. Four years later, in 1950, Nijinsky died of kidney failure. His body was shipped for burial to Montmartre Cemetery in Paris, where the brilliant dancer had first soared to fame—and madness. □

Nijinsky wears practice clothes to rehearse a New York theater date during a tour of the United States.

Engulfed

Walter Inglis Anderson was a Southern artist whose intense identification with nature was matched only by a profound alienation from his fellowman. The aversion to society of the quiet, moody man who called himself the Alienado was an obsession that bordered closely on schizophrenia and for three years crossed over that line. But it also led to a life of extraordinary artistic productivity, as Anderson tried with manic intensity to blend with, and observe, the nature he adored. "Those who have identified with nature," he said with characteristic understatement, "must take the consequences."

In his case, the consequence was almost total isolation. For nearly twenty years, Anderson walled himself off from the rest of humanity, including his wife and children, in a small cottage on the Gulf coast of Mississippi. For weeks at a time, he would camp on a barren scrub island without shelter, among stinging gnats and mosquitoes, rattlesnakes, and alligators, to sketch and paint the wildlife. Heat, drought, storms, and hurricanes did not deter Anderson from his rounds, as he lived out a vastly harsher version of

Henry David Thoreau's *Walden.*

Anderson's obsession with nature in the raw emerged gradually and only after he had suffered an extensive bout of overt mental illness. Born in New Orleans in 1903, Anderson came from a family with modestly distinguished roots: His great-grandfather had been a mayor of Glasgow. He was encouraged in his artistic interests by his mother and attended the Pennsylvania Academy of Fine Art, toured France for a year, and was much impressed with the Neolithic cave paintings at Les Eyzies. By the time he returned to the United States, the Great Depression was unfolding—not an auspicious time to begin an artistic career. Anderson joined with his brother in founding a pottery factory in Ocean Springs, Mississippi; his brother ran the business, and Anderson created a variety of lively pottery designs. Forever after, he listed his occupation not as "artist" but as "decorator." But he also kept up his painting and won several Work Projects Administration mural commissions.

Meanwhile, his mental condition was deteriorating. Moody as a boy, he became severely withdrawn, even after his marriage in 1933. Finally, in 1937, he asked to be institutionalized, for schizophrenia. Then he escaped and simply disappeared for a few months, wandering back to New Orleans, before returning to Ocean Springs. He was once again institutionalized in a Mississippi hospital for the mentally ill and once again escaped. Eventually, it seemed that his condition had stabilized at the point where he could function on his own but where human society would still sometimes become unendurably painful for him. When it did, he would disappear for long periods on journeys to such distant places as Central America and even China. After a while, he would reappear around Ocean Springs, usually dressed in shabby clothes, with a battered hat on his head.

Wanting to settle down, Anderson made a deal with his brother: He would decorate ten pieces of pottery a week, for one dollar each, and leave the business to his sibling. Anderson and his family moved to a small plantation owned by his father-in-law, where the painter began to bury himself in work. For most of the next six years, he ◊

During years of seclusion, Mississippi artist Walter Inglis Anderson vividly rendered such Gulf island denizens as the red-winged blackbird shown at left and the crab pictured above.

drew obsessively at night, transpos-
ing classic tales into line drawings.
He turned all of Alexander Pope's
translation of the *Iliad,* for example,
into 1,750 sketches and did much
the same for *The Legends of Charle-
magne,* the *Divine Comedy,* and
Paradise Lost. Sitting at the dining
table, he would place a copy of the
text on his left and a stack of typewriter paper on his right, and draw
as he read. As the pages turned, the
drawings would pile up, until they
slipped unheeded to the floor. As he
worked, Anderson would sing or listen to music. Occasionally he would
stop to feed scavenging insects
from a coffee spoon. Anderson's
wife collected his work in the morning, but he never offered any of it
for sale. "Man apparently lives the
life of some sort of draught animal," Anderson once observed, "as
soon as he begins to work."

Even with his eye on literature,
however, Anderson's aloof mind
turned more and more toward nature. He became focused on the
scattering of shifting, sandy islands
off the Gulf coast and one in particular, Horn Island, an unappetizing
stretch of piny dunes and brackish
lagoons that blistered with heat in
the summer and froze in the winter
Gulf winds. The only inhabitants
were ducks, shorebirds, wild hogs,
rats, reptiles, and raccoons. The
thought of painting those surround-
ings became Anderson's overriding obsession.

"Why does man live?" Anderson
wrote in one of his diaries. "To be
the servant and slave of all the elements." In 1946, he entered into
voluntary servitude by bidding his
family farewell and moving into a
remote cottage. It served as his
base and studio when he began his
miniature odysseys to Horn Island,

fourteen miles away. On each trip,
Anderson would take only his painting supplies and minimal food supplies, and sleep under his boat. He
would wade through marshes and
stumble over dunes in search of
specimens to sketch, using his hat
as a crude net to capture them.
Strongly mystical, Anderson gained
a kind of exultation from his utterly
marginal existence. "Everything
seems conditional on the islands,"
he wrote. "Out there, if I eat, I live,
if something stronger than I
doesn't destroy me."

That something turned out to be
lung cancer. After his death in
1965, at sixty-two, his relatives entered his studio for the first time in
years—no easy task, for Anderson
had trained a wild rose to grow
across all the pathways to the
house. Inside were more than
30,000 drawings, watercolors,
woodblock prints, and woodcarv-
ings of the beasts and landscapes
he had known so intimately in his
self-imposed exile. They were the
best reply to one of his own alienat-
ed musings: "One image succeeds
another with surprising regularity
on Horn Island. Whether they could
be shared is another matter." □

CROWDS AND CRAZES

Whatever their purpose, whatever the character of their members, crowds are less gatherings of individuals than composite creatures, with lives—and minds—of their own. They tap a deep human instinct to be part of a herd, to seek safety and anonymity in numbers, to abandon oneself to the moods of a larger body. These may be the gentle whims of fashion, light and ephemeral; groups coalesce even around kernels of mere silliness.

But crowds can also be destructive. Often, propelled by excessive emotion or fanatical belief, the collective mind moves dangerously out of touch with reality. A tranquil theater audience transmutes into a regiment of jeering goons; a questionable call turns an army of sports fans into an enraged mob; an epidemic-like perceptual disorder makes rock stars look like pop messiahs, transforms charlatans into saints, and attributes unexplained phenomena to extraterrestrials and devils. Underlying such aberrations are the ageless tensions between rich and poor, old and new, gods and demons—the larger crowd of a society breeds crazes that fit the times.

Suffer the Children

Holding crosses aloft, bands of children trudged southward from Germany's Rhine Valley toward the Mediterranean during the spring and summer of 1212. Their ranks were swelled by more young recruits—some no more than six years old—as they passed through villages and towns. Asked where they were going, they replied simply: "To God."

The children were the littlest crusaders, bound for the Holy Land. Their pious intention was to wrest Jerusalem away from its infidel Muslim rulers and restore it to Christendom. However, unlike the crusades that had gone before, theirs was not an armed pilgrimage. These children bore no arms but their crosses, believing that their greater innocence would attract God's favor and give them success where mighty armies had failed.

Under the leadership of Nicholas, a charismatic boy of about twelve from the German city of Cologne, some of the young crusaders and the scattering of adults who had joined them crossed the Alps into Italy. Exhaustion and summer heat took their toll, and discouraged deserters turned back toward home. But prayer and perseverance carried at least 7,000 through the mountain passes, and on August 25, Nicholas and his followers entered the Italian port city of Genoa, the presumed terminus of their 500-mile trek. There they had expected to find a miraculous conveyance to the Holy Land. Instead, they discovered disappointment. The Genoese were far less hospitable than the German peasants and townspeople who had cheered the youngsters along the way, and offered neither ships nor encouragement. Daunted, some stayed on in the unfriendly city, while others ventured to other ports, hoping for transport. A few turned toward Rome, where they managed to see the pope. One contingent of the splintering army was said to have embarked on two ships in Pisa, never to be heard of again.

Others turned wearily north, returning across the Alps in November to the jeers of those who had formerly saluted them.

Even so, the children who made their way to Italy fared better than their comrades to the west. Another party of youthful crusaders had made its way, at some cost, through southern France to the port of Marseilles. There, according to some accounts, fate played a cruel trick: Boarding ships that were provided by perfidious merchants, the children were shanghaied and sold as slaves to the very Muslims they had expected to conquer with their innocence. □

Horrorscope

The year 1523 saw thousands of Germans put aside their normal occupations for boatbuilding. The products of their labors, they hoped, would help them survive a flood of biblical magnitude, one that astrologers were confidently predicting would ravage the world in February 1524.

Astrological interest had been building since 1499, when one Johannes Stöffler published a widely circulated almanac citing a planetary happening in 1524 "well worthy of wonderment." According to Stöffler, February would bring twenty conjunctions—in astrology, intervals when planets, moon, or sun seem to occupy the same area of the sky simultaneously—"of which sixteen will occupy a watery sign, signifying to well nigh the whole world, climates, kingdoms, provinces, estates, dignitaries, brutes, beasts of the sea, and to all dwellers on earth indubitable mutation, variation and alteration such as we have scarce perceived for many centuries from historiographers and our elders. Lift up your heads, therefore, ye Christian men."

Stöffler's portentous prose left plenty of room for interpretation, but many astrologers concluded that the dread event to take place under the "watery sign" of Pisces—the fish—must be a catastrophic and universal flood. Spread by pamphlets and word of mouth, the prediction of disaster began to trickle across Europe in the early sixteenth century.

As 1524 drew closer, there was an outburst of publications about the impending deluge. Some writers, following the trend toward rationalism, declared that astrology was incapable of predicting anything, let alone a catastrophic flood. But others warned that humanity must brace not just for a great flood but for multiple disasters. Italian sage Luca Gaurico predicted not only heavy rain and snow but earthquake and lightning. At the Diet of Worms, a meeting of the council of the Holy Roman Empire, in 1521, delegates took time out from the business at hand—including the doctrine of renegade Martin Luther—to compare predictions. One of them, Alexander Seytz von Marpach of Bavaria, came out in favor of an enormous flood.

Agostino Nifo's contribution to the controversy carried special weight—he had recently been appointed official philosopher to Pope Leo X. In his multivolume *De Falsa Diluvii Pronosticatione* (On the False Prediction of a Deluge), Nifo professed his desire to give some peace of mind to frightened men who were ready to perch on mountaintops or build arks and ships to escape the flood. The predictions, Nifo noted,

were based on the movements of planets—bodies so inferior that they could not possibly supply portents of worldwide disaster. Such events could be predicted only from eclipses of the sun and the moon, he said. However, the subtle philosopher added, astrologers could read the planets for *local* disasters. Nifo believed that the watery sign of 1524 would bring floods all right, but only to the territories whose inhabitants were not faithful to the Holy See.

German astrologer Georg Tanstetter noted in 1523 that fear of the coming deluge "has already worked its way into people's souls." Some were so worried, Tanstetter wrote, that "they can no longer keep their affairs in order: they sell properties, fields and such possessions, or else they don't buy properties that are for sale, because they hope to be able to transport money more easily than castles or properties when they take to the hills."

As it happened, no one had to take to the hills when the sun entered the sign of Pisces in 1524—the weather in most of Europe was drier than usual. The need for an ark had not necessarily passed, some die-hards insisted: The flood might come after the ominous flurry of conjunctions. Johannes Carion, court astrologer for the elector of Brandenburg and steady believer that the planetary situa-

tion must eventually cause catastrophe, set the predicted date of the flood at July 15, 1525. As a precaution, on the day the elector and his wife rode in their coach to a mountain refuge. Not a drop of rain fell. By four in the afternoon, with no sign of rain to come, the elector's wife persuaded him to return to the castle. But Carion's dire prediction proved not altogether unfounded: As the coach entered the castle gate, the four horses and the coachman were struck by lightning.

The shocking accident in Brandenburg was as nothing compared to what nature had in store for the people of Bologna. On March 19, the next to last day before Pisces shaded into Aries, the city's residents were wakened by heavy rains. The weather continued wet and violent until December—there were great winds and thunderstorms, hailstones the size of hens' eggs, and overflowing streams. Not quite *the* deluge, these regional torrents were still attributed to planetary conjunctions, but with a nod to the primitive state of the astrologer's predictive art. How faithful the Bolognese were to the Holy See was not recorded. □

In 1876, Chinese men who sported braided queues—a mark of respectability—panicked over reports of hungry evil spirits. Queue wearers slept together in huge bands for mutual protection and paraded about banging gongs to scare the spirits away. After several worrisome months the panic died away.

Dating from 1521, this German woodcut echoes a 1499 prophecy of "terrible waters" to come in 1524, foretold by "great signs of wonder in the heavens in Vienna" in 1520.

In a Spin

During the Middle Ages and beyond, dancers crowded the streets and squares of southern Italian towns at summer harvesttime. Oblivious to the heat, they twirled and leaped with mad abandon, often dancing themselves to exhaustion. But this was no rapturous celebration: The gyrating mob of women, men, and children was driven by fear. They all believed that they had been bitten by tarantula spiders, whose incapacitating venom could be counteracted only by the frenetic dance they called the tarantella.

Both dance and spider were named for Taranto, the town in the heel of Italy's boot from which the hysteria spread in the last half of the fourteenth century. In the hottest months, the inch-long hairy tarantulas are especially plentiful, and bites are common. In reality, the spider's venom is not much worse than a bee's, producing little more than local pain and swelling. In medieval Taranto, however, the narcotic nature of the poison was beyond dispute. A tarantula bite—or an unexplained sharp pain that could be attributed to a spider bite—produced such alarming psychosomatic symptoms in the victim as fainting, giddiness, trembling, breathing difficulties, and profound lassitude. Apparently moribund patients reacted violently to certain colors—the same colors, it was believed, as those on the bellies of the imagined spiders. But if the music of the tarantella was heard, the victim would rush off to to join fellow sufferers in the dance.

The music—sometimes supplied by a pipe and tambourine, sometimes by one of the large itinerant troupes that hired themselves out in the summer to towns reeling with tarantism—had to continue until the dancers were exhausted. Otherwise, it was thought, the poison would not be fully distributed through the body and expelled through the skin. If a fraction of the poison remained, many believed, it would cause annual recurrences of the disorder when summer heat reactivated it. In such cases, some of the afflicted reportedly danced every summer for thirty years.

Despite its lunatic air, the convocation of dancers was usually a colorful affair, as tarantists were partial to clothing whose color matched that of the spider's abdomen. The passion for the color, which was believed to have curing powers, sometimes proved overwhelming. For example, when a tarantist Capuchin friar was visited by a concerned cardinal, he tried to throw himself on his superior's scarlet robe. Restrained by spectators, the friar fell into a swoon, alleviated only when the compassionate cardinal gave him the garment. The priest seized it, pressed it to his face, and resumed dancing in the greatest ecstasy, as though in the throes of love.

Besides refreshing the sweaty dancers, water exercised a peculiar influence. Some tarantists held on to glasses of clear water as they danced, but others felt impelled to hurl themselves into the sea itself. Spaces set aside for dancing were

A page from a 1641 encyclopedia shows the belly *(left)* and back of a tarantula and a banner reading "Music is the only medicine for my venom." Above a map of southern Italy is a curative tarentella melody.

often ringed by water vessels decorated with aquatic plants, and dancers would pause momentarily to bathe their heads and arms.

The annual appearances of tarantism took place against a backdrop of dreadful afflictions. By the mid-fourteenth century, bubonic plague—the so-called Black Death—had ravaged Italy sixteen times, killing half the country's population. Smallpox and measles were recurrent and often fatal, and Italians returning from the Crusades brought leprosy with them. Misery and fear were endemic, and the bite—or the imagined bite—of a poisonous spider could act, as one historian noted, like a spur to a horse that was already running. Moreover, tarantism could do more than psychological damage. It claimed thousands of lives through suicide and convulsions brought on by frenzied dancing.

Still, for some people—women in particular—the dancing and music provided some relief from lives of extraordinary drudgery. In some towns the season of the tarantella was called *carnevaletto delle donne*—"the women's little carnival." Women made most of the arrangements, saving up their household money to pay the musicians. One benevolent matron named Mita Lupa reportedly spent her entire fortune on the little carnival.

The dog-days disease returned year after year to southern Italian towns and villages until modern attitudes erased the last traces of medievalism, and the superstitious fear of the spider's bite declined. In the eighteenth century, the tarantella became what it remains today—music for lively and energetic dancing fools. The tarantula has almost been forgotten. □

Comet Tales

The fearful apparition arrived in May of 1456—a comet that glowed in the sky night after night, making people all across Europe wonder what ill fortune it boded. Such fiery visitors had long been feared as harbingers of war, flood, famine, plague, the death of kings—even the end of the world. This comet, however, was so enormous, with a tail stretching across a third of the heavens, that it seemed to portend the direst of catastrophes.

That catastrophe might be the triumph of the Ottoman sultan Fatih Mehmed II—Mehmed the Conqueror. Three years earlier, the Turkish ruler had conquered Constantinople, capital of the Christian Byzantine Empire that had been Europe's bulwark against Asia. The sultan's army had marched through the Balkans and, when the comet arrived, was menacing Belgrade. Rome was awash with fear. Deploying what weapons he could against the cosmic and terrestrial invaders, Pope Calixtus III ordered that church bells throughout Christendom be rung at noon, and in a papal bull he exorcised both the comet and conquering Turk.

The terrible events read in the comet did not materialize. Mehmed was repulsed at Belgrade. In July, the comet dimmed and disappeared. It returned three times more before English astronomer Edmund Halley, whose name the comet now bears, correctly predicted that it would reappear in 1758. After Halley's discovery, comets ceased to be supernatural, insubstantial harbingers in the popular mind. Nevertheless, they still inspired terror, and of something far worse than plague or war—people feared that a comet following an ▷

erratic orbit would crash into the earth and destroy it.

This flashed to panic in Paris in the spring of 1773. On April 21, the distinguished astronomer Joseph-Jérôme Le Français de Lalande described to the Paris Academy of Sciences sixty-one different comets whose orbits would bring them close to earth's orbit. Pressed for time, Lalande briefly mentioned the chance of a collision—without emphasizing its extremely low probability. The rumor that radiated from the lecture hall said that Lalande had cut short his talk to avoid precipitating panic over a comet on a collision course with the earth. Rumormongers even set a date for the catastrophic crash: May 20, only a month away. Fear mounted to a feverish pitch. Confidence men, claiming to have obtained tickets for seats to Paradise from priests, sold them to gullible citizens for exorbitant prices. Moved by the pleas of the devout, the archbishop of Paris resolved to order forty hours of prayer to avert the disaster. He was dissuaded from following through, however, by scientists who convinced him of the rumor's absurdity. And, sure enough, the fateful day passed uneventfully.

If there was a lesson in the debacle, however, later generations of Parisians forgot it. The great comet of 1811, still visible in European skies as the Napoleonic tide began its ebb, seemed a powerful portent of bad things to come. In 1857 the capital succumbed to yet another comet scare, based on as little substance as the first. Some scientists speculated that a comet seen in 1556 was identical with one reported in 1264. If the two were in fact one, its period would be some 292 years long, and the comet should

next appear around 1848. English astronomer John Russell Hind recalculated the comet's orbit around the sun and moved the date to 1858. This was further refined into an unequivocal prediction by a German astronomer: The comet would actually arrive in 1857—and smash into the earth on June 13.

Published in an almanac, the prediction spread throughout Europe, gaining particular credence in Paris. Frightened expectant mothers reportedly miscarried, and there was a surge in will writing—even at the end of the world, Parisians wanted their affairs in order. Churches and confessionals were filled with unaccustomed numbers worrying about their souls. One reporter wrote that "for a fortnight we have not been able to step out without hearing the cry, 'Here is the end of the world! A full description of the comet of June 13, only one sou!'"

The one-sou pamphlet was only one product spawned by the advancing comet. Entrepreneurs eagerly catered to the fears of the populace, offering comet-proof clothing and comet life-insurance policies—premiums fully paid in advance. The policies were pure profit for the underwriters: June 13, 1857, came and went without a sign of a comet. This puzzling departure from a cosmically ordained schedule was not explained for more than a decade. Then Dutch astronomer Martinus Hoek, who discovered that comet groups—actually fragments of comets—travel in the same orbit, showed why his predecessors' guesswork had missed the mark. The sightings in 1264 and 1556 had not been two visits by the same comet, but by two different comets, neither of which was likely to return. □

Bullish on Bulbs

Holland has long enjoyed a reputation as the tulip-filled land of solid business practices. The country's early experience with tulips and business, however, was anything but solid: In the early seventeenth century, speculation in the market for the plant's bulbs occupied so many Dutch citizens that ordinary business nearly ground to a halt.

At the height of what Hollanders called the *tulpenwoede*, or tulipomania, a single half-ounce bulb of Semper Augustus, a rare variety with a red-and-white striped flower tinted blue at its base, might sell for 5,500 florins—the equivalent of about eight pounds of gold. The bidders sometimes ran out of cash: Once, when only two Semper Augustus bulbs were to be found in all of Holland, one was bartered for twelve acres of building lots, the other for 4,600 florins, a new carriage, and a pair of gray horses, with harness. It was not unusual for an investor to sink a fortune of 100,000 florins into a collection of forty or fifty bulbs.

It was not the actual value of the tulips that drove prices to such spectacular levels—it was each buyer's speculative gamble that later buyers would pay still more. Tulip brokers seldom even saw their bulbs, which usually remained in the ground as they were bought and sold many scores of times. This commerce in invisible flora was aptly dubbed the *windhandel*—the "wind trade."

Although the floral objects of desire had always been considered rare and valuable, the

Holding a cornucopia of prize blossoms, Roman flower goddess Flora shares seventeenth-century artist Hendrik Pot's *Fool's Wagon* with a gaggle of tulipomaniacs.

market for tulip bulbs had not always raged quite so feverishly. When the flower was introduced to Holland from Turkey in the late sixteenth century, breeders found that its frequent mutations sometimes produced handsome new varieties. These showy flowers fetched good prices from the nobility and from merchants and professionals who were enriched by Holland's booming international shipping industry. But their interest in tulips centered on fine gardens and the status conferred by them, not by gain.

By the 1630s, however, the allure of the tulip had become less horticultural than financial. The outlay for a few breeder tulips was small, and the profits could be great. Fortune seekers of all types—nobles, seamen, farmers, chimney sweeps, and servants—turned their gardens, great or small, into virtual tulip plantations. Speculation in bulbs quickly followed; buying and selling in the wind trade was a

faster and easier route to riches than laboriously raising a conventional crop of real tulips for real gardens. The smart money cared nothing for pretty flowers.

The gamblers had guessed right—new players bought into the game all the time, and tulip prices spiraled upward. As the cost of playing the market rose, people risked everything to get a piece of the action: Small businessmen sold their enterprises for money to invest, landowners mortgaged their estates, and workers sold the tools they had used to earn a living. The lucky ones were soon able to plunge their tulip profits into houses, coaches, and horses.

Prices finally got so high that bulbs were sometimes sold in fractions, reckoned in a unit called the *aas*—seventeen ten-thousandths of an ounce. It took more than 9,000 of the tiny *aasen* to make a pound; a single one-ounce tulip bulb contained nearly 600 aasen. Even the smallest investors could get into the market for the price of a few hundredths of an ounce of their favorite variety. Of course, its weight could only be estimated, since the bulb remained underground.

The regulations that applied to ordinary business were inadequate

to cover the oddities of the tulip trade. It evolved its own specialized code, whose legalities were the province of the town tulip notary. These transactions were usually conducted in taverns, which profited handsomely from serving food and drink to the newly rich.

But Holland's cooler heads decried the tulpenwoede: Ministers preached against the evils of moral decline evidenced by the gambling mania; municipal governments tried, with little success, to pass tough laws against tulip speculation; and publications ridiculed the speculators. But the possibility of fabulous wealth—some speculators reaped as much as 60,000 florins in a single month—made ordinarily sensible citizens succumb to the tulip temptation.

The mania gripped the Dutch for three frenzied years. Then, in the winter of 1637, some wary investors began to pull out of the market with their profits. Prices softened with the reduced demand, then plummeted as people frantically tried to cash in some of their new wealth. Panicky buyers abandoned contracts negotiated months earlier, leaving some dealers with huge stocks of formerly priceless, but now worthless, bulbs; countless disputes arose over refusals to complete disastrous bargains, which the courts called gambling transactions and refused to enforce. In the ensuing chaos, many wind traders were ruined; a few managed to salvage enough from the debacle to return to their former occupations. The raging fiscal fever broke that winter and had vanished entirely by spring, when the first tulips of the year peeked out upon the lowland whose economy their beauty had nearly destroyed. □

Bulbs of Semper Augustus *(far left)* and Viceroy fetched top florin during Holland's tulip craze.

Convulsionnaire's Disease

The crowd overflowed the walls of Paris's Saint-Médard cemetery and spilled out into the district's run-down streets and alleys on an autumn afternoon in 1731. What drew them was not a funeral but the spectacle of mass hysteria: Dozens of people writhed on the ground in the throes of violent convulsions. Some foamed at the mouth or screamed in pain, while others were contorted by powerful spasms or fell into swoons.

At the center of the variously gawking and twitching mass of humanity stood the modest tomb of François de Pâris, an ascetic deacon of the Catholic church who had died in 1727. Pâris had preached and practiced extreme austerity. He had lived in absolute poverty in a shabby neighborhood, performing menial tasks for the poor and mortifying his body with a hair shirt and spiked belt. Weakened by self-inflicted tortures and a meager diet, Pâris had died at the age of thirty-seven.

Even before the deacon's death, he had come to seem a virtual saint because of his extraordinary piety. Within days of his demise, a miraculous story began to circulate that seemed proof of his saintliness. An elderly widow named Louise-Madeleine Beigney attended Pâris's funeral in the hope that with his intercession her right arm, paralyzed for twenty years, would be healed. After praying beside his body, she kissed and embraced the feet, then brushed her arm against the bier as priests prepared to carry it away. Only after re-turning home to her spinning did Madame Beigney realize that she had regained the use of her arm.

Soon Pâris's grave was the destination for the ailing faithful, who reported a steady succession of miraculous cures. The discarded crutches and bandages in Saint-Médard cemetery testified to the wonders supposedly wrought by François de Pâris.

These wonders annoyed the church hierarchy—Pâris was, from their point of view, a totally unwelcome candidate for

sainthood. He had belonged to the Jansenist sect, a reform-minded group whose teachings the Vatican had condemned as heresy. The deacon's growing reputation could only bolster the Jansenist position, and church officials and their secular allies worked assiduously to discredit the alleged miracles.

Such disapproval failed to discourage believers, whose ardor slowly hardened into fanaticism. In mid-July of 1731, the miracle seekers at the Saint-Médard cemetery witnessed for the first time a suppliant in convulsions. The woman, who was afflicted with a nervous disorder, twitched and jerked on Pâris's tomb every day until, in early August, she was apparently cured by her convulsions. Soon thereafter, a deaf-mute woman from Versailles declared that her graveyard convulsions had restored some of her hearing and speech.

The experience of the abbé Bescheran of Montpellier reinforced the belief in Pâris's mystic power. The abbé had a severely atrophied left leg, and he made his pilgrimage to Saint-Médard seeking a cure that would demonstrate both the reality of the miracles and the injustice of the church's opposition to Pâris. Bescheran went to the cemetery twice a day to lie on the tomb while others prayed for him. Without fail, and often for hours on end, his face was contorted by grimaces, and he writhed violently despite the attendants holding his arms.

Sympathetic doctors declared that Bescheran's sinews recovered their natural elasticity, but church leaders hotly disputed them, condemning the abbé's "indecent and obscene cavorting" and pointing out that he still limped as much as ever. Undeterred by his critics,

Bescheran continued his visits to Saint-Médard all fall and into the winter. His appearances drew ever larger crowds, and his convulsions were contagious. Every day more people fell into paroxysms at Pâris's tomb, filling the cemetery with "tears, groans and frightful screams," according to a police report. Some of these so-called "convulsionnaires" moved so wildly that their friends laid down mattresses and cushions to prevent injuries.

In short order, fits were felling people all over the cemetery, and the contagion began popping up beyond the graveyard's bounds. The long queues of people waiting their turn at the deacon's tomb contained many spectators drawn purely by curiosity, but they too were sometimes overcome with convulsions, along with the faithful.

The violence of the convulsions, critics claimed, proved that God had no hand in the goings-on at Saint-Médard. A police report even stated that there was evidence of a malign presence at the cemetery—convulsing girls, it was noted, "have their breasts and bosom exposed for up to three hours at a time. Their skirts are hiked up, legs in the air, which gives viewers the chance to examine some parts which women take care to hide."

In January 1732, Pâris's detractors finally convinced King Louis XV to order the cemetery closed. With the tomb off-limits and the riveting spectacles over, the convulsionary craze quickly faded. But there were fanatics among the deacon's followers, and they simply moved their activities into private homes. What had been a public practice quickly evolved into an underground cult that engaged in increasingly violent manifestations of its faith.

A typical gathering began with devotions to François de Pâris and scripture readings. Then, as the participants prayed ardently, at least one among them would be seized by convulsions even more bizarre than those seen at Saint-Médard. Thrashing in a frenzy, screaming and twitching, this first convulsionnaire usually catalyzed the onset of seizures in others, as intense emotion swept the room.

Because many convulsionnaires found the experience excruciatingly painful and beseeched their friends for relief, there arose a variety of procedures to assist them. Called secours—"aids"—the procedures were administered by cult members known as secouristes.

Secours could be quite violent. One manuscript relates an effort to straighten the limbs of a convulsed woman: "Each limb was tied with a long and strong piece of linen that allowed room for the placement of ten hands; and to augment our strength we each had one foot on the edge of the bed bracing ourselves. It took twenty-five men more than a half hour, pulling very hard, then less hard according to the strength of her contractions."

Other forms of secours were more violent still. The convulsionnaire was sometimes severely beaten with clubs, iron bars, or rocks with specially fitted handles. As many as a dozen people might stand or jump on a board placed on a convulsing body to control its movement. No matter how brutal the means, however, the convulsionnaires claimed to suffer little or no pain, and some even said that secours brought them great pleasure. Observers—perhaps not completely objective—reported that secours produced not so much ◊

In this eighteenth-century engraving, people caught in the throes of convulsions are beaten, trampled, and kicked by fellow followers of Parisian ascetic François de Pâris (inset).

as a bruise, leaving even the most delicate participants unscathed and grateful for their relief. Scarcely less than a convulsion, the more radical methods of secours signified high spiritual achievement.

The bizarre practices of the most devout Pârisites did nothing to mitigate official disapproval, and a few of them were arrested and imprisoned for public disturbance. Nevertheless, the movement continued to flourish, with hundreds or even thousands of participants in assemblies scattered around Paris. But only the Church cared. If Parisians had ever paid much attention to the hysterics in their midst, by the 1730s they had lost all serious interest in the aberrations of convulsionnaires. The popular mood surfaced in a string of gently mocking songs and poems that laughed at the papal bull, the alleged miracles, and the convulsions—religion was not the center of eighteenth-century Paris. Such enlightened philosophers as Voltaire considered the convulsionnaires personal enemies of understanding.

As public attention waned, the convulsionnaires splintered into ever-smaller cells, a few of them given to such extreme practices as crucifixion. Smelling leniency in the air, others emerged from underground to form religious communities where adherents, both men and women, could live together. But their days were numbered.

The French Revolution that began in 1789 broke the spell cast more than half a century earlier by François de Pâris. Years of revolutionary violence and chaos were more than the mystic movement could endure. The convulsions stopped and the moans and screams died away— without benefit of secours. □

The Rite Stuff

As the curtain opened on the second offering of Paris's new Théâtre des Champs-Élysées that spring evening in 1913, the orchestra had scarcely begun to play when members of the audience began to jeer and snicker. From the balcony, a group of indignant supporters, some hired for the purpose, responded with loud applause meant to silence the boors. But the din swelled, and the world premiere of the ballet *Le Sacre du Printemps* (The Rite of Spring) degenerated into what one critic dubbed *Le Massacre du Printemps*.

Sergey Diaghilev, the Russian impresario whose famed Ballets Russes company performed the ballet, and composer Igor Stravinsky had worried about a possibly difficult reception. Seeking to recapture the pagan spirit of ancient Russia, the revolutionary score was full of obsessive, primitive-sounding rhythms and powerful dissonances that conventional audiences could easily construe as strange and barbaric. Even fans of his music might be, Stravinsky admitted to an interviewer, "perplexed" by his new work. The choreography, by the celebrated dancer Vaslav Nijinsky

(pages 120-122), was controversial, substituting sudden, angular movements and idiosyncratic postures for the fluid smoothness and grace of traditional ballet.

Diaghilev had entreated his dancers and musicians to keep calm and carry on. "Whatever happens," he told them, "the ballet must be performed to the end." The impresario also took what had seemed a sensible step, hiring a band of young men to ensure friendly applause during the performance.

From interviews and accounts of dress rehearsals, the audience knew the evening would be an artistic first—and not one designed to please fashionable, but philistine, ballet fans. Snickers and loud laughing turned to shouts of indignation when the curtain rose on dancers who, a critic later said, appeared to be alternately afflicted with paralysis and seizures. Diaghilev's hired claque applauded vigorously and members of the audience eager to see the new production appealed for order, inflaming the opposition still more. The noise became deafening, drowning out

the music. The dancers could barely hear the orchestra, and in a desperate attempt to keep them in step, Nijinsky climbed onto a chair offstage and counted out the time.

When the first act ended, the agitated Diaghilev ordered the house lights turned on so that the police could round up the worst of the miscreants. This had no effect, for as the lights dimmed for the second act, pandemonium burst out anew. An elegant-looking woman slapped a jeering man, people shouted insults, and blows were exchanged among the most impassioned. Through all of it, conductor Pierre Monteux carried on stoically—as if, one observer put it, he was as heavily armored as a crocodile.

The wretched behavior and reactionary spirit of the ballet's detractors evoked scathing remarks from critics, even from those who disliked the ballet themselves. One firmly denounced "the stupid and systematic spitefulness of what is generally called the elite of Parisian society when faced with anything really new and daring." Another commentator sneered at the "overgrown children," adding that they "could find no other argument when faced with splendors so infinitely removed from their feeble understanding than that of stupidly laughing like babies."

Only Diaghilev seemed pleased by the furor, commenting to the unhappy Stravinsky, "Exactly what I wanted." The Parisians who turned out for the succeeding three performances of *Le Sacre du Printemps* behaved themselves. And when the Ballets Russes went on to London, it played to packed houses without any unseemly disturbances. After the scandal of the premiere, the ballet never again caused turmoil. □

Once in Love with Aimee

Trumpets blared and a hush fell over the vast auditorium. Then an appreciative murmur arose as the crowd saw a white-clad woman, balancing an armload of roses, descend a staircase to the stage. Moving to the strains of "The Stars and Stripes," she reached center stage and, raising the bouquet, flashed her radiant smile. Standing as one, the crowd of 5,000 burst into wild applause. The auburn-haired woman graciously bowed in response.

The adulatory opening to the show would have gratified the most jaded Broadway star. But this woman was no secular actress—she was Sister Aimee Semple McPherson, the voice of the Church of the Foursquare Gospel. Nine times a week, from 1923 through 1926 and intermittently through the 1930s, Sister Aimee presided over services at her Angelus Temple in Los Angeles—services that one reporter called "the most perennially successful show in the United States." Eager for a seat, her followers, along with throngs of the curious, arrived at the temple hours before every service, shoving their way to its doors. The thousands who were turned away stood in the street and a nearby park to listen to Sister Aimee over a loudspeaker. Thousands more heard her on her own radio station, KFSG.

One part revival meeting and one part vaudeville show, the service was an elaborately staged succession of singers and musicians, whose offerings, religious or profane, were the opening acts for the headline performance: Sister Aimee's message. The sermon, augmented with what McPherson called illustrations, gave full vent to her theatrical genius. Costumed actors, props, lights, sound effects, and such devices as cauldrons of fire and hot-air balloons reinforced her musings on heaven and hell, Jesus and Satan, and a modern world beset by jazz music and other temptations.

For a sermon with a nautical motif, Sister Aimee costumed herself as an admiral and narrated the tragic voyages of allegorical ships sailing against a backdrop of tossing waves. A heedless pleasure boat, overtaken by Satan's pirate ship, capsized and sank, and a proud ship of commerce fell afoul of pasteboard rocks. A submarine appeared, representing the critics of Angelus Temple and its founder; when its attack failed, the crowd broke into victorious laughter. People were so moved by Sister Aimee that doz- ◊

Pit Stop

In March of 1954, an odd epidemic of car trouble hit Bellingham, Washington, some eighty miles north of Seattle. Over several weeks, the windshields of more than a thousand cars had reportedly been cracked or disfigured with tiny pits. The police blamed unknown vandals for this damage, which cost Bellingham's insurers some $50,000. By April 14, newspapers in Seattle were reporting that "windshield-peppering hoodlums" were moving nearer to the city. They had struck in a town sixty-five miles north and at a naval air station just forty-five miles away. That night, according to the increasingly anxious reports, the mystery vandals targeted their first Seattle windshields. It was the beginning of a panicky deluge.

Over the next twenty-four hours, 242 people called the Seattle police to report damage to more than 3,000 cars—a toll far beyond the efforts of even the most industrious hoodlums. Some windshields were reported broken, but most showed pits no larger than a sixteenth of an inch. Many callers also described a sprinkling of sooty particles on their windshields. During the next week, the number of reported pitting incidents rose to 4,294. Worried motorists covered their windshields with rugs, newspapers, blankets, and floor mats and became increasingly alarmed that there was no obvious cause—the police had by then ruled out vandalism. The city's worried mayor telegraphed an appeal to President Dwight Eisenhower for federal assistance "on emergency basis."

Like a genie released from a bottle, the fear of pitting flowed out of the Pacific northwest, across the

ens of them trooped up to the stage at the end of her services to declare their conversion to her upbeat version of the Gospel.

But, like all commitments, their devotion was put to the test. In May 1926, the preacher suddenly disappeared from a beach near Los Angeles. The faithful prayed and offered a $25,000 reward to whoever found her. Some plunged into the Pacific to search for her body; one youth drowned in the effort and another died of exposure. Reportedly overwhelmed by grief for Sister Aimee, a girl in the congregation committed suicide. Then, five weeks after her disappearance, McPherson emerged from the desert near Douglas, Arizona, claiming to have escaped from a band of kidnappers who demanded a $500,000 ransom. The story did not wash with the authorities. They had evidence that her kidnapping had in fact been a clandestine fling with the Temple's radio operator, Kenneth Ormiston.

Volleys of charges and countercharges filled the newspapers for weeks, and Sister Aimee was indicted on charges of perjury, conspiracy to perpetrate a hoax, and obstructing justice. "I am like a lamb led to slaughter," the embattled evangelist announced. She faced what seemed to be an airtight case for the prosecution. Then, in a kind of judicial miracle, she was spared at the last minute: The district attorney, without explanation, moved for acquittal. Cynical observers were not surprised two years later when the same district attorney went to prison for accepting a $100,000 bribe in a stock-fraud case.

Even in the crucible of scandal, however, the faith of McPherson's followers remained largely intact. She continued to draw huge crowds through the 1930s, despite a series of well-publicized lawsuits with estranged associates and family members. During World War II, Sister Aimee was indefatigable, handing out Bibles, preaching to servicemen, and on one occasion selling war bonds at the astonishing rate of $150,000 in one hour. She died in 1944 at the age of fifty-four of an overdose of sleeping pills—ruled accidental. During the three days that Sister Aimee's body lay in state in Angelus Temple, mourners stood in lines stretching for blocks, waiting to file by her casket. In all, 50,000 of the faithful were able to share the last appearance of the impresario of evangelism. □

country. Reports began to come in from Ohio, California, and other points across the United States, and experts speculated that meteor dust, cosmic rays, or industrial ash might be responsible for the windshield plague. However, the most frightening—and soon the most widely accepted—theory blamed radioactive fallout from a series of hydrogen-bomb explosions at Bikini and Eniwetok atolls in the Pacific.

No one had experienced explosions of that size before, and their global effects could only be guessed at. Headlines in Seattle newspapers reflected people's fears and reinforced them with such cries as "Witness Says: Hydrogen Test Out of Control" and "3 H-Bomb Victims Face Death." One pitted-windshield story ran alongside a report on

the nation's first citywide nuclear-evacuation drill, in Spokane, about 200 miles east of Seattle.

Alarmed citizens found cold comfort in the fact that experts who examined pitted windshields with Geiger counters generally discounted the H-bomb hypothesis. They still did not explain the phenomenon. The search for an agent was still going on when, for no apparent reason, reports of damage suddenly began to decline. The police department disbanded its windshield detail. On April 21, the Seattle *Post-Intelligencer* ran a small story on page eight headlined: "Savants Absolve H-Bomb in 'Pit' Mystery."

The last official word about Seattle's pitted windshields was spoken on June 10. The University of Washington's Environmental Research

Laboratory reported that the soot was not Bikini fallout but mere coal dust. The samples of pitted windshields the lab studied showed nothing but the ordinary damage that is inflicted when pebbles hit the windshield of a car traveling at speed—nicks that usually go unnoticed. As for the epidemic of anxiety, it appeared to stem from the original act of vandals in Bellingham and its curious effect on the people of Seattle. Out of concern for the safety of their cars, people were suddenly moved to look *at* their windshields rather than *through* them—and saw for the first time the tiny nicks they had not noticed before. As these discoveries multiplied, it became an easy leap, for a panicked populace, from mysterious pits to hydrogen bombs. □

The Game of Life

The fans were in a festive mood on May 24, 1964, as they packed themselves like sardines into Lima's National Stadium for a match between Peru's soccer team and the visiting Argentine club. More than the usual national pride rode on the outcome: The winner of the game might be chosen to compete in the 1964 Olympics in Tokyo.

The hometown crowd lost none of its confidence in victory when the Argentines scored first; the Peruvians' spirited attack continued to elicit wild cheers. Then, with six minutes remaining, a Peruvian forward battered his way through the Argentine defense and booted home the tying goal. But the jubilant roar from 50,000 throats lasted only a moment. The referee, a neutral Uruguayan, signaled a foul against Peru and disallowed the score.

The crowd's delirium was instantly transformed into fury, and the stadium erupted in pandemonium. Matías Rojas, a burly fan widely known as Bomba for his explosive temper, scrambled over a nine-foot fence topped with barbed wire as onlookers roared, *"Ahí va Bomba!"*—"There goes Bomb!" A small police squad, dodging a hail of stones and bottles thrown from the stands, caught Rojas just before he reached the referee.

Following Bomba's lead, the fans surged onto the field. To continue playing was clearly impossible, and the terrified referee called the game. The crowd went berserk, and the police, in a vain effort to restore order, loosed clouds of tear gas. This set off a mass stampede for the exits, but the attendants had not unlocked three of the stadium's heavy steel gates. The first people to reach the gates were trapped there and crushed to death as the crowd continued to push forward, propelled by panic and unaware that the exits were blocked. Two gates buckled under the force exerted by the pushing, shoving, struggling mass, and survivors crawled out of the stadium over bodies piled six deep in some places. Thousands of people poured into the streets of Lima, and in the riot that ensued, cars and trucks were turned over and set on fire, offices looted, and windows smashed.

The official death toll was 318—the worst in the history of a sport notorious for the violent allegiance of its fans. But, as grieving families identified the victims, Peruvian observers came to see the tragedy as something more complex than the volatile psychology of spectators. The violence unleashed at the arena, some social commentators suggested, was partly the crowd's pent-up rage and despair: Despite the promises politicians had made, Peru's economy was undergoing a drastic decline, and to these people, most of them already poor, the future must have looked impossibly bleak. Thus, the stadium was packed with a great many Bombas, ready to explode when the referee made his call. □

Harmonic Hoedown

On mountaintops and seashores, in desert canyons, among the ruins of Machu Picchu in the Peruvian Andes, at the Great Pyramid in Egypt, and in places ordinary and extraordinary all over the world, thousands of people congregated to face the rising summer sun in a grand spiritual enterprise. Through meditation, prayer, music, and chants, they would purify the planet and lay the foundations of a new age of unity and peace.

It was Sunday, August 16, 1987, and the congregants believed that the positions of the planets on that day and on August 17 constituted a propitious "harmonic convergence." The term was the invention of José Argüelles, a Boulder, Colorado, art historian and student of Central American Indian prophecies. Argüelles had recently published *The Mayan Factor*, a book filled with nuggets plucked from ancient Mayan and Aztec calendars, Buddhist texts, and the author's forays into astrology, world history, and biochemical theory. From this miscellany Argüelles extracted the premise of his book: A 5,125-year historical cycle—in Argüellen terms, the time it takes the planet to pass through what he called a "galactic beam"—would complete itself between 1992 and 2012. The most exciting event in this period would be the return after many centuries of Mayan sages from what Argüelles termed their "transport into the farther reaches of the galaxy whence they had come." His meaning: The Mayans were extraterrestrials who had resided in Central America for a spell, returned to the outer-space homeland, and were now due for another stay on earth. The presence of the extraterrestrial Mayans would be felt for the first time during the harmonic convergence. According to Argüelles, the sages would be "perceived by some as an inner light and by others as feathered serpent rainbow wheels turning in the air."

Bringing in the new age required that at least 144,000 people—perhaps coincidentally, the number of converted souls the Bible requires for Judgment Day—travel to what Argüelles called "power centers" of the world to hold hands and meditate. The celebrants would, in the words of the art historian, "help awaken the rest of humanity" and begin to synchronize the earth with the rest of the galaxy. If the effort failed, Argüelles warned, "we are following a course leading to the extinction of many life forms including our own."

Scholars of the Mayan and Aztec cultures dismissed Argüelles's theories with phrases such as "really crazy" and "totally crackpot," and astronomers said that there was nothing very unusual about the planets' relative positions on the days in question. "The only cycle I see," said one astronomer, "is that a lot of people want to get back to hippie days." But such negative resonances were discounted, and word of harmonic convergence, fueled by Argüelles and other readers of the planetary portents, spread through a loose network of new age organizations that were interested in such events. By sunrise on the big day, a convergence had indeed occurred: Thousands of the faithful crowded the power centers, prepared to save all humanity and to change themselves forever.

The sounds of flutes and songs filled the predawn air as more than 5,000 pilgrims gathered on the rocky slopes of Mount Shasta in northern California. Other celebrants flocked to Chaco Canyon in New Mexico, the site of a 900-year-old Indian prayer ring, and the Great Serpent Mound, an ancient Indian burial ground in Ohio, also enjoyed an unwonted number of visitors. At noon Greenwich mean time, convergence participants around the world joined in thinking positive thoughts.

Since there were no official crowd counts, it was impossible to say whether the harmonic convergence activities passed the threshold of success with 144,000 in attendance. Nor could any feathered-serpent rainbow wheels manifesting the return of the Mayans be confirmed. But those who had taken part were convinced that their effort had not been in vain. One Wall Street banker who joined a ceremony on a Long Island beach spoke for many: "It's easy to pass off the group as certifiable, but the more people who are continuously working on overcoming conflict, the happier we'll be." □

On the summit of Hawaii's Haleakala Crater, new agers welcome the harmonic convergence at sunrise.

IN A SCENE that decorates a fourth-century-BC Greek vase found in the colonial city of Paestum in Italy, the goddess Mania rivets her mad gaze on Hercules as he cradles his son. Infected by Mania's madness, the hero throws the child into a fire. The vase's maker, Asteas of Paestum, drew the incident from the tragedy *Furious Hercules* by Euripides.

Elvis Lives

On August 16, 1977, Elvis Presley appeared at Claude Buchanon's Tennessee farm unannounced. The singer had visited twice before, and on one occasion he had helped Claude out when money was tight. But this meeting was very different. Elvis was wreathed in a thin, bluish fog as he walked up to his friend, smiled, and said, "I've come to say goodbye for a while." A moment later, Claude heard his wife calling: "Elvis has died! It's on the radio."

The forty-two-year-old Presley's death rocked his legions of fans— as one of them remarked, "every-one" was in love with Elvis. But their loyalty did not diminish; if anything, it grew. Statistics hint at the King's magnetism: In the twenty years between his first record and his death, Elvis lovers bought a half-billion of his recordings. In the eleven years following his death, another half-billion were sold.

But it is in experiences such as Claude Buchanon's that one sees Elvis Presley's extraordinary hold on people. Many besides Buchanon have reported similar ghostly encounters, and some of the Elvis sighters insist that it is not a spirit that they have seen. Their idol, they claim, is still alive—he faked his death in order to escape to a new life, perhaps in Hawaii, where numerous sightings have been reported. Such true believers find evidence in Elvis's very name—like *veils*, *Levis*, and *evils*, an anagram for *lives*.

Not all encounters with Elvis involve such fervid followers. Three months after his death, he supposedly visited a twenty-eight-year-old psychologist who considered herself a serious academic and only a lukewarm Presley fan. Using the pseudonym Hilda, she described the meeting to Raymond A. Moody, a psychiatrist investigating what he calls "unusual experiences concerning Elvis." The singer appeared to Hilda as she was working in her office. "I could tell he was aware that something was wrong in my life," she told Moody, "something that even I wasn't aware of, and that he was trying to be helpful to me." By the time Elvis left, Hilda felt he had accomplished what she saw as his mission—"to open me up more to myself and others and life."

A truck driver Moody called Jack Matthews said that he had encountered Elvis hitchhiking one December night in 1980 about a hundred miles west of Memphis. Although Matthews seldom picked up riders, he felt sorry for the man who was walking beside the road and pulled over to offer him a ride. The stranger accepted, and the two got along well, talking about trucking, their families, and problems that they had in common. Then, only a few miles from Memphis, roadside lights began to illuminate the truck cab so that Matthews could see his passenger's face. Matthews thought his rider looked familiar, but he did not know why until he thought to introduce himself. Responded the rider, "I'm Elvis Presley, sir."

"It was Elvis Presley, all right," the truck driver told Raymond Moody. "Or his ghost. He looked just like he did in his heyday. I was quaking in my boots."

One woman interviewed by Moody does not simply see an apparition of Elvis. She asserts that the singer lives in her house—in the flesh. Nancy Morgan claims that her son, Jeremy, who was born a year after Presley's death, is the star reincarnated. A devoted fan who was divorced during her pregnancy, Morgan remarked, "I missed Elvis a lot more than I missed my husband." She often played records from her huge Elvis collection for the little boy, who soon began to show an affinity for the music, bouncing in time and smiling. Morgan made an interesting observation: Jeremy's eyes, she said, were exactly like Elvis's eyes. When the toddler was eighteen months old, Morgan put the question to him directly: "Jeremy, are you Elvis?" His affirmative reply convinced her. "Ever since that day I have known in my heart that Jeremy is Elvis," she confided to Moody. "He is going to be a very important and popular person one day." Jeremy himself

added, "I've always known I was Elvis, since I was born. I came back to be with my mom."

A new incarnation apparently does not hamper Elvis's mobility. A checkout-counter tabloid reported a pair of 1991 sightings, one in front of a St. Louis movie theater in July, the other at an Augusta, Georgia, mall in December. There, Elvis was alleged to have told forty-five-year-old Margaret Moore, a lifelong fan, that he would return to Graceland on New Year's Day to do a coast-to-coast radio broadcast. Said Moore, quoting the King: "I'll say what I've been waiting fourteen years to say."

That broadcast was not made as predicted, but Elvis's acolytes have been able to get up-to-the-minute information about his posthumous appearances from a commercial telephone hotline. A caller on January 24, 1992, heard fellow fans describe these sightings: Elvis driving a white Cadillac through the parking lot of Service Merchandise in Tupelo, Mississippi; Elvis in the dairy section of a Chattanooga Foodland supermarket; Elvis materializing in a poster store in San Diego, then spectrally fading away right before a shopper's eyes. "In the past I always laughed at people who called in their sightings on the phone," said the woman who had witnessed that visitation. "Now I believe. Maybe he *is* alive." □

Holy Smoke

Rabbi David Rosen, a longtime Jerusalem resident, was surprised one evening to be called to the side of an old schoolmate who was visiting the Holy Land and who had begun behaving strangely. Rosen found him strange indeed. The "very stable, normal English public-school schoolboy" now stood outside one of the city gates dressed in sackcloth and ashes, urging passersby to redeem themselves from wickedness.

The case of Rabbi Rosen's friend is not an isolated one. Local psychiatrists treat an average of fifty tourists a year for similar behavior, a phenomenon that they call the Jerusalem syndrome. According to Yair Bar-El, director of the medical center that provides psychiatric treatment to foreign tourists, "Jerusalem can literally drive some tourists crazy."

Israeli psychiatrist Eli Witztum reports cases in which the afflicted have claimed to be Jesus, God, and Satan, among others. One woman, a vacationing British high-school teacher, insisted that she was pregnant with the son of Christ, despite medical (and theological) evidence to the contrary. A thirty-three-year-old American man exchanged all of his clothes for a sword in Jerusalem's Old City and ran off, convinced that God had told him to cure the blind. Most of those who succumb have had previous psychiatric episodes, but for some, including the naked swashbuckler, such bizarre notions and actions are an entirely new experience.

Bar-El, Witztum, and others who study the syndrome have no ready explanation for it. For deeply religious people, a visit to their holi- ◊

The inscription on the cross identifies a pilgrim on the road from Rome to the Holy Land in 1971.

can be devastating.

Jerusalem's power to convert ordinary people into delusional zealots is nothing new. In 1848, a Philadelphia Quaker named Warder Cresson came home so changed that his family had him committed. Shortly before World War I, there were no fewer than seven messiahs in Jerusalem. Five foreign consulates housed one messiah each, while two of the personages had to share dominion of the Austro-Hungarian consulate. After the war was over, only three messiahs remained, among them one Dr. Mussa, a Persian Jew who likened himself to Moses, Jesus, and Muhammad. Mussa once claimed responsibility for ending a drought in Jerusalem and thereafter incurred the wrath of officials by refusing to pay his water bills.

The Jerusalem syndrome seldom has a long-lasting or dangerous emotional effect, and the locals have learned to humor their deranged guests. Jerusalem resident Jim Gerrish recounts the possibly apocryphal story of a dinner party where two invitees, both of them tourists, claimed to be Elijah the Prophet. Says Gerrish: "They spent the whole dinner glaring at each other, accusing the other one of being an impostor." □

est of places may trigger overwhelming—and unbalancing—emotions. One site in Jerusalem is particularly potent emotionally. The Western Wall—familiarly, the Wailing Wall—is revered because it is close to the site of a temple built by the biblical king Solomon. Some people appear mesmerized by the wall, while others weep.

A role is also assigned to shock and disappointment. Many people come to Jerusalem expecting a city unchanged since antiquity, full of white-robed itinerants herding flocks of sheep. Instead, they find themselves in a metropolis replete with office buildings and noisy traffic jams. The contrast between expectation and reality, doctors say,

Dead Reckoning

The beat-up vans and buses festooned with tie-dyed banners are a village on the move: the Dead Zone. Part home, part carnival, part flea market, part alternate reality, the Zone is populated by 10,000 to 20,000 nomads familiarly known as Deadheads, zealous followers of the venerable Grateful Dead rock band. For as many as thirty weeks a year, they follow the band from coast to coast, carrying with them a kind of fossil culture that descends, like the graying band, from the mid-1960s flower child heyday of peace and love in San Francisco.

Set up near the concert site, the Zone is a beehive of commerce. Entrepreneurial Deadheads sell vegetarian food and Grateful Dead memorabilia to fans. In less open transactions, marijuana, LSD, and psyche-

A would-be concert goer in Washington, D.C., "looks for a miracle"—Deadhead jargon for a gift ticket.

Veteran Deadheads get a breath of fresh air at the window of a school bus turned mobile home. The Grateful Dead's spokesperson, Jerry Garcia *(below)*, has been the group's lead guitarist since 1965.

delic mushrooms change hands. After a concert, small crowds gather to hear village elders instruct the new generation in the tribe's history. They concentrate on the glory days of the sixties, when their "scene" seemed to be everywhere, on the verge of conquering the world.

The people of the Zone are only the most visible of the Deadheads, who number in the hundreds of thousands nationwide. For every Deadhead "on the bus"—that is, who follows the band—dozens lead relatively normal lives as security guards, diplomats, lawyers, carpenters, and the like. As often as they can, they go to a concert where they mingle with kindred spirits and renew themselves. Like the nomadic Deadheads, these people have a feeling akin to religious belief about their relationship to the band and its followers. One Deadhead whose credentials stretch back to 1965 says that they share a belief in "psychedelic awareness, the collective unity of consciousness." He adds: "The people that believe in those kinds of things identify the Dead as some kind of guide in life."

The devotion of Deadheads to their guides in life is fed by magazines and books. One of the most essential volumes is *Deadbase*, a compendium of facts and statistics about the Grateful Dead. Constantly updated, *Deadbase* contains a listing of every set the band has played

since 1965.

The band tries not to play the same songs in the same order twice, and for veteran Deadheads much of a concert's pleasure comes from comparing it to other performances and their often encyclopedic knowledge. They note differences in mood from show to show, determine when the band last played a song, and try to predict the opening song and the length of each set.

Some Deadheads supplement books and memory by recording concerts. Arriving early with gear that ranges from simple cassette recorders to sophisticated digital equipment, they jockey for the best spots in a special section. Some "tapers" ignore the boundaries and edge as close to the stage as they dare to get better quality—a practice called "taping mouth." In their endless quest for ever-better quality, tapers barter through ads in Grateful Dead magazines.

A Deadhead's knowledge of the Grateful Dead's vast repertoire comes into play once the music begins, as they wait for what is called

a resurrection—a song that the band has not played for years. When it comes, the resurrection is always a signal for celebration, its wildness in proportion to the time that has passed since the song was last performed. At a 1991 concert, the crowd erupted deliriously when the band launched into "New Speedway Boogie" for the first time in twenty-one years.

The music impels some members of the audience to begin spinning around in open spaces and hallways and to continue in a sort of spiritual ecstasy as long as the music lasts. The group of Deadheads who originated spinning travel together from concert to concert as a sign of their common inspiration.

The Deadhead phenomenon was spontaneous, springing up and persisting with no encouragement from the members of the Grateful Dead. Their spokesperson, Jerry Garcia, has his own explanation for the devoted following. "The good times get harder to come by," Garcia says. "We're like an alternative to two weeks at the beach, a little vacation spot where you can go to feel good about people again."

The youngsters who continue to swell the ranks of the Deadheads, Garcia suggests, crave escape from everything that smacks of the conventional. "You can't hop the freights anymore, but you can chase the Grateful Dead around. You can have all your tires blow out in some weird town in the Midwest, and you can get hell from strangers. You can have something that lasts throughout your life as adventures, the times you took chances. I think that's essential in anybody's life." □

ACKNOWLEDGMENTS

The editors wish to thank these individuals and institutions for their valuable assistance in the preparation of this volume:

Andrew C. Aronson, Silver Spring, Maryland; Jean Barman, University of British Columbia, Vancouver; Hugh Bowden, King's College London, University of London, London; Guido Buldrini, ANSA, Rome; Terence C. Charman, Imperial War Museum, London; Kathy Creely, Melanesian Studies Resource Center, University of California, San Diego; Emmanuela C. del Re, Rome; Rina Durante, Lecce, Italy; Hilary Evans, London; Sally Ferguson, Netherlands Flower Bulb Information Center, Brooklyn, New York; Michel Fleury, Paris; Cheryl Giannunzio, Wisconsin Public Television, Green Bay; R. A. Gilbert, Bristol, England; Ira Gitlin, Riverdale, Maryland; Sarah Heald, National Museum of American History, Smithsonian Institution, Washington, D.C.; Lyell Henry, Iowa City, Iowa; Michael Hittman, Long Island University, Brooklyn, New York; Istituto Archeologico Germanico, Rome; Peter Jonas, Cardinal Stritch College, Milwaukee, Wisconsin; Jean-Noël Kapferer, Paris; Richard Landis, University of Pittsburgh, Pittsburgh; Caroline Lucas, London; Anita Mancia, Istituto Storico della Compagnia di Gesù, Rome; Wolf-Dieter Mechler, Werner Heine, Stadtarchiv, Hannover, Germany; Sarah Moule, London; Marjorie Murphy, Swarthmore College, Swarthmore, Pennsylvania; Janet L. Nelson, King's College London, University of London, London; Herbert Ortstein, Zentralbibliothek der Bundeswehr, Düsseldorf, Germany; Eli Popoff, Grand Forks, British Columbia; Jean Richard, Dijon, France; Volker Schuhmacher, Institut für Grenzgebiete der Psychologie und Psychohygience, Freiburg, Germany; Ted Schwartz, Department of Anthropology, University of California, San Diego; Steven A. Seelig, Grateful Dead fan; Thomas Seiler, Medieval Institute Publications, Western Michigan University, Kalamazoo; Paul Sieveking, London; Paul Steeves, Stetson University, DeLand, Florida; Jeff Streed, Episcopal High School, Alexandria, Virginia; John Sullivan, *Livingston Enterprise*, Livingston, Montana; John B. Trevor, Grateful Dead fan; Marcello Truzzi, Eastern Michigan University, Ypsilanti; Alexander Viebig, VSB Unter den Linden, Berlin; Paula York-Soderlund, Arlington, Virginia.

PICTURE CREDITS

BIBLIOGRAPHY

Books

Allderidge, Patricia. *The Late Richard Dadd: 1817-1886*. London: Tate Gallery, 1974.

Allport, Gordon W., and Leo Postman. *The Psychology of Rumor*. New York: Russell & Russell, 1965.

Argüelles, José. *The Mayan Factor: Path beyond Technology*. Santa Fe, N.Mex.: Bear, 1987.

Arieson. *The Visitations: A Saga of Gods and Men* (Part 1). El Cajon, Calif.: Unarius Academy of Science, 1987.

Astin, Alan E. *Cato the Censor*. Oxford: Oxford University Press, 1978.

Austin, Alvyn. *Aimee Semple McPherson*. Don Mills, Ontario: Fitzhenry & Whiteside, 1980.

Ayto, John. *Dictionary of Word Origins*. New York: Arcade/Little, Brown, 1991.

Bach, Marcus. *Strange Sects and Curious Cults*. New York: Dodd, Mead, 1961.

Barnum, P. T. *The Humbugs of the World*. Detroit: Singing Tree Press, 1970.

Barrett, Anthony A. *Caligula: The Corruption of Power*. New Haven: Yale University Press, 1989.

Bartlett, John. *Familiar Quotations* (14th ed.). Boston: Little, Brown, 1968.

Benét, William Rose. *The Reader's Encyclopedia* (2nd ed.). New York: Thomas Y. Crowell, 1965.

Bett, W. R. *The Infirmities of Genius*. New York: Philosophical Library, 1952.

Bishop, Morris. *A Gallery of Eccentrics*. New York: Minton, Balch, 1928.

Blunden, Caroline, and Mark Elvin. *Cultural Atlas of China*. Oxford: Phaidon, 1983.

Blunden, Edmund. *Charles Lamb and His Contemporaries*. Hamden, Conn.: Archon Books, 1967.

Blunt, Anthony. *Borromini*. London: Allen Lane, 1979.

Blunt, Wilfrid. *Tulipomania*. Harmondsworth, England: Penguin Books, 1950.

Bolshakoff, Serge. *Russian Nonconformity*. Philadelphia: Westminster Press, 1950.

Boyer, Paul. *By the Bomb's Early Light*. New York: Pantheon Books, 1985.

Braden, Charles Samuel. *These Also Believe: A Study of Modern American Cults and Minority Religious Movements*. New York: Macmillan, 1949.

Brewer-Giorgio, Gail. *Is Elvis Alive?* New York: Tudor, 1988.

Briggs, Susan. *The Home Front*. London: American Heritage, 1975.

Cary, M., and H. H. Scullard. *A History of Rome Down to the Reign of Constantine* (3rd ed.). New York: St. Martin's Press, 1975.

Caute, David. *The Great Fear: The Anti-Communist Purge Under Truman and Eisenhower*. New York: Simon and Schuster, 1978.

Cavendish, Richard (Ed.). *Man, Myth & Magic*. New York: Marshall Cavendish, 1985.

Ceplair, Larry, and Steven Englund. *The Inquisition in Hollywood: Politics in the Film Community, 1930-1960*. Garden City, N.Y.: Anchor Press/Doubleday, 1980.

Charlton, D. G. *Secular Religions in France 1815-1870*. London: Oxford University Press, 1963.

Charteris, John. *At G.H.Q.* London: Cassell, 1931.

Chesneaux, Jean, Marianne Bastid, and Marie-Claire Bèrgere. *China from the Opium Wars to the 1911 Revolution*. Translated by Anne Destenay. New York: Pantheon Books, 1976.

Chick, N. A. (Comp.). *Annals of the Indian Rebellion: 1857-58*. Edited by David Hutchinson. London: Charles Knight, 1974.

Coben, Stanley. *A. Mitchell Palmer: Politician* (Civil Liberties in American History series). Edited by Leonard W. Levy. New York: Da Capo Press, 1972.

Cohn, Norman:
The Pursuit of the Millennium (Rev. ed.). New York: Oxford University Press, 1977.
Warrant for Genocide. New York: Harper & Row, 1967.

Connor, W. Robert. *Thucydides*. Princeton, N.J.: Princeton University Press, 1984.

Cooper-Hewitt, Debrett. *Designs for the Dream King: The Castles and Palaces of Ludwig II of Bavaria*. London: Debrett's Peerage, 1978.

Curran, Douglas. *In Advance of the Landing: Folk Concepts of Outer Space*. New York: Abbeville Press, 1985.

Dale, Philip Marshall. *Medical Biographies: The Ailments of Thirty-Three Famous Persons*. Norman: University of Oklahoma Press, 1952.

del Re, Emmanuela C. *Il Figlio di Ergos. Marcello Creti: Scienziato, Santo e Mago*. Florence: Pontecorboli, 1992.

Dohrman, H. T. *California Cult: The Story of "Mankind United."* Boston: Beacon Press, 1958.

DuBose, Hampden C. *The Dragon, Image, and Demon*. London: S. W. Partridge, 1886.

Edwardes, Michael. *Battles of the Indian Mutiny*. New York: Macmillan, 1963.

Ellwood, Robert S., Jr. *Religious and Spiritual Groups in Modern America*. Englewood Cliffs, N.J.: Prentice-Hall, 1973.

Empires Ascendant: 400 BC-AD 200. (TimeFrame series). Alexandria, Va.: Time-Life Books, 1987.

The Enterprise of War. (TimeFrame series). Alexandria, Va.: Time-Life Books, 1991.

Evans, Christopher. *Cults of Unreason*. New York: Farrar, Straus and Giroux, 1973.

Evans, Ivor H. *Brewer's Dictionary of Phrase and Fable* (Rev. ed.). New York: Harper & Row, 1981.

Fairbank, John King. *The Great Chinese Revolution 1800-1985*. New York: Harper & Row, 1986.

Feuerlicht, Roberta Strauss:
America's Reign of Terror: World War I, the Red Scare, and the Palmer Raids. New York: Random House, 1971.
Joe McCarthy and McCarthyism: The Hate that Haunts America. New York: McGraw-Hill, 1972.

Finley, John H., Jr. *Thucydides*. Cambridge, Mass.: Harvard University Press, 1955.

Finucane, Ronald C. *Soldiers of the Faith: Crusaders and Moslems at War*. New York: St. Martin's Press, 1983.

Fried, Richard M. *Nightmare in Red: The McCarthy Era in Perspective*. New York: Oxford University Press, 1990.

Friedmann, Claude T. H., and Robert A. Faguet (Eds.). *Extraordinary Disorders of Human Behavior*. New York: Plenum Press, 1982.

Fussell, Paul. *Wartime: Understanding and Behavior in the Second World War*. New York: Oxford University Press, 1989.

Gardner, Martin. *Fads and Fallacies in the Name of Science*. New York: Dover, 1957.

Germains, Victor Wallace. *The Truth about Kitchener*. London: John Lane The Bodley Head, 1925.

Gerrare, Wirt. *The Story of Moscow* (3rd ed.). London: J. M. Dent; New York: E. P. Dutton, 1910.

Grigoriev, S. L. *The Diaghilev Ballet 1909-1929*. Edited and translated by Vera Bowen. Harmondsworth, England: Penguin Books, 1960.

Grousset, René. *The Epic of the Crusades*. Translated by Noël Lindsay. New York: Orion Press, 1970.

Grunfeld, Frederic V. *The Princes of Germany* (Treasures of the World series). Chicago: Stonehenge Press, 1983.

Hall, A. Daniel. *The Book of the Tulip*. London: Martin Hopkinson, 1929.

Hall, Angus. *Strange Cults*. Garden City, N.Y.: Doubleday, 1976.

Harden, Donald. *The Phoenicians* (Ancient Peoples and Places series). New York: Frederick A. Praeger, 1962.

Harrison, J. F. C. *The Second Coming: Popular Millenarianism 1780-1850*. New Brunswick, N.J.: 1979.

Hecker, J. F. C. *The Black Death and the Dancing Mania*. Translated by B. G. Babington. London: Cassell, 1888.

Heckethorn, Charles William. *The Secret Societies of All Ages and Countries* (Vol. 1). New Hyde Park, N.Y.: University Books, 1965.

Henry, Lyell D., Jr. *Zig-Zag-and-Swirl: Alfred W. Lawson's Quest for Greatness*. Iowa City: University of Iowa Press, 1991.

Heuer, Kenneth. *The End of the World*. New York: Rinehart, 1953.

Hittman, Michael. *Wovoka and the Ghost Dance*. Edited by Don Lynch. Carson City, Nev.: Grace Danberg Foundation, 1990.

Hook, Donald D. *Madmen of History*. Middle Village, N.Y.: Jonathan David, 1976.

Hopkins, James K. *A Woman to Deliver Her People* (Dan Danciger Publication series). Austin: University of Texas Press, 1982.

Hoyt, Edwin P. *The Palmer Raids 1919-1920: An Attempt to Suppress Dissent*. New York: Seabury Press, 1969.

Humes, Edward. *Buried Secrets*. New York: Dutton, 1991.

Jacobson, David J. *The Affairs of Dame Rumor*. New York: Rinehart, 1948.

James, Edward T., Janet Wilson James, and Paul S. Boyer (Eds.). *Notable American Women, 1607-1950: A Biographical Dictionary* (Vol. 2). Cambridge, Mass.: Belknap Press, 1971.

Kagan, Donald:
The Archidamian War. Ithaca, N.Y.: Cornell University Press, 1974.
The Outbreak of the Peloponnesian War. Ithaca, N.Y.: Cornell University Press, 1969.

Kapferer, Jean-Noël. *Rumors: Uses, Interpretations, and Images*. New Brunswick, N.J.: Transaction, 1990.

Kaplan, Harold I., M.D., and Benjamin J. Sadock, M.D. (Eds.). *Comprehensive Textbook of Psychiatry/IV* (Vol. 2, 4th ed.). Baltimore: Williams & Wilkins, 1985.

Katz, Ephraim. *The Film Encyclopedia*. New York: Thomas Y. Crowell, 1979.

Keegan, John. *The Face of Battle*. New York: Viking Press, 1976.

Keen, Sam. *Faces of the Enemy*. San Francisco: Harper & Row, 1986.

Kilduff, Marshall, and Ron Javers. *The Suicide Cult*. New York: Bantam, 1978.

King, George, and Kevin Quinn Avery. *The Age of Aetherius* (Rev. ed.). Los Angeles: Aetherius Society, 1982.

Kittredge, George Lyman. *Witchcraft: In Old and New England*. Cambridge, Mass.: Harvard University Press, 1929.

Kodansha Encyclopedia of Japan (Vol. 8). Tokyo: Kodansha, 1983.

Koenig, Fredrick. *Rumor in the Marketplace*. Dover, Mass.: Auburn House, 1985.

Kreiser, Robert B. *Miracles, Convulsions, and Ecclesiastical Politics in Early Eighteenth-Century Paris*. Princeton: Princeton University Press, 1978.

Ladenheim, Jules Calvin. " 'The Doctors' Mob' of 1788." In *Journal of the History of Medicine and Allied Sciences* (Vol. 5). New York: Henry Schuman, 1950.

Landis, Mark. *Joseph McCarthy: The Politics of Chaos*. Cranbury, N.J.: Associated University Press, 1987.

Lapp, R. E. *Must We Hide?* Cambridge, Mass.: Addison-Wesley Press, 1949.

Larsen, Egon. *Strange Sects and Cults: A Study of Their Origins and Influence*. London: Arthur Barker, 1971.

Lawson, Alfred:
Fifty Speeches. Detroit: Humanity, 1941.
Lawsonomy. Detroit: Humanity, 1935.

Lerner, Michael G. *Maupassant*. New York: George Braziller, 1975.

Leroy-Beaulieu, Anatole. *The Empire of the Tsars and the Russians* (Part 3). Translated by Zénaïde A. Ragozin. New York: AMS Press, 1969 (reprint of 1902-1905 eds.).

Le Sacre du Printemps. Geneva: Editions Minkoff, 1980.

Lewis, Naphtali, and Meyer Reinhold (Eds.). *Roman Civilization. Sourcebook I: The Republic*. New York: Harper & Row, 1966.

Lodewijk, Tom. *The Book of Tulips*. Edited by Ruth Buchan. New York: Vendome Press, 1979.

Losada, Luis A. *The Fifth Column in the Peloponnesian War*. Leiden, Netherlands: E. J. Brill, 1972.

Love, John F. *McDonald's: Behind the Arches*. Toronto: Bantam Books, 1986.

Lunde, Donald T. *Murder and Madness*. Stanford, Calif.: Stanford Alumni, 1975.

Machen, Arthur. *The Angels of Mons: The Bowman and Other Legends of the War*. London: Simpkin, Marshall, Hamilton, Kent, 1915.

McIntosh, Christopher. *The Swan King: Ludwig II of Bavaria*. London: Allen Lane, 1982.

Mackay, Charles. *Extraordinary Popular Delusions and the Madness of Crowds*. New York: Farrar, Straus and Giroux, 1932.

McWilliams, Carey. *Prejudice: Japanese-Americans: Symbol of Racial Intolerance*. Boston: Little, Brown, 1944.

Madden, R. R. *Phantasmata or Illusions and Fanaticisms*. London: T. C. Newby, 1857.

Maire, Catherine-Laurence. *Les Convulsionnaires De Saint-Médard*. Paris: Gallimard/Julliard, 1985.

Majumdar, R. C. *The Sepoy Mutiny and the Revolt of 1857* (2nd ed.). Calcutta: Firma K. L. Mukhopadhyay, 1963.

Manuel, Frank E. *The Prophets of Paris*. Cambridge, Mass.: Harvard University Press, 1962.

Martin, Christopher. *The Boxer Rebellion*. London: Abelard-Schuman, 1968.

Mayer, Hans Eberhard. *The Crusades* (2nd ed.). Translated by John Gillingham. Oxford: Oxford University Press, 1988.

Melton, J. Gordon:
Biographical Dictionary of American Cults and Sect Leaders. New York: Garland, 1986.
The Encyclopedia of American Religions (3rd ed.). Detroit: Gale Research, 1989.
Encyclopedic Handbook of Cults in America. New York: Garland, 1986.

Michael, Franz. *The Taiping Rebellion: History and Documents* (Vol. 3). Tokyo: University of Tokyo Press, 1971.

Montgomery, John. *Abodes of Love*. London: Putnam, 1962.

Montgomery, Ruth. *Aliens among Us*. New York: G. P. Putnam's Sons, 1985.

Moody, Raymond A., Jr. *Elvis after Life*. Atlanta, Ga.: Peachtree, 1987.

Mooney, James. *The Ghost Dance Religion and the Sioux Outbreak of 1890*. Chicago: University of Chicago Press, 1965.

Moore, Patrick. *Can You Speak Venusian?* New York: W. W. Norton, 1972.

Morin, Edgar. *Rumour in Orléans*. Translated by Peter Green. New York: Random House, Pantheon Books, 1971.

Morris, William, and Mary Morris. *Morris Dictionary of Word and Phrase Origins* (2nd ed.). New York: Harper & Row, 1988.

Munro, Dana. "The Children's Crusade." In *American Historical Review* (Vol. 14, October 1913 to July 1914). London: Macmillan, 1914.

Murray, Robert K. *Red Scare: A Study in National Hysteria, 1919-1920*. Minneapolis: University of Minnesota Press, 1955.

1940-1950 (Vol. 5, This Fabulous Century series). New York: Time-Life Books, 1969.

1950-1960 (Vol. 6, This Fabulous Century series). New York: Time-Life Books, 1970.

North, Ernest Dressel. *The Wit and Wisdom of Charles Lamb*. Folcroft, Pa.: Folcroft Library Editions, 1974.

Odum, Howard W. *Race and Rumors of Race*. New York: Negro Universities Press, 1969 (reprint of 1943 ed.).

Onions, C. T., G. W. S. Friedrichsen, and R. W. Burchfield (Eds.). *The Oxford Dictionary of English Etymology*. Oxford: Clarendon Press, 1966.

O'Reilly, Patrick. *Hébridais: Répertoire Bio-bibliographique des Nouvelles-Hébrides*. Paris: Musée de l'Homme, 1957.

Oshinsky, David M. *A Conspiracy So Immense*. New York: Free Press, 1983.

Ostwald, Peter:
Schumann: The Inner Voices of a Musical Genius. Boston: Northeastern University Press, 1985.
Vaslav Nijinsky: A Leap into Madness. Secaucus, N.J.: Lyle Stuart, 1991.

Otten, Charlotte F. (Ed.). *A Lycanthropy Reader: Werewolves in Western Culture*. Syracuse, N.Y.: Syracuse University Press, 1986.

Palmer, J. A. B. *The Mutiny Outbreak at Meerut in 1857*. Cambridge: Cambridge University Press, 1966.

Payne, Robert, and Nikita Romanoff. *Ivan the Terrible*. New York: Thomas Y. Crowell, 1975.

Plutarch. *The Lives of the Noble Grecians and Romans*. Translated by John Dryden and revised by Arthur Hugh Clough. New York: Random House, no date.

Ponsonby, Arthur. *Falsehood in War-time*. New York: Garland, 1971.

Price, Harry. *Leaves from a Psychist's Case-Book*. London: V. Gollarcz, 1933.

Reiterman, Tim, and John Jacobs. *Raven: The Untold Story of the Rev. Jim Jones and His People*. New York: E. P. Dutton, 1982.

Riley-Smith, Jonathan. *What Were the Crusades?* London: Macmillan Press, 1977.

Rosen, Barbara (Ed.). *Witchcraft*. London: Edward

Arnold, 1969.

Rosnow, Ralph L., and Gary Alan Fine. *Rumor and Gossip: The Social Psychology of Hearsay.* New York: Elsevier, 1976.

Roueché, Berton. *The Medical Detectives.* New York: Times Books, 1980.

Rovere, Richard H. *Senator Joe McCarthy.* New York: Harcourt, Brace, 1959.

Runciman, Steven. *The History of the Crusades, Volume 1: The First Crusade.* Cambridge: Cambridge University Press, 1954.

Sann, Paul:
Fads, Follies and Delusions of the American People. New York: Bonanza Books, 1967.
The 20s: The Lawless Decade. New York: Crown, 1957.

Setton, Kenneth M. (Ed.). *A History of the Crusades, Volume II: The Later Crusades, 1189-1311.* Madison: University of Wisconsin Press, 1969.

Sherer, Joel. "Wovoka." In *Twentieth-Century Shapers of American Popular Religion,* edited by Charles H. Lippy. New York: Greenwood Press, 1989.

Shirley, Ralph. *The Angel Warriors at Mons.* London: Newspaper Publicity, 1915.

Simkins, Peter. *Kitchener's Army: The Raising of the New Armies, 1914-16.* Manchester: Manchester University Press, 1988.

Sinnigen, William G., and Charles Alexander Robinson, Jr. *Ancient History from Prehistoric Times to the Death of Justinian* (3rd ed.). New York: Macmillan, 1981.

Stauffer, Vernon. *New England and the Bavarian Illuminati.* New York: Russell & Russell, 1967 (reprint of 1918 ed.).

Steeves, Paul D. "Skoptsy." In *The Modern Encyclopedia of Russian and Soviet History* (Vol. 35), edited by Joseph L. Wieczynski. Gulf Breeze, Fla.: Academic International Press, 1983.

Sugg, Redding S., Jr. *A Painter's Psalm.* Memphis: Memphis State University Press, 1978.

Sugg, Redding S., Jr. (Ed.). *The Horn Island Logs of Walter Inglis Anderson.* Memphis: Memphis State University Press, 1973.

Thorndike, Lynn. *A History of Magic and Experimental Science* (Vol. 5). New York: Columbia University Press, 1923.

Thucydides. *History of the Peloponnesian War.* Translated by Rex Warner. Harmondsworth, England: Penguin Books, 1954.

Todd, Janet (Ed.). *British Women Writers: A Critical Reference Guide.* New York: Continuum, 1989.

Tracts of Medical Jurisprudence. Philadelphia: James Webster, 1819.

Train, John. *Famous Financial Fiascos.* New York: Clarkson N. Potter, 1985.

Treece, Henry. *The Crusades.* London: Bodley Head, 1962.

Troy, Sandy. *One More Saturday Night.* New York: St. Martin's Press, 1991.

Turner, E. S.:
Dear Old Blighty. London: Michael Joseph, 1980.
The Phoney War on the Home Front. London: Michael Joseph, 1961.

Tyng, Sewell. *The Campaign of the Marne 1914.* New York: Longmans, Green, 1985.

Walk, Wastrand (Ed.). *Daniel McNaughton: His Trial and the Aftermath.* London: Gaskell Books, 1977.

Wallace, Irving. *The Square Pegs: Some Americans Who Dared to Be Different.* New York: Alfred A. Knopf, 1957.

Werner, Herbert A. *Iron Coffins: A Personal Account of the German U-Boat Battles of World War II.* New York: Holt, Rinehart and Winston, 1969.

Werstein, Irving. *The Boxer Rebellion: Anti-Foreign Terror Seizes China, 1900.* New York: Franklin Watts, 1971.

The World Almanac Book of the Strange. New York: Signet, 1977.

Worsley, Peter. *The Trumpet Shall Sound: A Study of 'Cargo' Cults in Melanesia* (2nd ed.). New York: Schocken Books, 1968.

Yeomans, Donald K. *Comets: A Chronological History of Observation, Science, Myth, and Folklore.* New York: John Wiley & Sons, 1991.

Periodicals

Achiles, Marcus. "Vale do Amanhecer: Contatos Imediatos com a Fé." *Manchete,* March 16, 1991.

"Africa Illness Laid to Mass Hysteria." *New York Times,* August 9, 1963.

Allan, James. "Mystery Illness at Carnival Hits 230 Children." *Daily Telegraph,* July 14, 1980.

Allderidge, Patricia H.:
"Criminal Insanity: Bethlem to Broadmoor." *Proceedings of the Royal Society of Medicine,* September 1974.
"Richard Dadd (1817-1886): Painter and Patient." *Medical History,* July 1970.

Axthelm, Pete, et al. "The Emperor Jones." *Newsweek,* December 4, 1978.

"Baby's Bleeding Hands Nearly Revive Terror of Razor-Blade Cuts." *China Post,* May 14, 1956.

Bar-El, I., et al. "Psychiatric Hospitalization of Tourists in Jerusalem." *Comprehensive Psychiatry,* May-June 1991.

Barr, Robert A. "Glass Pits Due to Ash, Say Police." *Seattle Daily Times,* April 16, 1954.

Bennett, Raymond. "The Box that Contains the Answers to the World's Problems." *Bedfordshire Times,* October 13, 1967.

Billiter, Bill. "Satanic Messages Played Back for Assembly Panel." *Los Angeles Times,* April 28, 1982.

Bissell, Shelton. "Vaudeville at Angelus Temple." *Outlook,* May 23, 1928.

Blumenfeld, Laura. "Procter & Gamble's Devil of a Problem." *Washington Post,* February 4, 1991.

Bowman, Robert. "Robert Schumann's Life." *Psychiatric Communications,* 1970, Vol. 13, No. 1.

Brackett, Ed. "Enigmatic Cultist Chose to Die in Blue Ridge." *Asheville Citizen-Times* (North Carolina), March 18, 1990.

Brenner, Marie. "East Side Alien." *Vanity Fair,* March 1990.

Budlong, Julia N. "Aimee Semple McPherson." *Nation,* June 19, 1929.

Burnett, John. "Magic and Murder in Matamoras." *Christian Century,* September 13-20, 1989.

Campion-Vincent, Véronique. "The Baby-Parts Story: A New Latin American Legend." *Western Folklore,* January 1990.

Cartwright, Gary. "The Work of the Devil." *Texas Monthly,* June 1989.

Carvalho, Sandra. "No Vale do Amanhecer, O Sobrenatural." *O Globo,* November 19, 1987.

Cellario, Alberto R. "El Trágico Fin de un Partido de Fútbol en Lima." *Life en Español,* July 6, 1964.

"The Cloud over Paradise Valley." *People,* June 4, 1990.

Coben, Stanley. "A Study in Nativism: The American Red Scare of 1919-20." *Political Science Quarterly,* March 1964.

"Command Performance." *Time,* April 2, 1951.

Comstock, Sarah. "Aimee Semple McPherson: Prima Donna of Revivalism." *Harper's,* December 1927.

Conley, Robert. "Laughing Malady Puzzle in Africa." *New York Times,* August 8, 1963.

"Control Yuan May Take Up Question of Razor-Blade Cuts." *China Post,* May 17, 1956.

Crane, Joanna. "Bishop Warns 'Steer Clear'. " *Bedfordshire Times,* June 1, 1990.

"A Crashing of Mountains." *Time,* June 5, 1964.

Critchley, Macdonald. "Four Illustrious Neuroluetics." *Proceedings of the Royal Society of Medicine,* July 1969.

"Curbs for Trojan Horses." *Fortune,* July 1940.

"Earthlings to Take Spaced-out Cosmic Pause." *Harrisburg Patriot News,* August 15, 1987.

"Fatigue Caused Carnival Illness, Doctor Claims." *Daily Telegraph,* July 16, 1980.

Flynn, Pat. "Parade Is for Brothers from Space." *Union* (San Diego), October 13, 1986.

Freedman, Alix M. "Rumor Turns Fantasy into Bad Dream." *Wall Street Journal,* May 10, 1991.

Gerstell, Richard. "How You Can Survive an A-Bomb Blast." *Saturday Evening Post,* January 7, 1950.

Gloyne, Howard F. "Tarantism." *American Imago,* March 1950.

Goodman, Fred:
"The Rolling Stone Interview: Jerry Garcia." *Rolling Stone,* November 30, 1989.
"The End of the Road?" *Rolling Stone,* August 23, 1990.

Goshko, John M. "Nailing Disinformation: The Slum-Child Tale." *Washington Post,* August 26, 1988.

Harris, Michael P. "Paradise under Siege." *Time,* August 28, 1989.

Henican, Ellis. "Dads Battle 'Cult' for Children." *Newsday,* May 31, 1988.

Hersey, John. "Behind Barbed Wire." *New York Times,* September 11, 1988.

Hoban, Phoebe. "Psycho Drama: The Chilling Story of How the Sullivanian Cult Turned a Utopian Dream into a Nightmare." *New York,* June 19, 1989.

Hodson, Millicent. "Nijinsky's Choreographic Method: Visual Sources from Roerich for Le Sacre du Printemps." *Dance Research Journal,* Winter 1986-87.

Horsnell, Michael:
"Blame Laid on Stress for Collapse of 300." *Times,* July 26, 1980.
"Crop Spray Doubted as Cause of Illness." *Times,* July 15, 1980.
"Jazz Festival Illness Still Unexplained, Experts Say." *Times,* July 24, 1980.

Huckerby, Martin. "300 People Collapse at Jazz Band Competition." *Times,* July 14, 1980.

"Hum If You Love the Mayans." *People Weekly,* August 31, 1987.

" 'Hysteria Hit Children'." *Daily Mail,* July 15, 1980.

Illis, L. "On Porphyria and Aetiology of Werewolves." *Proceedings of the Royal Society of Medicine*, January 1964.

Jacobs, Norman. "The Phantom Slasher of Taipei: Mass Hysteria in a Non-Western Society." *Social Problems*, Winter 1965.

Johnsrud, Byron. "Windshield-Peppering Hoodlums Strike Whidby Naval Air Station." *Seattle Daily Times*, April 14, 1954.

Jonas, Peter. "Alfred William Lawson: Aviator, Inventor, and Depression Radical." *Old Northwest*, Summer 1983.

Kapferer, J. N. "A Mass Poisoning Rumor in Europe." *Public Opinion Quarterly*, 1989, Vol. 53, pp. 467-481.

Kulick, Aaron R., Harrison G. Pope, Jr., and Paule E. Keck, Jr. "Lycanthropy and Self-Identification." *Journal of Nervous and Mental Disease*, 1990, Vol. 178, No. 2.

Lacayo, Richard. "Heading for the Hills." *Time*, March 26, 1990.

Landes, Ruth. "The Abnormal among the Ojibwa Indians." *Journal of Abnormal and Social Psychology*, January 1938.

Legge, Gordon. "Doukhobors Talk Peace." *Maclean's*, October 10, 1983.

Liu, Melinda. "Beware of Headhunters." *Newsweek*, December 11, 1989.

Long, Rebecca. "Speculation Continues to Grow on Weather Modification." *News* (Frederick, Md.), July 23, 1991.

"Man Dies, 6 Hurt as Hailstorm Hits Metro Area." *Toronto Star*, June 14, 1976.

Marcus, Amy Dockser. "Jerusalem Syndrome Makes Some Visitors Believe They're God." *Wall Street Journal*, December 30, 1991.

Marcus, Amy Dockser, and Arthur S. Hayes. "CBS Is Found Blameless in Music Suicides." *Wall Street Journal*, August 27, 1990.

"Mass Burial Rite Held for Peru Riot Victims." *New York Times*, May 27, 1964.

"Mass Hysteria: The Facts." *Times*, July 26, 1980.

Mathews, Tom, et al. "The Cult of Death." *Newsweek*, December 4, 1978.

"Mayor Wires Ike and Langlie: President's Aid Asked in Windshield Mystery." *Seattle Post-Intelligencer*, April 16, 1954.

Medalia, Nahum Z., and Otto N. Larsen. "Diffusion and Belief in a Collective Delusion: The Seattle Windshield Pitting Epidemic." *American Sociological Review*, April 1958.

"Messiah from the Midwest." *Time*, December 4, 1978.

"Mighty I AM." *Time*, February 28, 1938.

"Moon Wars." *Time*, July 19, 1982.

"More Red Than Herring." *Time*, June 4, 1951.

"Mystery Illnesses: The Hollinwell Incident." *Fortean Times*, Issue no. 33, no date.

"Mystery Windshield Damage Spreads in Seattle and County." *Seattle Daily Times*, April 15, 1954.

"Naked Women Convicted of Mischief in Setting Fires." *Vancouver Sun*, May 9, 1991.

Nicol, Susan C. "Investigation Reveals Weather Modification in Frederick County." *News* (Frederick, Md.), July 15, 1988.

Nicolas, Jean. "La Rumeur de Paris: Rapts d'Enfants en 1750." *L'Histoire*, December 1981.

"Nightmare in Jonestown." *Time*, December 4, 1978.

"No Laughing Matter." *Newsweek*, August 26, 1963.

Norris, David, and Robert Turner. "Poison Cloud Riddle of 305 Sick Children." *Daily Mail*, July 14, 1980.

"Northwest Mystery." *Newsweek*, April 26, 1954.

Novakovsky, Stanislaus. "Arctic or Siberian Hysteria as a Reflex of the Geographic Environment." *Ecology*, April 1924.

O'Brien, R. Barry. "Domino Idea in Mass Illness." *Daily Telegraph*, July 15, 1980.

O'Hara, Jane. "The Embers of Defiance." *Maclean's*, December 16, 1985.

O'Harrow, Robert, Jr. "Act of Nature, or Plain Old Theft?" *Washington Post*, August 11, 1991.

"On Comets." *Harper's Weekly*, June 6, 1857.

"100 Cars Reported Damaged by Windshield Vandals Here." *Seattle Post-Intelligencer*, April 15, 1954.

Parker, Seymour. "The Wiitiko Psychosis in the Context of Ojibwa Personality and Culture." *American Anthropologist*, August 1960.

"People Urged Not to Get Excited Over Rumored Razor-Blade Terror." *China Post*, May 7, 1956.

"Peru Will Assist Riot Victims' Kin." *New York Times*, May 26, 1964.

Pickford, Elizabeth, Neil Buchanan, and Sherryl McLaughlan. "Munchausen Syndrome by Proxy: A Family Anthology." *Medical Journal of Australia*, June 20, 1988.

Podolsky, Edward. "The Syphilitic Brain and Human Destinies." *Medical Annals of the District of Columbia*, July 1955.

" 'Positive Proof' of Windshield Damage Sought." *Seattle Daily Times*, April 19, 1954.

"A Pox on Windshields." *Newsweek*, May 3, 1954.

"Profit's Prophet." *Time*, May 21, 1945.

Rankin, A. M., and P. J. Philip. "An Epidemic of Laughing in the Bukoba District of Tanganyika." *Central African Journal of Medicine*, May 1963.

"Razor-Blade Terror Ebbing, Police at All-Out War to Solve Mystery." *China Post*, May 6, 1956.

Reinemer, Vic. "Is Fluoridation a Marxist Plot?" *Reporter*, June 16, 1955.

Relix, December 1991.

"Reports of Damage to Car Glass Taper Off." *Seattle Daily Times*, April 16, 1954.

Rowsome, Frank, Jr. "The Great Windshield Mystery." *Popular Science*, July 1954.

"The R.S.P.C.A. and the War." *Animal World*, October 1939.

Rudloe, Jack. "The Nature of a Painter." *Natural History*, February 1990.

"Savants Absolve H-Bomb in 'Pit' Mystery." *Seattle Post-Intelligencer*, April 21, 1954.

"Secret Society Sits on Fence." *Bedfordshire on Sunday*, September 27, 1987.

Shah, Kumar A., Mitchell D. Forman, and Howard S. Friedman. "Munchausen's Syndrome and Cardiac Catheterization: A Case of Pernicious Interaction." *Journal of the American Medical Association*, December 10, 1982.

Silverman, Jon. "The Faithful Few Who Will Never See Success." *Evening Echo*, August 8, 1973.

Span, Paula. "Cult or Therapy: Parents at War." *Washington Post*, July 27, 1988.

"Spokane Sets Biggest U.S. Air Raid Test." *Seattle Post-Intelligencer*, April 18, 1954.

Steele, Richard, Tony Fuller, and Timothy Nater. "Life in Jonestown." *Newsweek*, December 4, 1978.

Sugg, Redding S., Jr. "Southern Gentleman and Pope's Homer." *Smithsonian*, February 1977.

"300 Dead in Lima as Rioting Erupts at Soccer Match." *New York Times*, May 25, 1963.

Tuttle, Alexandra. "Did You Hear the Rumor . . ." *Time*, March 11, 1991.

"U. Scientists Skeptical in Glass Puzzle." *Seattle Post-Intelligencer*, April 17, 1954.

"Voices from Beyond: The Channelers." *People*, January 26, 1987.

Wangh, Anne Wilson. "Vaslav Nijinsky: Genius and Schizophrenic." *American Imago*, Fall 1978.

"What Hit the Windshield." *Business Week*, May 1, 1954.

White, Elizabeth. "Doom in 30 Years if Bishops Don't Open Joanna's Box." *Bedfordshire Times*, August 21, 1970.

"Windshield Blemish Spreads South; Ohio Cars Also Marred By Pox." *Seattle Post-Intelligencer*, April 18, 1954.

"Windshield Dilemma: Mayor's Call for U.S. Aid Answered, Reports Vary on Cooperation." *Seattle Post-Intelligencer*, April 18, 1954.

"Windshield Front Quiet in Northwest." *Seattle Daily Times*, April 17, 1954.

"Windshield Vandals Strike in Anacortes." *Seattle Post-Intelligencer*, April 14, 1954.

Witztum, Eliezer. "Am I So Short of Madmen that You Have To Bring This Fellow Here To Carry On in Front of Me?" *Teva v'Aretz* (Nature and Land, Jerusalem), November 1987.

Yellowlees, Peter M. "Werewolves Down Under—Where Are They Now?" *The Medical Journal of Australia*, December 4-18, 1989.

"Zigzag & Swirl." *Time*, September 6, 1943.

"Zigzag & Swirl." *Time*, March 24, 1952.

Other Sources

"I Wear the Morning Star: An Exhibition of American Indian Ghost Dance Objects." Catalog. Minneapolis: Minneapolis Institute of the Arts, July 29-September 26, 1976.

Jacobson, Kenneth. "The Protocols: Myth and History." Pamphlet. New York: Anti-Defamation League of B'nai B'rith, 1981.

Korey, William. "The Soviet 'Protocols of the Elders of Zion': Anti-Semitic Propaganda in the U.S.S.R., August 1967-August 1977." Pamphlet. New York: B'nai B'rith International, Division of Public Affairs, 1977.

"Phobias and Panic." Pamphlet. U.S. Department of Health and Human Services Publication No. (ADM) 88-1472. Rockville, Md.: National Institute of Mental Health, 1986.

"Sea, Earth, Sky: The Art of Walter Anderson." Catalog. Jackson, Miss.: Mississippi State Historical Museum, no date.

Teicher, Morton I. "A Study of a Relationship between Belief and Behavior among the Indians of Northeastern Canada." In "Proceedings of the 1960 Annual Spring Meeting of the American Ethnological Society." Edited by Verne F. Ray. Seattle: American Ethnological Society, 1960.

To Elvis. Telephone service providing updates on Elvis sightings. National Enquirer, January 28, 1992.

INDEX

Numerals in italics indicate an illustration of the subject mentioned.

Time-Life Books is a division of Time Life Inc.,
a wholly owned subsidiary of
THE TIME INC. BOOK COMPANY

TIME-LIFE BOOKS

PRESIDENT: Mary N. Davis

Managing Editor: Thomas H. Flaherty
Director of Editorial Resources: Elise D. Ritter-Clough
Director of Photography and Research:
John Conrad Weiser
Editorial Board: Dale M. Brown, Roberta Conlan,
Laura Foreman, Lee Hassig, Jim Hicks, Blaine
Marshall, Rita Thievon Mullin, Henry Woodhead
*Assistant Director of Editorial Resources/Training
Manager:* Norma E. Shaw

PUBLISHER: Robert H. Smith

Associate Publisher: Ann M. Mirabito
Editorial Director: Russell B. Adams, Jr.
Marketing Director: Anne C. Everhart
Production Manager: Prudence G. Harris
Supervisor of Quality Control: James King

Editorial Operations
Production: Celia Beattie
Library: Louise D. Forstall
Computer Composition: Deborah G. Tait (Manager),
Monika D. Thayer, Janet Barnes Syring, Lillian Daniels
Interactive Media Specialist: Patti H. Cass

**Library of Congress
Cataloging-in-Publication Data**
Manias and delusions / by the editors of Time-Life
Books.
p.   cm.   (Library of curious and unusual facts).
Includes bibliographical references.
ISBN 0-8094-7731-9
ISBN 0-8094-7732-7 (lib. bdg.)
1. Psychology, Pathological—Popular works. 2. Hys-
teria (Social psychology)—Case studies. 3. Delu-
sions—Case studies.
I. Time-Life Books. II. Series.
RC460.M26 1992
616.89—dc20   91-43017 CIP

LIBRARY OF CURIOUS AND UNUSUAL FACTS

SERIES EDITOR: Carl A. Posey
Series Administrator: Roxie France-Nuriddin
Art Director: Cynthia Richardson
Picture Editor: Sally Collins

Editorial Staff for *Manias and Delusions*
Text Editor: Sarah Brash
Associate Editor/Research: Susan E. Arritt
Assistant Editors/Research: Ruth Goldberg (princi-
pal), Jennifer A. Mendelsohn
Assistant Art Director: Alan Pitts
Senior Copy Coordinator: Jarelle S. Stein
Copy Coordinator: Juli Duncan
Picture Coordinator: Jennifer Iker
Editorial Assistant: Terry Ann Paredes

Special Contributors: Sue Allison, Eliot Marshall,
Peter Pocock, George Russell (text); Catherine B.
Hackett, Debra Diamond Smit (research); Louise
Wile Hedberg (index)

Correspondents: Elisabeth Kraemer-Singh (Bonn),
Christine Hinze (London), Christina Lieberman (New
York), Maria Vincenza Aloisi (Paris), Ann Natanson
(Rome). Valuable assistance was also provided by Mia
Turner (Beijing); Barbara Gevene Hertz (Copenhagen);
Clement Masenas (Dubai); Marlin Levin (Jerusalem);
Caroline Alcock, Judy Aspinall (London); Trini Ban-
drés (Madrid); Elizabeth Brown, Katheryn White (New
York); Wibo Van de Linde (Netherlands); John Maier
(Rio de Janeiro); Leonora Dodsworth, Ann Wise
(Rome); Don Shapiro (Taiwan); Dick Berry, Mieko Ike-
da (Tokyo); Moira Farrow (Vancouver); Roderick Con-
way Morris (Venice); Traudl Lessing (Vienna).

The Consultant:
William R. Corliss, the general consultant for the
series, is a physicist-turned-writer who has spent the
last twenty-five years compiling collections of anoma-
lies in the fields of geophysics, geology, archaeology,
astronomy, biology, and psychology. He has written
about science and technology for NASA, the National
Science Foundation, and the Energy Research and Development Administration (among others). Mr. Corliss
is also the author of more than thirty books on scientific mysteries, including *Mysterious Universe, The
Unfathomed Mind,* and *Handbook of Unusual Natural
Phenomena.*